More Praise For *For*

"*Fortunate Soldier* is the compelling n
service in the Vietnam War. Moffett epitomizes the universal sensitiv-
ity of the Vietnam experience when he says, 'We had lived together,
shared the fear of dying and the joy of surviving the turmoil of
Vietnam together. Brothers all, those men who surrounded me that
last night.'"
— Rep. Steve Israel, United States Congress

"One word: IRREVERENT! Now the other words: The most engaging, hilarious book about wartime experiences since M*A*S*H or
Catch-22. Wonderfully hilarious factual account of life in the rear
during the Vietnam War."
— Billie Marie Zal, author, *The Fabric of our Lives*

"Smoothly written but not glib—the natural humor flows from the
all-to-true stories of life in the rear. More than just a funny wartime
memoir, this book illustrates how looney the wartime military estab-
lishment can be. Best of all, it provides a marvelous look at the social
mores that prevail during war."
— Father James Sheehan, author,
The Father Who Didn't Know My Name

"In the short and often maudlin pantheon of Vietnam literature,
Fortunate Soldier is a stand-out that's bound to be called heretical and
it's author, Pat Moffett, an apostate. The reason? It's FUNNY! But
you know what else? It's FUNNY! This could be the book that
changes everybody's mind about Vietnam. Armed with gun, typewriter, and a lethal sense of humor, this young American was determined to live to tell about it. It's BRILLIANT!"
— Eldon Thomas, author, *Table For Three*

"You have never read a war story like this one: an achingly comic
memoir about Vietnam. Moffett turns his wartime experiences into
an uproarious, biting, and irreverent look at Vietnam: Earnest
young soldiers in ridiculous circumstances, trying to do their best.
Lost in an outrageous, baffling, war zone that bears no resemblance

to the war they planned to fight. The characters are genuine, funny, compassionate and hopelessly confused. Not your traditional war story. Not even close."

— Cal Kirby, author, *Business Battle Plan*

"The most provocative book of the season–guaranteed! The smart-ass style of the memoir's construction makes the Vietnam War seem all the more screwy and terrifying. The episodes border on the slapstick, but the clever writing reminds you that you're in a combat zone. Offbeat, hilarious, Pat has the ability to find the funny side of uniformed life— the more by-the-book, the clearer a target for our hero.."

— Arthur Reinherz, author, *Father, Dear Father*

"Hilarious episodes and savage wit sure to offend many—especially those still insistent on re-fighting the Vietnam War and who just won't let it go. Penetrating as slugs from an M16 with humor sharp as a bayonet. If you're ready for a whole new take on the Vietnam War, this is definitely your book."

— Paul Gordon, author, *Concrete Solution*

"An insider's look at the kind of tour of duty most of GIs served in the military during the Vietnam War. No better book has been written about that time and place than Fortunate Soldier. Funny as hell and with an eye for the absurd, this book is very different than any other book about Vietnam."

— Captain Edward M. Brittingham, USN (Ret.), author, *Operation Poppy, Sub Chaser*

"A breakthrough antidote to the mostly macho literature of Vietnam. Often stark, always darkly humorous portrait of war. There have been many combat books about Nam, but almost none with the MASH-like sense of hilarity that can be even more powerful than all the sturm and drang. Lively people, non-stop action, gifted writing. Moffet's book is absent all the war cliches and *Fortunate soldier* isn't pointless or tragic. This might be the first grown-up version of Vietnam. He gives it the maturity and serious dignity it deserves—by treating it with liberal doses of hilarity and zaniness."

— Joyce Egginton, *NY Times* bestselling author, *From Cradle To Grave, Circle of Fire, Day of Fury*

"Pat has an appreciation for the absurd procedures, the twisted rituals, the over-the-top seriousness that's endemic to any barely-controlled institution like the military. And he's got the razor wit to skewer it all. A masterful story-teller with an eye for action and a knack for choosing only the most entertaining scenes, Moffett's book is richly descriptive, murderously zany. He can flush out the rear guard details of the history of the Vietnam conflict but with a sense of humor. Moffett is right up there with Philip Caputo, Stewart O'Nan, and Tim O'Brien. An excellent book by a first-rate writer."

— Mathias B. Freese, author, *i*

"*Fortunate Soldier* abounds in the same inventiveness, benevolence, and love for the asinine and absurd found in the best of Vonnegut and Heller. This book is among the most compelling Vietnam war documentaries ironically because it lacks the blood and guts. Pat relates his tales with laughing-out-loud hilarity. The honesty in this book is compelling. It is a young man who adapts to a world where the rules aren't worth the paper they're written on and so decided to write his own very entertaining book. *Fortunate Soldier* is unique in its poignancy and humor capturing as it does all the people, places and lunacy that are part and parcel of all wars."

— Gary Anderson, Syndicated Columnist

"The politically incorrect Pat Moffett, an utter pragmatist, completely irrepressible and wholly unapologetic has written about a side of Vietnam that most people have no idea about. Here's a guy with no ax to grind who has produced a masterpiece of the genre. Puts to lie General Robert E. Lee's axiom that War seldom avails anything to those unfortunate enough to have to fight it. What a book!"

— Rev. Basil Sharp, author, *The Adventure of Being Human*

"A delightful and wickedly funny book. I thoroughly enjoyed it."

— Lieutenant Colonel Patrick O'Toole, United States Marines (Ret.)

"This is simply a terrific book! Pat Moffett shows us a side of the Vietnam War we rarely gear about: the amusing, often hilarious tales of pranks, parties, unofficial missions and end-runs around rules that were a part of daily life for thousands of soldiers stationed in Vietnam."

— Peter Tirschwell

FORTUNATE SOLDIER

Karen

Pat Moffett

All the Best,

Pat Moffett

Garrison-Savanna Publishing, LLC
New York

Garrison-Savanna Publishing, LLC
15 Cutter Mill Road, Suite 164
Great Neck, NY 11021

website: www.fortunatesoldier.com
email: fortunate@optonline.net

ISBN: 0-9742278-0-3

LCCN: 2003107303

Book design by:
The Floating Gallery:
244 Madison Ave, #254, New York, NY 10016
877-822-2500   www.thefloatinggallery.com

Printed in Canada

This book is dedicated to

ARNOLD P. SARNA

I didn't forget

I would like to thank the following people for their contribution to this book:

Tom Brasfield
Patrick O'Toole
Jeff Reznak
Rich Kitzen
Vinny Calandra
Mike Brunetti
Rick Walsh
Mike Thach
Carl Peters
Charlie Alben

Special thanks to;

Larry Leichman at The Floating Gallery for keeping me focused and on track during this entire process.

Brian Smart, Senior Editor, for bringing a semblance of order to my rambling writing style.

Pat Bengtsson for lending me her artistic talent to create a cover that is a story in itself. I am profoundly grateful.

Contents

Dedication vii

Acknowledgments ix

Time To Go to Nam or The End of Life, As We Know It. 1

April Fools 23

Typographical Error 39

Hello Goodbye 55

Cinderella 73

Dear John 90

House of the Rising Sun 109

Unfair Trade 126

Rank Has Its Privileges 144

Midnight Confessions 161

Saigon Pizza to Go 178

Easy Money? Maybe Not 194

Trip to Vung Tao 212

A Day of Peaks and Valleys 233

Leaving On A Jet Plane...Not So Fast 248

Ticket To Ride 263

Welcome Home 281

TIME TO GO tO NAM
OR THE END OF LIFE,
AS WE KNOWN IT

Ever notice how war can really inconvenience your life? Let me tell you, it's true. It's the middle of October, 1967, and I was a twenty-year-old Brooklyn guy looking for a job in New York City. There's just something not quite right about being young, male, physically fit and modestly handsome…and hearing the same questions asked again and again at every job interview.

"When are you going to get drafted? When are you going to Vietnam?"

This was the era of the Draft, and I was 1A "eligible for military service." Don't ask me how the local draft board managed to leave my name undetected for two years. I wasn't in college, wasn't a conscientious objector, and definitely wasn't physically disqualified. I have to assume it was a bureaucratic blunder, or perhaps Uncle Sam was just holding onto my name for special reasons.

Whatever those reasons were, it was ruining my life. My fiancé Gretchen and I wanted to get married, have a handful of kids, and live the American Dream. Of course, tradition says that you have to have a stable job before taking that next step. Tradition, in this case, is another word for Gretchen. She was quite adamant about that condition.

Yes, the Vietnam War was definitely inconveniencing my life. My girlfriend wouldn't get married until I had a good job, yet no employer would hire me. I was too much of a risk. They could invest thousands of dollars into training me, and then one day I might be whisked away by the draft. Businesses don't like to waste money, and so they screened guys like me with that question. "When are you going?"

I couldn't live in limbo. I had plans for my life, and I wasn't going to let something like a war get in the way. So I did what had to be done…I asked the round middle-aged clerk at the draft board office the same question that the business owners were asking me.

"When am I getting drafted?"

"Well, son," he replied, "there's really no telling. But with that 'Nam thing going on, well. I'd say a year at most."

It was like hearing a doctor diagnose cancer, as if the "'Nam thing" was incurable and I only had a year left before the Grim Reaper announced my number was up.

I couldn't wait a year! There were things to do, money to earn…an entire life to live! This was my life, and I wasn't going to waste another day of it sitting around waiting for someone else to tell me what I was going to do with it. I had plans. Besides, Gretchen wouldn't wait forever.

I got a job as a clerk at a Japanese steamship line for $85 per week. It wasn't much, but it provided Gretchen and me with beer money. That was enough to satisfy my desires, but Gretchen wanted more. She wasn't going to marry me until I found something solid in the way of a job.

So I did what had to be done. I volunteered for my own draft number. The clerk at the draft board was shocked when I signed the papers surrendering two years of my life to the US Army. I'm surprised that he didn't change my draft status to 4F, "not qualified" due to mental disorder. The look on his face said that he seriously thought I was nuts. He gave me instructions on where to be and when. I left him sitting behind the desk still shaking his head like he had water in both ears.

My mother wasn't too happy about it, believe me. My father, well, he simply said that I should walk my own way in life. If it's what I thought was best, then he was behind me.

Gretchen wasn't very pleased at first. It took quite a bit of convincing—involving a great deal of loose garments and squeaky springs—before she came to understand it was for the best. Afterwards, she promised to wait for me. Did I already mention that I'm modestly handsome? It comes in handy sometimes, especially when negotiating the future with your nineteen-year-old fiancé.

My first taste of military life was the Whitehall Examining and Entrance Station in Manhattan, New York. Here I learned the military term, "hurry up and wait." It means to run from one place to another and then wait for your name to be called. This training held me in good stead during my time with the Army. After the usual poking, prodding and the traditional "turn your head and cough," the doctors pronounced me fit for service.

I left New York the next day on a train bound for Fort Jackson, South Carolina. Are you familiar with the joke about the difference between a fairy tale and a war story? A fairy tale begins, "Once upon a time." A war story begins, "No shit, there I was…."

No shit, there I was at Fort Jackson, going through Basic. It was a little ironic that Halloween occurred during the first week of training. We got to wear green uniforms and get our hair shaved. Whatever way you looked at it, that Halloween we could be mistaken as cue balls, pickles or—as the Drill Sergeants were happy to call us—Sad Sack soldiers.

The Drill Sergeants definitely didn't need any costumes. I kept waiting for that week to end, just to see if one of them would remove their mask. You know, show me that there was really a human being under that "rip your head off" disguise of theirs. Sad to say, they never did take off their masks.

After the first week of training, it came time for our first night of guard duty. A two and a half ton truck—commonly called a "deuce and a half"—dropped twenty of us trainees at different spots throughout the base and would pick us up in the morning.

My sentry post was ridiculous. Fort Jackson had an eighteen hole golf course. Somewhere in the middle of it was a refreshment stand that served soft drinks to golfers during the day. My duty was to guard that stand for eight hours during the night. It made no sense.

I took my military training seriously, though, and said to myself, "If someone thinks they're going to steal a batch of lemonade out of this stand, they can forget it 'cause it's not going to happen on my watch!"

That was my original intention. After several hours of walking around, circling the stand, I started to get bored. There was nothing to listen to and—except for constantly moving—there was nothing to keep me awake. The drill sergeants already told us the horror stories of what happened to trainees caught sleeping at their post. I wasn't going to let that happen. It was my goal to be the best soldier who ever graduated Basic Training, and I sure wasn't going to get caught sleeping on the job.

I needed something to keep me awake, though. That's when I remembered the transistor radio that I'd stuffed into my pocket as the drill sergeants harassed us out of the barracks for guard duty. "It won't do any harm," I told the lemonade stand. "Besides, it'll keep me awake, and that's the important thing."

A peddler on Wall Street sold me the radio for five bucks, complete with battery and an ear plug. I turned it on and picked up some southern station that was playing Neil Diamond's song, "Kentucky Woman." I think down south they thought Neil was a "good old boy" farmer turned musician when in fact he was just a nice Jewish boy from Long Island.

I put the strap of my M-14 rifle around my neck so the weapon would fall at my waist just like a guitar. With the music playing in one ear, I strummed away with the song like I was having my own little concert. It was just me and Neil playing to an audience of golf course holes and the lemonade stand.

Now, we were all told that we might get a visit from the sergeant of the guard sometime during the night to make sure we weren't goofing off at our guard post. Ah, but who was going to waste their time coming all the way out to a golf course to check on the refreshment stand?

Bad thought! Little did I know that a Master Sergeant felt like playing Airborne Ranger that night. He crawled about a hundred yards of fairway to throw a surprise attack on my lemonade post. With Neil crooning in my ear, I never heard my attacker coming until he grabbed me around the neck and started choking me with my M-14 strap. He took my radio and stomped it to bits on the ground. Damn! I thought, I'm here a week and I'm in trouble already.

One thing to be said about the Army, it definitely presses home the point of discipline and punishment. The next night, when everyone else was sleeping in the barracks, I was sent to join the ranks of the kitchen police, or "KP," to pay for my little concert on the golf course.

"Alright, Private," said the Mess Sergeant as he led me past a long row of stainless steel pots and pans. "You're the back sink man this morning. Grab a Brillo pad and start cleaning up all of this. Oh, and don't cut yourself...then we'd have to move you somewhere else."

The "back sink man" is a lousy duty. You're stuck cleaning all the pots and pans used to prepare breakfast. KP may sound easy...it's just washing dishes, right? That's true, but when the mess hall cooks for several hundred people, that's a lot of dishes. The cooks don't use kitchen-size pans, either. I started cleaning thirty gallon pots filled with the dry remnants of pancake batter, ten gallon pots of dried grits, and five gallon bowls with raw egg inside.

My hands were raw within minutes. It's odd to realize the batter for the soft pancakes that I'd eaten every morning could dry into sharp needles that burrowed under my short fingernails. It didn't take me long to regret my solo performance by the lemonade stand, but there was no relief in sight.

That's when I remembered the subtle suggestion from the mess sergeant. Some guys might put up with washing dishes, but not a guy from Brooklyn. Give me the knife! Now most people would be squeamish about slicing their hand with a knife, but cuts were nothing to me. I grabbed a handful of utensils and tossed them in the wash water and then ran the sharp edge of a knife across my forefinger.

"Hey Sarge," I yelled. "I cut myself!"

The mess sergeant walked over and inspected the wound. "That didn't take long, Private. Most troops spend an hour or so before figuring it out. Put a band-aid on that and then get back here. You're DRO now."

That didn't sound promising to me. I wondered what the next level of punishment would be as I pulled a bandage from the handy first aid box. Behind me, the mess sergeant was yelling at another soldier. "Hey Private! Get your butt over here, you've just been promoted to back sink man!"

It turns out that DRO meant "Dining Room Orderly." The DRO's spotless white jacket instantly turned me into a fancy waiter.

My job was to stand near the officer and NCO—noncommissioned officer, or Non-Com—tables. Rank has its privileges, and I had to wait on the senior soldiers. They would yell "DRO!" and it was my job to get them whatever they wanted.

Oddly enough, the first guy who yelled "DRO!" was the same Master Sergeant who had destroyed my radio and put me on KP. He recognized my face immediately and barked, "What the hell are you doing here?"

"I'm DRO, Sergeant!"

He glared at me. "I can see that, Private. How did you manage that? You're supposed to be washing dishes!"

I showed him my hand and with a voice full of childlike innocence I replied, "I cut my widdle finger right here, Sergeant."

"You stupid shit, ain't there nothin' you won't do to get out of work?"

"Why yes, Sergeant," I replied with my best customer service smile. "What can I get for you?"

That did it. "You can fucking eat shit and die, troop! Now get the hell away from me before I rip your head off and shit down your throat!"

One thing to be said for sergeants, they definitely have a way with words. Lucky for me, an officer picked that moment to yell "DRO!" I hastened away from the beet-faced Master Sergeant and did my best to keep the grin off my face.

I've learned over the years that basic training is like a good war story…if you've been there, you already know about Drill Sergeants, sleep depravation, inhaling your chow, and twenty-seven hours of PT every day. If you haven't been there, then go talk with your closest recruiter…I'm sure the nice Sergeant there will be very happy to discuss Basic Training with you.

Let's just say that Fort Jackson was my home while I survived eight weeks of Basic Training hell. We finished the tortuous training the week before Christmas, and I was looking forward to spending a few weeks leave with my family.

There were several small details left before the Army would let us put on civvies again. The last few days, we cleaned weapons and turned in equipment. Any free time was spent rehearsing for the graduation ceremony. There was one last thing...each soldier was called to Company Headquarters to receive his orders. There are three types of orders in the Army. The first is a written order, like the one sending me to Fort Jackson. The second is a verbal order, where an officer or a NCO would tell you what to do. The third is the impractical order, one that is physically impossible to carry out. You know, like when the jerk private beside you tells you to go to hell. The Army doesn't require that you obey the third type.

The other two, though...there's no arguing with them. You follow the order. The Army has different levels of hell waiting if you don't obey, depending on how serious the officer or NCO was about the order. If it's minor, you could end up painting rocks with a toothpick. If the Army wants to get your attention, there's always the Article 15...you lose some pay, maybe a stripe, and you still paint rocks with a toothpick. If it was something really serious—like going Absent Without Official Leave (AWOL) all the way up to desertion or murder—then the Army has several vacation spots for you, like the military prison at Fort Leavenworth.

I walked into the Personnel Administration Center and took a chair alongside five other trainees. The unit clerk told us why we were there. Once again, war was getting ready to inconvenience my life. A slip of paper—a written order—was going to tell me what the Army thought I should do for them. It would say where I was going for Advanced Individual Training (AIT). It would also tell me the Military Occupational Specialty (MOS) that best fit my numerous abilities.

The MOS is a code for your job category, and there are tons of these number-letter codes in the Army. Any "Zero" series MOS is nice to have, like 02J—pronounced Zero Two Juliet—the code for Clarinet Player. Anything after the teens is relatively safe, like "Ninety-one Tango" (91T), the MOS for a Horseshoer. Now why the Army needs a horseshoer is beyond me, but it sure sounded like a nice safe Stateside job. I never heard anybody mention Vietnam and horses in the same sentence.

The unit clerk handed over my Military Personnel Records Jacket, commonly called the "201 File." I held it in my hands, afraid to open it. This was another opportunity for someone else to tell me what I was going to do with my life, and I resented that. Inside the brown folder would be copies of my orders telling me what MOS the Army—in its infinite wisdom—assigned to me. My next duty station would be determined by that MOS.

I'm not a devoutly religious man, but I considered prayer at that moment. Of course, it wouldn't do any good. Some clerk in Personnel already determined my fate. Prayer wasn't going to change it. I took a deep breath and opened the file.

The MOS jumped right out at me. It read 11B, or "Eleven Bravo." In their dark military humor, soldiers have an affectionate nickname for that MOS. It's "Eleven Bullet-Stopper," for the guys who stand up and collect bullets from the enemy. Infantry grunts normally get stuck with that detail.

That's right, I was destined to become an infantryman. With Vietnam still making the nightly news, I had little doubt about where I was going. Europe didn't have a great need for inexperienced infantrymen. Vietnam, on the other hand, seemed to have a chronic shortage.

The good news was that my orders granted two weeks holiday leave between Basic and AIT. I used mine productively by flying home. The flight seemed a little strange to me…I kept hearing a crackling in my ear. I didn't smell any smoke so after awhile I forgot about it.

Mom force-fed me with Christmas sweets and massive dinners in a vain effort to replace all the weight I lost. Gretchen satisfied other hungers; after numerous episodes of spring squeaking, she again promised to wait for me.

Leave ended too quickly, as it always does in the military. On the flight back to Fort Jackson, I had an unpleasant surprise. The crackling that I'd heard flying home was the first warning that I had an ear infection. I thought my ear was going to explode during the trip back to Fort Jackson.

The first thing I did after we landed was to visit the base hospital. It wasn't good; the doctor gave a Christmas list of drugs and antibiotics, then stuck me in bed for five days. The only problem is that he didn't notify my unit that I was in the hospital. The drill sergeants thought I'd gone AWOL. They even called my parents, who replied that they'd watched me board the plane to Fort Jackson. Then somebody thought of calling the base hospital.

Luckily there weren't any repercussions from my ear infection. I left the hospital and reported to the training company. The clerk took care of the inprocessing paperwork and then sent me to the barracks.

That's when I discovered several pleasant surprises. The first was that I would be completing AIT with my two friends from Basic, Glenn Queen and Ritchie Quinn.

The second bit of good news was that Glenn drove his car back from his home in Virginia. With wheels available, we wouldn't be stuck on the base. The world—well okay, Columbia, South Carolina—would be our oyster. We just needed to be subtle about it, as you were supposed to have a pass anytime you left post overnight. I'm pretty sure that the unit clerk told us "supposed to," so it wouldn't be breaking any regulation. Right?

The last positive thing was that we were billeted in new quarters. During Basic, we lived in wooden barracks. Rumor had it they were built during World War I, and they definitely looked it. Imagine fifty recruits mashed together in one forty-foot room. Only thing holding the panes in the windows were years of accumulated paint. The cold winter wind blew through thin walls and around gaps in the windows and doors. An old coal furnace on the back wall was the only source of heat. We took turns pulling "furnace duty" all night, keeping it stoked and praying it wouldn't blow up.

As AIT trainees, we rated luxury housing by comparison. Our new barracks were brick buildings with central heating and spacious rooms. We only had to share the room with seven other men. Glenn and Ritchie laid claim to one side of the same room and then saved a bunk for me. Putting us together was trouble just waiting to happen.

The utilitarian room needed something to make it unique, special…to make it home. The three of us discussed various options as I unloaded my duffel bags and transferred things into my footlocker. It needed to be something that matched our lifestyle, benefited the group, and didn't violate Army regulations. The third point was negotiable, of course.

Quinn suggested a record player, but we each enjoyed different types of music. We wrangled and haggled awhile, trying to find something all three could agree on. The answer was very simple, once we thought about it. If there was one thing we had in common, it was drinking. Glenn's car made it possible for us to run by the Class Six store which sold beer. The only thing left was finding someplace to keep it chilled. Leaving it outside in the January cold was not an option. After all, we wanted to be the ones drinking it. The unanimous decision was to buy a small refrigerator from the Post Exchange, or PX.

A Staff Sergeant barged in before we could put our plan into action. In the stern voice of a drill sergeant, he bellowed, "Listen up! There's an orientation briefing tonight at eighteen-hundred. Unpack your shit, then bust ass over to the auditorium across the street. Attendance will be taken, so make sure you're there!"

When you're a Private facing a NCO, there is only one response. All three of us made it in unison. "Yes, Sergeant!"

After being in the military eight weeks, we were old hands at this stuff. We assumed it was the usual Army hype on training. Barely curious, the three of us sauntered in fifteen minutes early, discussing where our next assignment might be. The rest of the 250-man class was milling around, doing much the same thing as they waited for the briefing to get underway.

The rumor mill had it that not everyone in AIT would go to Vietnam. That made sense to the others. There was a need for infantry soldiers in other parts of the world as well. We could go to Germany to keep the Soviets from attacking down the Fulda Gap. Korea was still a hotspot, with Kim Il Sung threatening daily to unite the two Koreas. However, I didn't buy into that idea.

"Hey, listen!" I argued. "I don't think the US Army sends two hundred men into advanced training to go anywhere but Vietnam."

"That's not what I heard," countered Ritchie. "The vast majority may go to 'Nam, but I've been told that thirty percent are assigned to other countries."

A trainee sitting in front of us interrupted our discussion. "I know someone from the last cycle here at Jackson who told me ten guys went to Korea, ten to Germany, and believe it or not, five to Hawaii."

That's how fairytales begin in the army. "I knew a guy who knew a guy who heard that"...might as well start it off the right way, with "once upon a time." I wasn't buying it, but it offered some pleasant possibilities to my compatriots.

"Wow!" Ritchie was stunned. "Can you imagine the three of us stationed in Honolulu?"

"Yeah," added Glenn. "Coconut drinks, hula girls, sex on the beach. It'll be great."

My counter-argument was drowned out by someone yelling, "ATTENSHUN!"

Two hundred and fifty pairs of heels locked together in unison. We stood in the silent position of attention, heels locked and eyes forward as an officer made his way to the podium.

"Good evening, men!" he said.

Two hundred and fifty voices responded in one chorus. "Good evening, sir!"

"My name is Captain Blakenship. I am your senior training officer during your stay here at Fort Jackson. You'll hear more from me as the days go on, but right now I would like to introduce you to the Battalion Commander, Major Westwood. He would like to say a few words. Major." He nodded and moved away from the podium.

"At ease, men. Take a seat!" the Major began.

That was a verbal order. We complied automatically, according to the training grilled into us during Basic. There were no side conversations, no goofing around. Two hundred and fifty men sat down quickly and quietly.

At nearly six and a half feet tall, Major Westwood was an impressive figure in full dress greens. He had lots of fruit salad—decorations and awards—on his chest and a combat patch on his right sleeve.

"You are now going to see a film which is exactly eight minutes in length," he explained. "It will give you some important inspiration for your training over the next nine weeks. I suggest you pay close attention. After the film, I will be available to answer any questions. Roll the film, Sergeant."

The auditorium lights faded until we sat in complete black. Somewhere behind us, a buck sergeant at the projector hit a switch.

The typical Department of Defense emblem appeared on the cinema-sized screen before us.

"Told you," Ritchie whispered. "Just another stupid training film."

He was wrong. The film had no sound. That would've only made it worse. Everyone in the auditorium pushed back into their chairs as we were flung into the middle of the Vietnam war.

In stark black and white, we watched soldiers in the middle of a firefight. The film kept nothing hidden. The screen was filled with blood and dying. Medics rushed forward to patch up severely wounded men. The battle ended and the MEDEVAC helicopters came in. Some GIs were loaded onto stretches and carried to the choppers. Others were zipped into body bags while a chaplain gave them last rites.

This was the real thing. It was the longest eight minutes any of us had ever endured. It went on and on, until we could scarcely bear to look at the screen.

Mercifully, it finally ended. As the house lights came up, no one moved a muscle. The silence was so intense I could hear my heart beat. The film reached a deep place in each of us.

Major Westwood resumed his post at the podium. He stood in silence for a moment as his eyes roamed over us. Several men jumped as his voice cracked through the still air like a whip. "Gentlemen!"

Every one of us sat straight in our seat.

"I hope you were paying attention to that film." The battalion commander paused for effect, then continued. "Because ALL of you are going to Vietnam. If you don't want to end up in a body bag, I suggest you concentrate on your training for the next nine weeks. Any questions?!"

There was nothing left to question.

"Very well," he acknowledged. "DIS-MISSED!"

The troops that walked out the auditorium on that bleak January evening were a somber bunch indeed. We knew our future was cast in stone. There was no turning back. We were going to Vietnam.

I felt as sullen as everyone else did, but it is my nature to try and put some levity into any experience. The drill sergeants in Basic accused me of being a wise-guy. That wasn't it at all. I just believe that humor can get you through even the darkest situation.

Catching up with Queen and Quinn, I quipped, "Well, boys! I guess this puts a damper on our Hawaii plans, don't you think?"

They didn't even look at me, let alone speak. The pessimists had won this round.

There was only one thing to do after that…we bought our refrigerator and kept it well stocked. It was against the Training Battalion's regulations but we didn't care.

Neither did our platoon sergeant, who always popped a top with us whenever he came by inspecting the billets. He served his tour in Vietnam already and figured we should enjoy our time in "The World," as he called it. His stories, always told after we handed him a second beer, let us know what we could expect.

Glenn, Ritchie and I threw ourselves wholeheartedly into the training. It was tough. After the Tet Offensive occurred later that month, it became even tougher. The goal of survival was vivid in our minds. We worked conscientiously to learn everything we could to achieve that goal.

The three of us started using our free weekends to hit the bars in Columbia. The last week of February, we learned that there was no "supposed to" when it came to having passes to leave post. We rolled in late Sunday night to find Captain Blakenship waiting for us outside the barracks.

He chewed on us for ten minutes, tossing out suggestions about Article 15s and rock painting. Then he got the wickedest grin on his face. "Tell you what, boys. I have a better idea. Your platoon sergeant says you're the best of the bunch, so I'm going to put you to work."

"Yes, sir!" was our reply. Funny how officers always seem to calm down when you toss a lot of those replies their direction.

"I need some volunteers for the seventy-two hour problem. They're going to get up at oh-dark early to ambush the officer's class." His eyes watched our reaction carefully to see if we would object. We didn't; we knew better. He nodded once, then continued. "Thanks for volunteering. You guys are going to give up your time off next Sunday, and you're going to give me a hand."

There's a ritualistic pattern to conversations like this. We responded, "Yes, sir!"

"The three of you will ambush their patrol. Your sergeant will get with you later about the details. Now get your asses inside and get to bed!"

It really is too easy to make an officer happy. You just have to know what to say. Of course, we told him what he wanted to hear. "Yes, sir!"

The following Sunday at four in the morning, the three of us were in the field, ready to ambush a bunch of officers. March in South Carolina isn't the warmest month to be laying on cold ground, believe me. Especially not when you're dressed in the uniform of a Vietnamese soldier. Black pajamas and a conical straw hat just aren't thick enough to keep you warm.

Add the fact that we returned from another night in Columbia just a few hours earlier, and you have the recipe for disaster. Hung over, freezing, without any sleep over the previous twenty-four hours, and waiting for a squad of soldiers who were supposed to appear sometime before dawn…we did exactly what one would expect. We fell asleep.

My first warning was the rifle butt that slammed through my straw hat and glanced off the top of my head. A cold of a different type raced through me as a voice whispered into my ear, "Son, you're dead."

I rolled over and looked at the silhouette kneeling beside me. The Major grinned and held one finger up to his lips. Seconds later I heard two more grunts nearby, and then a loud voice. "That's all of them, sir."

I could tell by their wide eyes and shocked faces that Glenn and Ritchie felt the same way I did. It didn't really matter to us that Captain Blakenship would go ballistic when he found out we'd fallen asleep. What terrified me was the fact that a squad of men managed to sneak up on us. If it had been for real, then I'd be really dead.

The Major smoothed things over for us with the Captain by complimenting him on an excellent "search and destroy" mission. He applauded us on our site selection, use of available ground cover for camouflage, and dispersal. It helped that the Major was a combat vet who laced his compliments with lessons about Vietnam. Captain Blakenship accepted the praise, as if what occurred was just part of his plan. The remaining squad of officers dispersed, leaving the Major to give the three of us some advice.

"You did good, thinking like the enemy, boys. Just one thing to remember," he said, smiling. "VC don't snore."

That was the highlight of AIT. The past five months—eight weeks of basic training and nine weeks of advanced infantry training (AIT)—were grueling. I often felt like I was outside my own body, watching it all happen to somebody else. I don't know how many times I awoke from deep sleep thinking about the bad dream I just had, only to realize it was real and the nightmare was only beginning.

Glenn, Ritchie and I went to Company Headquarters together to receive our orders. No surprise, they read "Vietnam." The orders granted us leave, and then told us to report to Fort Lewis, Washington. All three of us were flying out on the same plane.

We went our separate ways for leave, enjoying the time to kiss parents and girlfriends and say goodbye to friends. It was a strange feeling. I walked familiar streets in civilian clothes, waved at people I'd known for years. Yet the entire time, there was a nagging thought in the back of my mind that it wasn't real. It felt temporary, like the calm before the storm.

One little fact kept dispelling my illusion that everything was normal. I was an infantry grunt who was leaving for Vietnam. The nightly news showed me glimpses of what I was in for...nothing like the eight-minute Army film, but vivid enough to worry me.

I was young, male, physically fit and modestly handsome. I wasn't going to let my fears worry my family, and definitely not Gretchen. It was a lonely thing to do, but I kept it all bottled up inside. On the outside, I was having a wonderful time—Gretchen made no complaints, believe me—but it was all a façade. I was terrified.

The fears remained with me during the flight to Fort Lewis. I reported in to the reception station, received instructions, and lugged my duffel bag to the barracks. I claimed my bunk and waited for Quinn and Queen to arrive.

Now I was among a couple hundred GIs at Fort Lewis, just outside Tacoma, Washington. We jumped through the "hurry up and wait" drill, processing through one station of bored civilians or soldiers after another. It was well organized, with only a few snafus, as the Army readied us for embarkation to Southeast Asia. The bored looks on the clerks' faces said it all. I wasn't a person to them...I was just another one of the many "fortunate" souls going to Vietnam.

During our two days at Fort Lewis, we were confined to base. The Army wouldn't let guys like Queen, Quinn and me off-post for a night in Tacoma. We were accustomed to a few cold beers before hitting the sack. It wasn't fair.

Even worse, at first I thought it was insulting. The guys who were going to bug out had already gone AWOL by missing their flight to Fort Lewis. Then I found myself constantly glancing up at the clock on the wall. As the minute hand clicked closer to the departure time, it seemed that something squeezed tighter around my heart.

The brass must've thought that if they let us off-post for a few beers, they'd never see us again. After awhile, I had to admit that they were probably right. There's just something about sitting there waiting, watching the time slowly creep forward. It's the not knowing that gets to you...the unknowns about the final destination, whether that brunette nurse is the last American woman you'll ever see, or if someone like that chaplain will be speaking the last words you'll ever hear as everything fades to black.

I felt like a condemned man heading for the electric chair, not knowing if the Governor would call with a last-minute pardon. In all my years of life, I've never been that scared before or since. Waiting there—not knowing what my future held—taught me a valuable lesson. It isn't being immune to fear that makes a man brave...no, true courage is being able to continue on when you're really too terrified to move.

We had just one night left on American soil before heading out, and we occupied our time with card games and jokes. It was all false bravado to disguise what everyone was thinking and feeling, but it worked. In that room full of strangers, we had one thing in common. Fear. We faced it as a group and kept it at bay with raunchy jokes and laughter.

With the exception of Glenn and Ritchie, I can't remember the names of any of those men now. That night, though, they were the closest thing to brothers I've ever had. We shared everything together, made promises we knew wouldn't be kept, and laughed until our sides ached. Nobody lost it, and not a one of us followed our instincts to run far away from the army base.

Lights out was at 2200 hours. Tomorrow was the big day...on to 'Nam. I knew I'd better get some sleep, but in the darkness it was impossible. I could hear the low hum of the fan at the end of the barracks and the restless rustle of my companions around me. My pulse pounded heavy in my head as the fear arrived to claim me once again.

It's strange, sometimes, how the mind works. All of my questions about why and how and what...my subconscious answered them with music. It surprised me, but it really shouldn't have. That's how I always relaxed, headphones on and music cranked so loud I could barely hear myself think.

The Byrds song playing in my mind was already outdated; they released it in 1965. Yet the simple rhythm and words gave a strange sense of comfort as I laid there in the dark.

> To Everything (Turn, Turn, Turn)
> There is a season (Turn, Turn, Turn)
> And a time for every purpose, under Heaven
>
> A time to be born, a time to die
> A time to plant, a time to reap
> A time to kill, a time to heal
> A time to laugh, a time to weep

I barely closed my eyes when the harsh bawl of a drill sergeant assaulted my ears. "Okay! Everybody up. It's time to go to 'Nam!"

With one eye open, I unhappily looked in his direction. Sure enough, it seemed a small sadistic grin flitted across his face. He actually enjoyed waking us up and sending us off to this miserable war. I checked my watch. It was not quite 0100 hours. That's one o'clock in the morning for civilians and Reservists.

"Get dressed and make it fast!" the sergeant roared. "I want every swinging dick outside in twenty minutes!"

Drill sergeants had such a way with words. Then he continued, fracturing the Spanish language. "And for you Spanish boys, arndelay, arndelay! No monyarna!"

We scurried like rats to get ourselves together. Just once, I would like to be an observer during a barracks wake-up call instead of a participant. Anyone watching through the windows would think it was as slapstick and hilarious as a Jerry Lewis movie. Guys in their underwear danced on the cold bare floor as the sergeant kept up the verbal abuse.

"Move it, move it, move it!" he ranted. "Jody is already makin' it with your girlfriend, so no point in thinkin' about "home now."

In my five months in the army, I still hadn't figured that one out. Who the hell is this Jody guy, anyway? The drill sergeants credited him with everything. The cadence songs were called Jodies. If you believed them, this character was the best at everything. "Ain't no use in going home," one song went, "Jody's got your girl and gone. Ain't no use in looking back, Jody's got your Cadillac." See what I mean?

It had to be a Southern thing. If you wanted to make a point with a guy like me from Brooklyn, you'd use names like Tony, Vinny, or Nicky. But Jody? I don't think so. In fact, any guy named Jody in our neighborhood would have to change his name or move. There were knuckle sandwiches aplenty for any pansy named Jody who showed up in our turf.

But I was far away from my neighborhood. Chances were, I wouldn't see my old stomping grounds for a very long time— maybe never. In the last twenty-one weeks, my life had been altered forever. I was an army grunt now, and Jody was out there courting my Gretchen. Not much I could do about it, either.

In the face of the sergeant's insistent heckling, we tripped over each other as we grabbed our gear and rushed down the steps. We quickly formed up in ranks as he stomped to his position in front of the formation.

"All right, at ease!" he said. "The buses hauling your sorry asses to the airport are running a half hour late. So stay in position 'til they get here."

Just like the army, I thought. Another "hurry up and wait" drill. On the other hand, none of us were truly in a hurry to get to 'Nam. We formed a cluster near our duffel bags, smoking and joking while we waited for the buses. When they passed the thirty-minute deadline, we started hoping that they wouldn't show at all.

Regrettably, the buses did eventually arrive. We boarded and made our way through the pre-dawn hours to the Seattle-Tacoma International Airport. The buses didn't head toward the well-lighted terminal. Instead, they rolled past and headed to the dark end of a deserted runway.

We peered through a fine mist of early morning fog. There in the darkness, barely discernible, was the outline of an airplane. The buses rolled up to the ramp, and once again the sergeant began bellowing. "Alright, listen up! I need volunteers for baggage detail...you, you and you! The rest of you, drop your duffels on the white line and get your butts on the plane!"

We trudged up the stairs of the Northwest Orient 747 by flashlight. It truly felt as if we were sneaking out of the country and didn't want anyone to catch us.

Once we were airborne, with eight and a half hours of flying time to Japan, I settled into my seat and actually dozed off a couple of times. My thoughts were disoriented and jumbled each time I awoke. I suffered from a hope similar to the death row inmate...like I expected the President to call and say it was okay, the plane could turn around and head back home now. I was in complete denial regarding my ultimate destination.

We were bound for a layover at Yokota Air Base in Japan but—like our minds—it was fogged in. We were diverted to Haneda Airport near downtown Tokyo. As the plane taxied to the gate, the pilot apologized for more bad news. The flight crew taking us the rest of the way to Vietnam would be three hours late. The good news...we would be allowed to wait in the terminal.

My mind created a wonderful vision. We arrived in the middle of the night, so naturally the terminal would be almost vacant. Low lighting and a plush lounge were ready for us. A courteous bartender waited behind the open bar. After several drinks, I would plop onto one of the numerous couches and stretch my legs. Perhaps I would even prop my boots on a table. Then I would settle down for a really comfortable snooze.

The trip commander, Colonel Bowers, stripped away my enticing vision. He stared at us without an ounce of compassion and outlined the conditions under which we could occupy the terminal. "All right, you grunts! On my left you'll see a large roped-in area with a marble floor. Get behind that rope and stay there until our flight is announced over the PA system. The only time you can leave the area is to use the latrine."

He watched as we walked in sullen silence to the designated area, feeling like rounded-up cattle. No plush lounge seating here, not even a folding chair. Tentatively I raised my hand and ventured a question.

"Excuse me, sir. Why do we have to be confined to a small space in such a large terminal?"

The colonel's answer didn't offer any comfort, though his tone was a bit less strident. "Son, the Japanese government is neutral when it comes to Vietnam. They just don't want you roaming around their airport."

I wondered about that. Where is it written that, for a country to maintain neutrality, American GIs had to be hidden out of sight? Why were we only allowed to refuel the plane, take a piss, and not sit on the furniture? Was Switzerland like this in World War II? But I kept those thoughts to myself.

After about half an hour of standing around in our cattle pen and feeling our muscles grow stiff, Queen and Quinn and I asked permission to use the latrine. The Master Sergeant in charge agreed with a gruff, "Go ahead. But be back here in ten minutes!"

The men's room was about fifty yards from our enclosure. We took our time covering the distance and doing our business. It wasn't until we ambled back that trouble tapped on our shoulders.

We noticed an enticing stairway nearby that led down and out of the watchful Master Sergeant's line of sight. There was no need for any words…we simply looked at each other and nodded. The

Master Sergeant was conveniently looking the other way. Like escaping convicts, we quickly slipped down the stairs.

Aha! This was more like it—an expansive waiting area with soft couches and comfy chairs. There were no passengers, just a cleaning man with a mop and pail. As we sank into the cushioned comfort of the long couches, an announcement sounded over the PA system. It didn't matter that it was in Japanese. We knew the PA worked and we would be able to hear our flight when it was called.

"Perfect!" I exclaimed to my buddies. "Now, let's get some sleep."

It seemed that I barely closed my eyes when I felt someone jostling me. I cracked open one eyelid, ready to give an impractical order to Glenn or Ritchie. I outranked them, having been promoted to Private First Class on finishing AIT. To my amazement, it was the Japanese cleaning man.

"GI!" he cried urgently. "Your plane! Your plane!"

He pointed to the window. Fully awake now, I stared in disbelief. Sure enough, there was our plane, taxiing out to the runway for take-off.

Oh my God, I thought. We're really in big trouble now. I quickly shook Queen and Quinn awake and told them the news.

"What's the punishment for missing movement?" asked Glenn as he lunged to his feet.

"It's either execution or twenty-five years in Leavenworth," I replied, not sure which and not eager for either sentence.

Our Japanese friend perceived our dilemma. His reaction restored my faith in how a neutral country should act. "GI, I help! I help!"

What could he do, I wondered…a mop and pail jockey inside the terminal? But his help was our only option. We were rapidly being left behind.

The wizened little Japanese man motioned for us to follow him. We soon found ourselves on the tarmac in an area where planes pull into the gate. He summoned a coworker with a two-way radio and they conversed quickly in Japanese. The second helper disappeared for a moment, then reappeared driving one of those clunky trucks with a portable stairway attached.

"Climb, climb," he urged while indicating with hurried hand motions that we should line up on the stairs.

I ran to the top as Queen and Quinn jumped aboard behind me. The helpful Japanese worker hopped behind the wheel and raced that clunky stair truck across the field faster than any of us would have guessed it could move. He talked frantically into his radio as he drove with one hand.

I hung on for dear life, silently asking myself how this crazy chase could accomplish our goal. We neared the idling plane. It sat on the main runway, ready for takeoff. I allowed myself to hope.

We' drew within a hundred yards when the 747's giant engines roared into life, signaling imminent take-off. The plane began moving. Without us!

"Oh, man," I whispered to myself, "we're cooked."

But just as suddenly, the engine noise dropped to a whistle and the plane's forward progress ceased. What now, I wondered.

I shouldn't have doubted our Japanese genies. Like something out of a dream, the door of the plane opened. A flight attendant guided the stairs into place. Our Japanese friends had done it!

We used all kinds of hand motions to offer thanks—many thanks—and goodbye to our "neutral" Japanese friends. After exchanging relieved grins, we strolled nonchalantly onto the plane as if we did it every day.

We headed up the aisle toward three empty seats and then our panache diminished quickly. Colonel Bowers stood with arms crossed and legs planted firmly across the aisle. He glared at us with fire in his eyes.

"I gotta good mind to bust the three of you and throw you in the stockade soon as we arrive in 'Nam," he growled. "But you know what? Dummies like you usually get shot up by Charlie anyway and never make it back alive. So I'm gonna leave you to your own destinies. Now go sit down, and don't move for the rest of the trip!"

We hunkered down meekly in our seats. It was a strain for us—trouble kept tapping us on the shoulder, egging us on—but we behaved ourselves for the rest of the flight. Our destination promised a bounty of trouble. We could wait. The biggest adventure in our young lives was about to unfold.

APRIL FOOLS

Seattle to Vietnam is a long haul. When your bird is a military charter and your destination a war zone, there's nothing fun about that trip. At first we GIs talked in subdued voices. It was small talk, mostly…wondering where we were going to wind up, how our families and friends were handling it, and how things would be when—we skipped the "if" part—we came back. Eventually, the talk drifted off. By twenty-two hours into the trip, most of us—me included—were sleeping soundly.

We were jarred awake by sudden turbulence. I sat up and stifled a yawn, then rubbed my eyes. I peered out the window, looking for the cause of the disturbance. It didn't take long for the entire plane full of GIs to rouse as we saw our first sign of war. Cruising right next to us was the streamlined form of a U.S. Air Force F-4 Phantom jet fighter.

Our pilot confirmed our suspicions. "Gentlemen, the plane you see outside is our escort to Cam Ranh Bay. We will be landing in approximately forty-five minutes." There was a slight chuckle in his voice as he continued, "For your information, the weather in Vietnam is sunny and ninety-five degrees with scattered ground fire."

Easy for him to joke. He wasn't staying for a year.

About thirty minutes later, the plane banked and began its descent. I looked across the soldiers beside me and through the small porthole-like window. Below us was Cam Ranh Bay, a deep-water port used by the U.S. and Vietnamese navies. It was my first sight of Vietnam.

Cam Ranh Bay was the logistics center of Vietnam. The buildings and docks that I could see through the window were new…the United States had built the majority of infrastructure, changing Cam Ranh from a jungle town into a small city. All branches of service had bases near the bay. We were landing at the Air Force base, where we would be loaded onto buses and taken to the nearby Army base for in-processing.

The landing was so normal and uneventful that it was somehow frightening. No missiles or tracers reached up from the ground, no waves of Viet Cong rushed across the tarmac. There was just the squeal of tires and the roar of the engines. The plane taxied toward several large metal Quonset huts, and then the engines fell silent. The only sound was the whisper of air conditioning from the overhead vents.

There's a funny thing about cushioned seats on airplanes...the cushion seems to disappear sometime around four hours into the flight. After twenty-four hours in transit, it's like sitting on a church pew during a day-long sermon. I rubbed my rear as I stepped into the aisle, trying to get circulation back into my cheeks.

I was the first grunt in line to get off that plane. The stewardess barely had the door opened before I stepped onto the portable stairway waiting outside. That's when reality set in. There was movement at the bottom of the stairs. A Vietnamese guy in black pajamas and a straw hat was half hidden behind the stairwell, making curious sweeping motions.

My heart pounded in panic as my hand closed around the warm stairway railing. I was thinking that I would rather be groping for a gun. According to our training back in boot camp, you should prepare to fight whenever you see that outfit. That's how Viet Cong guerrillas dress. In fact, I'd worn a matching outfit when I was assigned the role of "enemy" during exercises at Fort Jackson.

As I stood riveted to the spot, a captain stepped up behind me. He must've noticed my alarm because he put his arm around my shoulder and said, "Don't worry, son. Not everyone wearing those clothes is a VC...just the ones carrying weapons. Brooms don't qualify."

I felt like such a cherry.

Hoping nobody else had noticed my little rookie incident, I managed to move myself down the steps. I didn't even look at the Vietnamese man as I walked past, and I hoped he wasn't looking at my beet-red face. He said something that sounded like "dzhow ong GI!" I simply nodded and ignored the greeting as I walked past.

A sergeant stood at the edge of the flight line. I didn't really pay any attention to what he said. I just followed the direction of his pointing finger and walked the fifty feet to the line of buses going to the clearance center. After a deep breath that helped remove embarrassment and tension, I turned to watch the other recruits disembark.

Chuck Dressel, one of the guys I met on the plane, reached the bottom of the stairs. He retrieved his Kodak Instamatic camera from his carry-on bag and quickly snapped a picture of the Vietnamese man with the broom.

When the sweeper realized Chuck was taking his picture, he went berserk. He began hitting Chuck with his broom as he chased Chuck across the tarmac. The man was swinging his broom so wildly he rarely made contact with the fast-moving GI. In rapid order, two military police—MPs—joined the chase, lending a Marx Brothers air to the scene. Within half a minute, the MPs grabbed the Vietnamese sweeper and hauled him away. Catching his breath, but none the worse for wear, Chuck joined me in line.

"What the hell was all that about?" I asked.

"He didn't want his picture taken," Chuck explained. "The MPs said it was some kind of Buddhist belief. They think the camera steals their souls and they'll go straight to hell."

"If that's all it takes, we should just let the Air Force snap photos of everyone!" joked one of the nearby privates.

We had a good laugh about the affair, and then laughed about another incident. Quite a few soldiers had jumped onto the buses, hoping to claim one of the prize seats near the front. The Air Force sergeant in charge had different ideas. He boarded each bus and pleasantly informed every soldier he saw that they were now part of the baggage detail. Standing outside the buses watching Chuck and the sweeper turned out to be a good thing as we watched the baggage detail offload our luggage of hundred-pound duffel bags.

After all of the bags were "dress right, dress"—in straight rows and columns—each of us found our duffel and loaded onto the buses. I had just settled into my seat with the duffel in my lap when the Air Force sergeant sprang up the bus steps.

"All right, listen up! There's been a mistake, and you guys need to get back on the plane. You're needed in Germany!"

The look on his face was deadly serious, and so was the roar of approval from the soldiers surrounding me. That's when I saw the grin slowly appear on the NCO's face.

"April Fools, guys! Welcome to Vietnam!" The sergeant jumped out of the bus and motioned for the driver to follow the line of moving buses.

It's probably a good thing that he left so quickly. If he hadn't, I'm sure that long afterwards—perhaps during some thoughtful moment in Leavenworth prison—all of us on that bus would've realized that he was only joking. At that moment, though, we were all ready to rip him into tiny little pieces.

Instead, we were saved by the bus driver. He closed the door quickly and pressed the gas pedal to the floor. The guys who were fast enough to actually stand up soon found themselves sitting back in their seats. There was quite a bit of grumbling at first, but it gradually changed to laughter. We finally had to admit…it really was a good April Fools joke.

The bus ride to the U.S. Army Processing Center was our first introduction to this country we'd come to defend. It didn't look so bad. The first bunch of GIs we saw didn't seem concerned about fighting. They were hanging out at a roadside stand near a beautiful beach, sipping on straws sunk into coconut shells and talking with very attractive Vietnamese girls. Hmmm.

The guy sitting next to me followed my gaze and took the words right out of my mouth. "Maybe this war stuff won't be so bad after all."

But the rational side of my brain knew this would be the exception rather than the rule. It was just like the excitement in AIT when Queen and Quinn had dreamed about being stationed in Hawaii. The beautiful beach with its raven-haired women and coconut drinks was just an illusion. Unless I lucked out in a major way, I knew this tour of duty was going to get a lot worse.

We arrived at the processing center and offloaded our bags. There were no screaming sergeants waiting to tell us what to do and where to go. Instead, it was almost quiet and passive.

"Find a bunk and secure your gear in one of those barracks," a Specialist told us in a bored, monotonous tone. He pointed toward several three-story buildings, then pointed in another direction. "That's the supply room where you'll get your linens and pillow. It closes in thirty minutes. Chow is between seventeen hundred and eighteen thirty over there."

The soldier—a Specialist Fifth Class, commonly called a "Spec Five"—continued pointing toward different buildings and explaining what was where. When he was finished, he turned and walked away.

We all looked at each other. If you want to panic a group of soldiers, all you have to do is talk in a bored, monotone manner as if you have all the time in the world. That's not the way that the Army works. Not yelling at soldiers is abnormal, and not giving specific instructions and a deadline is cruel and unusual punishment. Soldiers aren't used to it. It's frightening.

A Staff Sergeant stepped forward and saved us from our confusion. In his drill sergeant voice, he barked, "All right, you heard the man! Grab your junk and get into those barracks! Move it, people. We ain't got all day!"

That was a routine that everyone understood...we were supposed to hurry up and wait! There was a flurry of activity as soldiers grabbed their duffels and carried them quickly into the buildings. Each of us found a bunk, threw our gear into the wall lockers between the beds, ran to the supply room to grab our linen, and then waited for our next instructions. When it became obvious that we were in for a long wait, several of the guys dug out their cards.

We spent two days at the processing center, filling out forms and getting squared away with our jungle gear. The unit running the in-processing center didn't seem to have a great sense of urgency. They quietly and efficiently went about doing their job. I guess cataloging and inspecting over four hundred soldiers in two days was routine for them. That was fine with me. Every day spent filling out paperwork was one less that I'd spend walking in the bush looking for the enemy.

Some things in army life do not change, regardless of where you are stationed. One of those is the latrine. In the real world, we would call the latrine a "bathroom." Whether it's Vietnam, Germany, or

Fort Jackson, you will find the same utilitarian style of latrine construction on every army post.

There are long metal tubs on the outside walls; these are used as urinals. A waist-high wall normally runs through the center of the room, and on either side of this wall are rows of thirty or more bowl toilets. Unlike civilian bathrooms, the military latrine doesn't have stalls or partitions separating the toilets.

Privacy is not a word in the Army vocabulary, as I discovered during Basic training the first time I used the latrine. It can be a little disconcerting at first…to sit down on a toilet to do your thing and have the guy beside you ask the guy beside him to pass the sports section of his newspaper. After awhile, though, you get used to it. Just like the open showers—which have are no partitions between the showerheads either—it's just part of Army life.

I was one of the first to finish the paperwork drill the first day, and I was enjoying my free time with a little light reading. It was a unique moment of privacy…just me, my newspaper, and an empty latrine.

The swish of a broom didn't bother me at first. I figured it was some private on detail, cleaning the latrine. It was normal, and the soldier would be done in a few moments. I flipped the page of the newspaper and continued reading.

That's when I felt the broom brush against the inside of my legs. I lifted my legs as was customary so the poor private could clean around the toilet. There was quite a bit of thumping and swishing as the broom scraped against the bowl. After a few moments, my legs were getting tired of being held in the air.

"Are you about done?" I asked from behind the privacy of my paper.

The swishing stopped, so I put my feet down again. Then I felt hard bristles rub against my legs once more. I shifted the paper and leaned forward, looking down to see what the problem was. A small piece of toilet paper was stuck on the base of the toilet.

"Listen," I said, slowly closing the paper and folding it in half. "Just leave it and I'll get it later."

I raised my head, intending to glare fiercely at the young private. The glare never appeared, though. Instead, I was mortified as I looked into the eyes of an elderly Vietnamese woman.

"What in the…?!!" I yelled so loud that anyone in the barracks could hear me. "What in the hell is a woman doing in the men's bathroom?!"

Nobody came to my rescue. Instead, the Vietnamese woman simply continued swiping at the piece of toilet paper between my legs. I covered myself with the newspaper and did the strangest sort of dance—jumping on one leg, then the other as I tried to move out of the woman's way.

She finally nabbed the toilet paper with her broom, pinning it securely to the floor and then sweeping it out from under my dancing feet. The elderly woman then bowed slightly before turning her back on me. She continued sweeping the latrine floor as I slowly sat back down on the toilet. I didn't move the newspaper out of my lap until several minutes after she had swept her way out of the latrine and down the hall.

I told Chuck Dressel later that evening about the attack of the cleaning woman and her broom. After the camera incident at the airport when he evaded the maniac sweeper, we both had to laugh. He said it must be a conspiracy by the North Vietnamese.

"Yeah, they call it Operation Clean Sweep!" I replied.

So far, I had been in-country for two days and I already knew this was going to be a strange war. I remembered the captain's warning at the airport—that we only needed to worry about guys in black pajamas with guns, not brooms—seemed funny now. The only action I'd seen so far had been from Vietnamese with brooms!

The next day was full of medical briefings about malaria and sexually transmitted diseases. The medics gave us several days worth of Dapsone tablets to combat the first, and offered condoms to prevent the second.

Finally, the moment we were all dreading arrived. We were summoned as a group to learn our individual destinations…what unit we would be assigned to during our tour in Vietnam.

An overweight Master Sergeant waddled into the briefing room and stepped behind the podium. "Men! Atten-shun!"

The fact that his hips were wider than the podium caused a few snickers. That this overweight excuse for a noncommissioned officer wanted us to stand up for him raised a few eyebrows. We took our time standing, and most of us assumed the position of "Rest." That's where you can talk and move around…you just couldn't move your right foot.

"Before we reads your division assignments, I wants to remind youse of one things." The Master Sergeant seemed oblivious to our disrespectful attitude. "While youse are in this country, youse are the guests of the Vietnamese people. Make sure youse acts like it."

"What a loser," muttered one of the soldiers near me.

"Yeah, the pride of the R.A.," commented another.

There was a definite barrier between R.A.—Regular Army—soldiers and us draftees. Regular Army soldiers volunteered to serve in the Army. They signed up for four years instead of the draftee's mandatory two-year term, and many of them re-enlisted to make a career of it. That meant they received the prized positions far away from Vietnam…leaving us draftees to fill the vacancies in the war-torn country.

I didn't say anything. After all, I had technically volunteered to join the Army. I wasn't interested in giving up four years of my life, though. Gretchen would never wait for me that long, and being R.A. wasn't a guarantee that I wouldn't be shipped off to Vietnam anyway.

Instead, I kept my thoughts to myself. Okay, I mentally said to the Master Sergeant. I get your drift. But "guests?" Invited to a war? I never received an engraved invitation, that's for sure. And where was he when they taught the difference between singular and plural back in grammar school?

A more fit looking sergeant with a clipboard made his way to the podium. He didn't say a word, just glared at the room full of soldiers. That was enough to motivate everyone into assuming the position of attention.

I remembered my father telling me, "If you ever want to look important in the Army, just walk around with a clipboard." Now I understood what he meant. This guy actually was important, at least for us. That clipboard held our names and unit assignments…our destinations in Vietnam.

He barked out the first name, "MOFFETT!"

Me! I stood straighter and replied, "Yes, Sergeant!"

"101st Airborne Division!"

What? How could that be? I started waving my arm to get his attention. He looked at me with one of those "what the hell is it now, Private" looks on his face.

"Hey, Sarge!" I shouted. "There must be some mistake. I'm no paratrooper. How can I be going to an airborne unit?"

The sergeant glared down at me. "Don't worry, boy. The old One-Oh-One will take good care of you."

"So," I mumbled quietly, "they're going to teach me how to pull the ripcord, then kick me out of a plane?"

Apparently I wasn't quiet enough because the sergeant answered my question. "No, son, they won't waste time teaching a leg to jump. They'll just push you out the door!"

I wasn't certain, but I had the feeling that I had just been insulted. "Leg?"

"I don't see no jump wings on your chest. That makes you a leg, not AIRBORNE!" The sergeant's glare was becoming a little wild and crazy at that point. It suddenly disappeared as he smiled. "You should be grateful to be with the 101st."

"Yeah," whispered a guy near me. "But you don't get the extra fifty dollars a month jump pay like all the other Airborne troops. You're just a leg."

There's an old axiom in the Army that you should never skyline yourself…that's when you stand on top of a barren hill with the sun behind you. It makes you an easy target for the enemy. I realized that I was skylining myself with the sergeant. It was time to beat a hasty retreat and let him focus his attention on someone else.

"Yes, Sergeant," I replied.

The sergeant waited for me to say anything else, then nodded. He glanced down at his list, then barked out the next name. Every time he called out "101st Airborne," he would pause for a moment as if waiting for something. Then he would say, "Leg!" and call out the next name. It wasn't until he was halfway through the list that we learned what he was expecting to hear. The soldier whose name he had just called replied, "Airborne, Sergeant!"

I was still concerned about being tossed out of an airplane, though. I later found out from someone standing next to me that nobody jumped out of airplanes with parachutes in Vietnam. The jungle was too thick to use airborne soldiers except as straight-leg infantry. That made me feel better…although it started to gall me that everyone else in the 101st got an extra fifty bucks a month for being on jump status without ever needing to jump. What a rip off.

The sergeant worked his way through the list. Of the four hundred men who had flown in with me, two hundred of us were going to the 101st training center in Bien Hoa…the name of the base is pronounced as "Ben Wa."

Once we received our unit assignments, it seemed as if the lackadaisical attitude of the in-processing center changed dramatically. We were pushed through the final stations and then jumped on a C-7A Caribou airplane for the flight to Bien Hoa.

The 101st training center was located a few miles away from the Air Force base at Bien Hoa. The R.A. sergeants placed us into training platoons and ran us through four days of mini-Basic Training. We spent what seemed like eighteen hours a day reviewing and relearning the combat training we had received in the States.

Since my MOS was 11 Bravo—light weapon infantryman—I spent most of my time on the firing range with the M-16, shooting at dirt. The M-16 was different from the M-14 rifle I had lugged around and fired in Basic, but I had fired the M-16 during AIT. It was lighter and used a smaller bullet.

I still didn't believe that the M-16 was a better weapon. It seemed to have a weak report compared to the bark of the M-14, and there was little recoil. Even if it did carry more bullets, the plastic weapon just didn't inspire any confidence. I felt like I was carrying a pea-shooter to a Wild West shoot-out.

Apparently I wasn't the only one feeling that way, because a sergeant took the time to clear up the misperception. It seems that the rifling on the M-16 causes the bullet to be off-balance when it leaves the barrel. Instead of spiraling like a football, the bullet would tumble a little. When it hits, the tumble causes the bullet to do strange things…for example, hitting the enemy in the shoulder and having the bullet come out his foot.

That was a little too technical for most of us, so the sergeant explained it another way. "Imagine a fly in a jar, spinning around and around trying to get out. That's what the M-16 round does when it hits the ribcage. Now, any questions?"

We didn't have any, and we all considered the M-16 a better weapon after that.

On the fifth day, we learned our permanent unit assignments. We formed up in our training platoons after morning chow, expecting another day of training. Instead, we were told to grab our gear and report to a nearby dry and dusty field. Four buses were already waiting for us when we arrived, their engines idling.

Yet another overstuffed sergeant addressed us. "Alright, you cherries! When I call your name, climb on of those buses that will take you to the airport. You'll be going to Phu Bai, where all the fun and games are."

"Oh, no," I thought. It hadn't taken us long in country to learn all about Phu Bai. It was to the north, near the demilitarized zone. Action there was heavy.

But the sergeant didn't give us any time to ponder. He called out names quickly, one after another, dispatching men to the buses. This time, I was not the first name called. In fact, I watched the group around me shrink away. Finally there were five of us, then four, then three, and two. The sergeant paused ominously.

Finally, he shouted, "Moffett!"—as if there were anyone else around to talk to—"You're going to Phouc Vinh." He pronounced it as Fook Vin.

Where the hell was Phouc Vinh? I yanked out my copy of the small map we'd all been given and ran my finger across towns near Phu Bai. I assumed it would be close, but it wasn't there. I looked up at the sergeant, ready to ask my question.

"You can jump on one of the buses and ride to the airport with your buddies," the sergeant added.

But first, I needed to know the answer to my burning question. "Sarge," I said, "how come I'm not going with the rest of the guys—"

He interrupted me. "Soldier, I have no idea. You'll find out when you get to Phouc Vinh."

I grabbed my duffel and slung it over my back. This didn't make any sense. The dry brown grass brushed the dusty reddish-clay soil off my boots as I walked toward the bus.

"Hey, Moffett!" yelled Glenn Queen as I boarded the bus. "What took you so long? Think you're special or something?"

"Yeah," I replied, scratching my head. "Seems I'm not going to Phu Bai with you guys. They're shipping me to Phouc Vinh."

"Phouc Vinh?" Glenn waved for me to take the seat beside him. "Where the hell is that?"

"Don't ask me."

The ride to the airport was full of questions. Glenn and I tried to find Phouc Vinh, but the small map sheet we had been given didn't show it anywhere. It kept us busy, though, and neither of us said anything about the approaching separation. Glenn and Ritchie were going one direction, and I was going another. I kept wondering, "Why am I being singled out?"

Except for being young, male, physically fit and modestly handsome…I had no special talents. My training was pretty standard; no more or less than what Quinn and Queen had received. Why was I getting special treatment? Had I pissed somebody off at the in-processing center? Or could it be Colonel Bowers, the trip commander on the flight from Fort Lewis…could this be his way of getting even for us missing the plane?

Once we got to the airport, I watched my hundred and ninety-nine buddies board three C-130 transports. I waved goodbye as Glenn and Ritchie boarded and didn't stop waving until the three giant airplanes had lifted into the air.

I felt lost. I had made a lot of friends among that group. Some, like Queen and Quinn, had been with me as far back as basic training. The planes disappeared into the clouds and I was overcome by a deep feeling of sadness. Now I knew nobody in this mess of a country. I was all alone.

My self-pity was interrupted by a tap on the shoulder. I turned to look at the Air Force sergeant behind me.

"Hey, you the one goin' to Phouc Vinh?"

"Yes, Sergeant," I replied.

He pointed a large twin-engine prop plane just outside the terminal and handed me a boarding card. "That's your transportation. Give this card to the crew chief and you're on your way. Good luck."

"Excuse me, Sergeant," I said before he could walk away. "Why am I going to Phouc Vinh?"

The Air Force sergeant shrugged his shoulders and grinned. "I can't tell you that. You'd better get movin' though. That plane can't leave without you."

I tossed the heavy duffel bag over my shoulder and started walking toward the plane. I was beginning to feel like I had landed in the middle of someone's mystery thriller. Even the plane—a C-47—was tantalizingly mysterious. My father had flown one of the twin-engine cargo planes during World War II. I thought the Air Force had retired all of the old birds.

The crew chief waited by the door as I climbed the stairs and stepped into the plane. He took the boarding pass, then thumbed over his shoulder. "Buckle in. We're taking off shortly."

The C-47 could hold about forty passengers, yet I was all alone. I crouched on one of the long bench seats that ran from nose to tail, and I waited. No one else got on. It was just me, the pilot, co-pilot and crew chief. This was getting really spooky.

There was a brief explosion from the left side of the plane, and then a loud roar as the engine gathered speed. The right engine started without any backfire and was soon running smoothly.

My ears popped as the rear door slammed shut behind me. I turned and watched the crew chief work his way forward. He paused at certain points to check different parts of the plane or glance out the window.

He grinned as he walked past me, then paused. His voice barely rose above the noise of the engines, even though I could tell he was yelling "Hey, PFC, looks like you've got yourself a private plane to Phouc Vinh! You must be someone special!"

From the shaking of his shoulders as he made his way to the cockpit, I could tell that he was laughing. I couldn't see the humor. So far, I hadn't learned anything new to tell me where I was going or why.

I looked out the window as the C-47 began taxiing toward the runway. A TWA 747 sat at the edge of the landing field. GIs were boarding the plane, the smiles on their faces telling me their destination. They were going home.

"One more year," I muttered to myself. "Then that will be me, going home."

The twin engines roared. I was forced to grab the bench with both hands just to keep from being thrown to the rear of the large cargo bay. I could feel the rough concrete rumbling beneath the wheels, and then a free-fall sensation as the plane lifted into the air.

The TWA 747 grew smaller as I watched through the window. I made a promise to myself at that moment. "Three hundred fifty-eight days and a wakeup. Then I'm heading home…and the first thing I'm going to do is kiss the ground back Stateside."

Once we'd reached cruising altitude, the crew chief walked back toward me. "Pilot sez you can come up to the cockpit if you want. You look lonely sitting back here by yourself."

He didn't know how right he was. I looped the carrying straps of my duffel around the bench so the bag wouldn't shift during flight. Then I followed the crew chief forward to the cockpit.

Up front, there were brief introductions and the traditional offer of a cup of coffee. With the way the plane was bouncing and shaking, I decided it was wisest to decline the steaming cup of java that the pilot extended toward me. I could just see us hitting turbulence and myself tossing scalding coffee on the back of the pilot's neck. That wouldn't make my father happy, to learn that his son was killed by crashing the same plane he had flown during WWII. He always loved the "Gooney Bird," as the C-47 was affectionately named. I'm not sure which one he would mourn more, the plane or me.

I sat on a stool just behind the pilot and kept my hands in my lap. The crew and I made small talk for a while, but it was difficult to hear over the constant noise of the airplane. The conversation consisted of short sentences. I soon realized that I wasn't going to learn any more about my destination or reason for being singled out.

Then the pilot tapped my Boonie hat to get my attention. He pointed out the window, then down. Over the roar of the engines, he yelled, "Phouc Vinh!"

I stood up from my seat and looked out the window. There wasn't much on the ground below us except for a bunch of hooches—thirty-foot long metal barracks—on both sides of a dirt road.

The rutted dirt road turned out to be our runway. I sat down quickly as the pilot and crew started their descent. My father had told me many times that the Gooney Bird could land just about anywhere…and now I was going to find out if he was right. The road didn't look like it was long enough or wide enough to handle an airplane. Matter of fact, it didn't look like it was wide enough for two cars to drive without one having to head for the ditch!

We bounced down on the hard clay surface. The engines screamed as the pilot reversed the throttle and used both engines and brakes to slow the aircraft. It looked as if the pilot was riding a bucking bronco, the way he was pushing pedals and fighting the wheel.

The plane finally pulled to a stop. My face was probably a little green as I smiled at the pilot. He gave me a thumbs-up, as if the landing that raised hair on the back of my neck was simply another routine landing for him.

I staggered back to retrieve my duffel bag. It had untied itself from the bench and lay against the back wall of the cargo plane. I think I found my heart and stomach back there as well. I grabbed my belongings and made my way forward again to thank the crew.

The crew chief held the door open for me. "Whatever reason you came here for," he said, "I hope it all works out."

"Thanks," I said. I was fervently hoping so, too.

As I walked down the stairs and toward the hooches, I heard the door slam shut behind me. The C-47 revved up. I turned and watched it power down the runway, then take off and disappear into the glare of the midday sun.

Well, I was here—wherever here was—for better or worse, and I still didn't know why. I walked through dusty grass and red dirt on the edge of the runway, and made my way toward the metal buildings.

A sign hanging by a nail read "U.S. Air Force." Might as well try that one, I thought, and walked inside. I pulled out my orders and handed them to the Airman sitting behind a small counter. "Can you tell me how I can get to—"

"Yeah, I know," he said. "The 101st, right? We heard you were coming."

They'd heard I was coming? How? More important, why? This was getting more and more bizarre.

"I'll call over there," the airman said, "and they'll send somebody to pick you up. Wait outside. It should only take a few minutes."

The airman turned away and busied himself talking on the phone. I still didn't have any answers, and I could tell that the young Air Force kid behind the desk wasn't going to be very helpful.

So I did what I was told. I stepped outside, threw my duffel down onto the reddish-brown soil and sat on it. My ears still hummed with the vibration of the Gooney Bird, and so it seemed as if there were no other sounds around me. It was a strange feeling, as if I was completely alone in the world.

I stared out across the runway, wondering what would happen next.

TYPOGRAPHICAL ERROR

I saw it approaching on the far horizon, obscured by a cloud of dust. Several moments passed before I could make it out clearly. It was a flatbed truck roaring straight toward me across the dual-purpose runway and road.

This was not some dinky little vehicle. The bed on this truck must have been fifty feet long. The cab was painted olive drab and black, the standard camouflage colors of a military vehicle. The truck was the type used to haul construction equipment...but there was nothing on it.

I turned away, knowing that it wasn't the ride I was expecting. It took me by surprise when, a few minutes later, the truck stopped in front of me with the sound of screeching brakes.

There were two guys in the cab. One leaned his head out and said, "This is the only vehicle we could find. Get in."

There was still something very mysterious about all of this. First I was singled out to go to Phouc Vinh instead of Phu Bai, then I was the only passenger on the Gooney Bird. Now I was being picked up in a giant truck that was the only one they could "find," as if the two soldiers in the cab had to steal it instead of simply using one of the unit's jeeps. It just didn't make any sense. What was I being pulled into here?

"Come on, leg! You're the guy sent from Bien Hoa, right?" The assistant driver didn't wait for me to reply. "We ain't got all day. Get in."

The two guys in the cab made no move to make room for me inside. I slung the duffel over my shoulder and asked, "You mean 'get on,' don't you?"

"Whatever," the assistant driver replied, shrugging his shoulders.

I threw my bag on the flatbed, then jumped on. There were no rails or barriers on the side of the truck. I found a spot in the center of the truck just behind the cab where I could sit without rolling off.

The Airman hollered from the doorway of the small Air Force shack that there was another plane coming in. The driver barked some kind of response, then ground the gears as he shifted. The truck lurched forward, and I wondered how I was going to stay seated on the flatbed. It was enough of a challenge to keep myself in one place as we bounced across the rough terrain. Keeping the duffel with me was almost impossible. I finally wrapped the duffel bag straps around my leg and braced myself with my arms. Then I held on for dear life.

The dust, humidity, ninety-five degree heat, and sweat steaming from every pore made it feel like I was making mud pies on my face. I'd heard my mother say mud packs were good for the complexion, but I didn't think this was quite what she meant. I opened my mouth to yell at the driver. That was a mistake. Chewing on dirt and grit is definitely not the most satisfying meal I've ever had.

The truck was moving fast enough to generate a breeze, so the ride wasn't bad when we were in the open. It became oppressive every time we drove into the shade of a tree-lined lane. The trees were tall and gnarled, and their branches didn't really start until eight feet or higher. One would think that the wind could easily move through the thin stands of trees, but it didn't. Waist-high undergrowth grew between the tall trees, blocking the wind. It felt like we had driven into a steam bath.

I had already spent seven days in-country, yet most of what I had seen of Vietnam was from the air and from the sterile security of military installations. My first opportunity to truly experience Vietnam came as we reached the village of Phouc Vinh.

The main road was a dirt street. Single-story white wooden buildings with corrugated tin roofs lined both sides. We had to slow down and finally came to a complete stop because a farmer was herding his water buffalo across the street. Young children played barefoot in the streets, their laughter loud against the otherwise serene scene.

There was a distinct odor in the air. It was a strange collection of modern technology and the dark ages. The scents of gasoline and diesel intermingled with water buffalo manure and compost. I could also catch the occasional whiff of something that smelled like rotting fish.

The sidewalks in front of the stained, patchwork buildings were reddish-tan dirt. I saw an occasional discarded wooden pallet that the pedestrians used to cross the deep drainage ditches running parallel with the road. A young Vietnamese woman caught my eye as she walked on the hard-packed dirt sidewalk. She was dressed in traditional clothing called the Ao Dai.

It was the first time I had seen a young Vietnamese woman up close, and the combination of her beauty and the Ao Dai was very striking. The outfit was a simple design, really…it consisted of a pair of pants and tunic. The pants were long, wide-legged, and they glistened like white silk. Yet there was something about the clothing that made the young woman stunning. Perhaps it was the high-collared white tunic that fit tightly against her body, or maybe it was the provocative slit running from the knee-length hem up to her slender waist. Long raven-black hair flowed smoothly over her shoulders, making her somehow appear eternal and beautiful.

I guess the farmer finally moved his snorting water buffalo across the intersection because the truck started to move. As we slowly bounced through the village, I began to feel like I was sitting on a float in a surreal single-vehicle parade. Merchants came out to cheer and applaud. Everyone waved. A young boy—in a short-sleeve white shirt, black trousers and sandals—jumped onto the trailer and gave me a warm can of Coca-Cola.

"GI number one!" he announced, then jumped back onto the street.

The truck had only moved a few more yards when another girl in the traditional Ao Dai dress clambered onto the trailer. I barely had enough time to notice the bright pastel pink tunic and white pants before she maneuvered herself onto my lap. After that, I completely failed to notice anything about her except for soft, smiling lips and those dark brown eyes.

She held an open bottle of Ba Muoi Ba beer to my lips and started pouring the beer into my mouth. I grabbed the bottle and swallowed before she managed to drown me. Then she kissed me on the cheek and said, "GI come back Phouc Vinh. Buy me one Saigon Tea. I love you too much!"

It was a good thing that she jumped off the flatbed after that, considering that she managed to raise my morale faster than my fiancé ever had. The assistant driver chose that moment to lean out his window and jokingly yell, "Hey, cherry, hands off! You ain't earned that yet!"

Phouc Vinh is a tiny village, and it didn't take long to drive through it. The unusual welcome and parade-like atmosphere only added to my feeling of strangeness. It took us another ten minutes to reach the perimeter gate of the army base. A guard in the tall watchtower tracked us with his M60 machinegun until the gate guard waved us through. The truck rumbled down several narrow roads before finally stopping in front of a large tin-roofed building.

"Here's where you get off, buddy," said the assistant driver. Strange that the driver never said anything to me during the entire trip.

I grabbed my duffel bag and jumped off the flatbed. The truck was already moving away as I raised my hand to wave thanks. I turned to face the screen door of the large building, then paused. Here was where I would discover the answer to the mysterious orders assigning me here instead of Phu Bai.

Music drifted through the open windows as a radio played "Daydream Believer." It seemed appropriate, considering that the day so far seemed like a daydream. I dropped my duffel on the ground and rummaged through it, pulling a handkerchief from the depths before I resealed the bag. I used the army-issued green cloth to rub all of the dust and grime from my face.

It wasn't the best, but I was presentable. I walked up the steps and into the building, then reported to the sergeant working behind the front desk. He told me to follow him and lead me toward an office in the back. My escort left me as I knocked on the doorframe.

A voice barked, "Come in!"

I entered the room and stopped in front of the gray metal desk, then locked my heels at the position of attention. I reported with my best and snappiest salute.

"At ease, son!" the massive officer behind the desk commanded.

"Welcome to Echo Company, 3rd Battalion, 187th Infantry, 101st Airborne Division. I'm your CO, Captain Torres. Now, which mortar would you prefer to work with?"

The mystery deepened as I looked at my new commanding officer. Why would I be working with a mortar? But all I said was, "Mortar, sir?"

"That's right, mortar!" he replied sharply. The captain pantomimed with his hands as he spoke. "You know…where you drop a round down a tube, then the projectile comes out and goes boom on the enemy?"

I knew what a mortar was, but it still didn't make any sense. "I guess I'll work with any one you'd like to take a chance on, sir. But I've never seen any of them."

"What did you say?" he demanded, rising from his chair. He slammed his fists onto his desk and pushed his face near mine.

"Sir, I'm infantry light weapons qualified. I've never been trained on a mortar."

He gave me a glare that could chisel paint, as if expecting me to recant my story. The room suddenly felt very hot and sticky to me. I knew the normal way to appease an officer wouldn't work here, and so I kept quiet.

"Soldier! Look at your orders. It says right here that your MOS is 11-Charlie." His index finger tapped menacingly next to my name on the orders. "11-Charlie MEANS MORTARS!"

There had to be a special training course for officers that teaches them how to go ballistic in a heartbeat. One of the sub-courses must be how to effectively spray spittle so that it strikes the face everywhere except for the eyes. I didn't even blink as I looked down at my orders. Sure enough, they read 11C, not the 11B I'd trained as at Fort Jackson.

I offered the only explanation I could think of. "Sir, I guess it must have been a typographical error."

The safest position for a soldier in this situation is at attention, with your hands at your sides and face straight forward. I gripped the seam of my jungle fatigues with sweaty hands as I watched the Captain's face turn beet red. His cheeks looked like they would explode with his fury.

"I can't believe this! You mean to tell me that I called those idiots in Bien Hoa and asked for one experienced mortar man...that out of two hundred guys, they sent me a TYPOGRAPHICAL ERROR?!"

I couldn't find any hole to crawl into, so I shrugged my shoulders and said, "It looks that way, sir."

Captain Torres slowly drew away from me. It was like watching a raging bull step back...I didn't know if he was going to charge me or attack something else. It didn't take long to find out.

"Son of a bitch!" he swore, slamming his hand on the desk so hard he upended a cup of coffee. The black liquid poured across a number of documents on his desk, making matters worse. He grabbed the papers and waved them around, trying to remove the coffee stain. On realizing the futility of the gesture, he tossed the papers back onto the desk. In a frustrated, angry voice he muttered, "Damn it."

We both stood in silence for a moment and watched the coffee seep into the paperwork. I was still trying to figure this whole thing out, so I broke the silence by asking, "So the private plane bringing me here, and the parade through the village...?"

"Just coincidence," he replied in an empty voice, his eyes never shifting from the papers on the desk. "None of that was planned."

There is a funny thing I had already learned in my time in the army. There is a difference between sergeants and officers. Sergeants are physical, always jumping into the action with a shove or a quick boot to motivate their soldiers. Officers, on the other hand, are more mental and they thrive on reports and paperwork. From the way that Captain Torres stared at the soggy documents on his desk, one would think that his best friend had just been shot.

"Sir?" I asked.

"Huh," was his only reply.

"Was that important?"

"Yeah." He exhaled heavily, then ran his fingers through bristle-brush hair. "It has to be in the colonel's office within the hour. I don't have anyone to retype it. My company clerk is on R&R in Bangkok!"

I reviewed my options. When the shock of the coffee mishap finally wore off, there were two things the captain could do. Either he would go into a blue funk for the rest of the day, or he would get angry at missing his deadline and look for a target to vent on. The commander hadn't dismissed me yet, so I was stuck in the office. That's called a target of opportunity. I needed to get out of there, and fast.

There was an opportunity to perhaps ease the situation a bit. I grabbed a deep breath to calm my own nerves. "Begging the captain's pardon—"

He raised his eyes to face me. From the glare, I knew what direction the officer was heading. Time had run out, and I was about to become the focus of his attention and anger.

"—but if you have more of those blank forms, I can retype that stuff in about five minutes."

"Really?" he asked with a wary, questioning look on his face.

I nodded affirmatively. "Yes, sir."

There was a wicked smile on his face as he handed me the forms. He pointed toward a rickety typewriter just outside his office. It sat on an equally shabby table that looked ready to collapse. His voice promised dire things if I failed as he said, "Start typing."

I finished the job, error free, in less than five minutes. The captain's eyes followed me as I walked into his office and handed him the papers. He checked them thoroughly. From the way his forefinger ran across the pages, I knew that he really wanted to find at least one mistake.

"Not bad," he said, once again calm and cool.

Then he gazed up at me with a look that was hard to define. I wondered what was going through his mind, and what thunderbolt was coming next. He requested a mortar man, and he got me…my future was completely under his control. I expected the next words to be an order to gather my gear and head north, into the action.

"Ya know," he began thoughtfully; I waited for the bomb to fall. "Most of the guys from Fort Campbell are gonna DEROS outta here in about two months."

Fort Campbell was home of the 101st, and most of them were stationed at Phu Bai. I didn't say anything, just waited for the bomb to fall. He glanced down at the freshly typed pages in his hand, then up at me. Here it comes, I thought.

"I can use a guy like you when that happens," he stated. "But right now, I want you to go into the field with RECON platoon. I'll call you in when I need you."

It wasn't a combat assignment like Phu Bai, but RECON platoon sounded like field duty to me…yet there was hope that I would be recalled to help the commander in the office. I was pleasantly surprised. "Thank you for the opportunity, sir. I look forward to it."

"That will be all, Private. Dismissed."

I snapped a sharp salute, then marched smartly out of the office. My duffel bag still leaned against the wall near the dilapidated typewriter where I left it. I grabbed it by the straps, threw it over my shoulder and left the office in search of RECON platoon.

The nice thing about the Army is that it is very orderly. The base camp followed this principle; all of the buildings were laid out in straight columns and rows. They followed the same construction design of lap-board walls and corrugated tin roofs. Doors were placed at the front and rear of the buildings. Windows consisted of a two-foot high wire screen just below the eaves that ran the entire length of both long walls. Each building was about thirty feet long, and sandbags were piled waist-high around every wall.

The engineers laid the camp out so that the first building of each row was the Headquarters building. The next building was the company supply room, followed by the platoon barracks. I figured that the motor pool would be located at the far end of the row.

It wasn't that hard to find RECON platoon. They were a battalion asset, so they were located on the first row and almost the last building. I reported to the platoon sergeant, who assigned me a bunk and told me to stay out of the way. He had a mission to plan and didn't need a cherry leg bothering him.

I spent the rest of the day becoming familiar with base camp. Some things in the army are critical to a young soldier, and I determined that I would find them on my own. The first, of course, was the mess hall. Any soldier who can't find the mess hall doesn't need to be in the army; it's typically the building with the long line of people going into it three times a day. Very hard to miss.

The next is the supply room. There's an old army saying that there are only two people you don't ever want to cross…that's the mess sergeant and the supply sergeant. Even officers respect this unwritten rule. Irritating both sergeants occasionally resulted in a soldier being bent over with diarrhea from food poisoning and not having any toilet paper available. I always ensured that I stayed on their good side.

Finance also plays an essential part in every soldier's life, since that's where they draw their pay. I opted to have part of my pay sent home to my mother to save for me. While Gretchen wanted us to save money for the wedding and honeymoon, I planned on buying a new Cutlass Supreme when I returned home. Priorities are important; I figured I had time to persuade her that mine was the highest priority.

Instead of dollar bills, the finance office issued Military Payment Certificates, or MPCs. Any purchase made at the PX—the Post Exchange—was paid for using bills that looked like they were printed for a strange Monopoly game. MPCs came in just about every denomination, ranging from a penny to ten dollars. Undoubtedly some general at echelons above reality determined that these fake bills were the wisest way to go. I guess he was concerned that a bunch of GIs would spend US dollars on the local economy and undermine the value of the Vietnamese piaster. After the finance officer briefed me on using MPCs, I concluded that it was a waste of time. There was little chance that I would ever get to spend them in this outpost.

All of these services—chow, supply, and finance—affected a soldier's daily life. There was one last section that had a far greater impact…the personnel administration center, or PAC section. This small group of clerks and typists determined where a soldier went in-country. A simple mistake caused by a missed keystroke sent me to Phouc Vinh instead of Phu Bai, and that was an accident. I didn't want to think about what could happen if I annoyed one of the clerks. Sometimes the power of the pen—or in this case, the typewriter—is mightier than the sword.

The next few days were spent getting acquainted with the guys in RECON platoon. A reconnaissance unit is typically the eyes and ears of a combat battalion; they patrol far forward of the line companies and report on enemy activity. While they carried a significant amount of firepower, the RECON platoon wasn't supposed to engage the enemy. Instead, they called back to tell Headquarters where the enemy was and what they were doing.

The RECON platoon would leave the base at Phouc Vinh on five-day non-resupply missions. I was terrified the first time that I went out on one. Each one is the first time, because you don't know what to expect. As the platoon sergeant joked, "It's the not knowing that kills you."

We rolled out of the gate in jeeps with enough firepower to start a small war. Several jeeps carried the mortars, others had recoilless rifles, and anything else mounted a M60 or a fifty-caliber machinegun.

I manned a M60 machinegun. Standing behind that heavy weapon was both reassuring and scary at the same time. I knew that if Charlie—the enemy—missed with his first shot, I could mow down small trees with my weapon. That was the catch, though. He had to miss first.

RECON platoon spent the next five days driving around the perimeters of the outlying company base camps and listening/observation posts. It was a strange game of hide-n-seek, really. We knew there were VC in the area and they knew we were there as well, yet neither side managed to find the other. I guess Charlie didn't care for the way RECON platoon could reach out with mortars, machineguns and recoilless rifles to say, "Tag! You're it!"

In three weeks time of going out on recon missions, we never made contact with the enemy. Each time we came in from the field, we cleaned our weapons and bundled our laundry. I was doing just that when Harry Melick, a Spec 4 from Battalion PAC, came into the "hooch," the common nickname for our tin-roofed barracks.

"Hey, Moffett," he said. "CO wants to see you on the double."

"Alright, I'm on my way," I replied. I washed up quickly and headed for the company orderly room.

I had already heard about Melick. If you ever wanted to know what was happening around base camp, just ask Harry. The lanky clerk was a strict by-the-book type when it came to his job, but he was an entrepreneur in another way. Information is a commodity in the Army, and Harry was one of the best at marketing it. He didn't mind running errands for the officers because it opened doors that were normally inaccessible. He seemed to know everyone...and everything about everyone. It wouldn't have surprised me if I walked into Captain Torres' office to hear him say, "Moffett, I was just thinking about calling for you." Harry was that good with information management.

I walked through the orderly room to the commander's office and rapped sharply on the doorframe. A voice called out, "Enter!" I reported to the commanding officer in true military fashion...snappy salute and locked heels. Captain Torres put down the paperwork in his hands and returned the salute with the practiced ease of a professional Regular Army soldier.

"At ease, Moffett," the officer said. "An opening for a typist has come up in our company morning reports group. I recalled your typing ability when you helped me out a few weeks ago, so I thought I'd give you a shot."

"Thank you, sir. I'm sure I can handle it," I replied.

"Good." The same wicked grin appeared on his face. "It could be only temporary, depending on your performance."

"Yes, sir. Understood, sir. You won't be disappointed."

The captain nodded. "Step out into the next office and report to Spec 5 Richard Leisure. He'll take you through the routines today. You'll start full time tomorrow. Any questions?"

"No, sir."

"Dismissed!"

I offered another sharply executed salute and moved out quickly, eager to learn about my new assignment. The sooner I mastered this challenge, the sooner Captain Torres would forget about it being "temporary."

There was something about Spec 5 Leisure that immediately made me feel welcome. I don't normally warm up quickly to strangers, but Leisure was somehow different. I felt that I could even become friends with him, and the feeling seemed to be mutual.

"Where you from, Moffett?" he asked, rising from his chair to shake my hand.

"Brooklyn, New York, Specialist."

"Call me Rich."

Now that was something. A Specialist Fifth Class was the same as a buck sergeant except that he couldn't lead soldiers into combat. I'd never had a sergeant tell me to call him by his first name. I decided to see how casual Spec 5 Leisure was willing to go. "So, where are you from, Rich?"

He grinned and replied, "Washington Court House, Ohio."

That sounded like a joke waiting to be made. I teasingly asked, "Did you actually live in a courthouse, or is that just the name of the town?"

"It's a town in Ohio, you idiot!" he retorted, and we both laughed.

He motioned for me to follow him, and asked a few questions about my background as we walked out of the orderly room. Just up the dirt road from Captain Torres' office, he escorted me into a Quonset hut and introduced me to battalion adjutant. Captain Dowling was the Battalion S-1, or Personnel Officer, who ran the battalion's personnel administration center. The Captain welcomed me onboard, then turned back to the paperwork on his desk.

Outside Captain Dowling's office stood five wooden desks. Four of them were occupied by GIs plunking away on some very old Remington manual typewriters. Leisure made the rounds and introduced me to the other guys, including Spec 4 Melick.

We ended up at the vacant desk. I plopped down gracefully in front of my typewriter, which looked like the worst of the bunch. I didn't care. This was a rear area job, and that was all that mattered.

Leisure then explained the morning reports process. "It's real simple, Moffett, kinda like basic accounting. If you have a debit, you must have a credit and vice versa. The morning report tracks every soldier. Once a GI is assigned to a company, we keep track of his whereabouts whenever he leaves the company on R&R, leave, sick call, whatever. This prevents units going into the field without a full compliment of personnel.

"As an example, if a soldier gets sick and goes to the hospital, you type his name, reduce the company strength by 1 and add 1 to the hospital column. When he returns, you type the same information in reverse."

"I understand. It seems pretty cut and dried," I said.

"Good. Now I hate to start off on a sad note, but we have to do this one right away." Leisure reached into an index card box, pulled out a 5 x 7 card and handed it to me.

I read the name out loud. "Sarna, Arnold Paul, Specialist 4th Class."

Leisure rolled a morning report form into the typewriter and lined it up evenly as I reviewed the card. The information typed there said that Sarna was from Livonia, Michigan. His MOS was 71H20, Clerk Typist.

I prepared to start typing, then paused. Something about this seemed odd, so I asked my new boss. "Okay Rich, what happened to Spec 4 Sarna? Has he taken ill or something?"

The humor in Leisure's voice was absent as he replied in an emotionless tone, "I am afraid it's worse then that. He was killed two nights ago."

That was a shock. I raised the index card where he could see it and pointed toward the important line. "What? How can that be? It says right here that Sarna's a 71H20 clerk typist. How could he have been killed?"

Rich just shook his head. "I guess someone back in the world told you that clerks don't die in Vietnam, right? Well, Arnold is proof that there's no truth to that."

I stared at the card in my hand. It was a tiny thing to carry the story of a soldier's life. It was also the closest I'd come to knowing someone killed in Vietnam. "Sorry, Rich. I'm just a little stunned. How'd it happen?"

"A VC rocket meant for the airport fell short and hit Sarna's hooch." Leisure stood straight, his eyes watching my face. "The rocket went through the tin roof and exploded on the rafter right above his bunk. The only thing between him and the blast was a mosquito net, which didn't provide any protection. He never knew what hit him."

I sat motionless, forming a mental picture of everything Rich had told me.

"Now here's some more news you may not like," Leisure continued. "You're Sarna's replacement, and you're now sitting at his desk."

He slapped me on the back. "So shine bright, Brooklyn boy, and make us all proud. I gotta go to see Captain Dowling for a minute."

I must've looked pretty shell-shocked. Rich clapped me on the shoulder and squeezed with a firm grip, then started walking away. Over his shoulder, he said, "Finish up this report and I'll take you into Phouc Vinh village for lunch and a massage."

It was a strange twist of fate that brought me here. That was first thought in my head as I looked down at the tiny white card. I had come to Phouc Vinh totally by accident…all because of someone's typographical error. That mistaken keystroke caused Captain Torre's outburst of anger which resulted in spilled coffee all over his papers. The mishap gave me the opportunity to demonstrate my typing ability. Somewhere in North Vietnam, a factory produced a faulty rocket; instead of hitting its target, the rocket landed short and killed one soldier asleep in his bunk. Because of that, I was pulled from recon patrols and assigned to a desk job.

My good fortune was altogether unbelievable.

I typed the morning report slowly and with great care as I moved Arnold Sarna off the active list of Echo Company. Given the circumstances, I didn't want to make any mistakes. Doing so would seem irreverent. Arnold Sarna died in order for me to sit here. The least I could do was ensure that everything was perfect as I typed the last document that showed his name in this battalion.

The report was finished when Rich returned. He nodded his satisfaction, then told me to grab my headgear. Lunch and whatever waited for us in Phouc Vinh.

When we got to the restaurant, the little appetite I had left quickly diminished. Several Vietnamese citizens sat on the ground outside the steel-gated entrance to the restaurant. They begged for money, their sad plight obvious by their various missing limbs.

Following Rich's lead, I climbed over them to the front porch of the restaurant only to find a woman openly breast feeding her baby. Next to her, two crouching Vietnamese were eating something with such an awful odor it made my eyes tear.

I waited until we were past them before asking my new boss, "Rich, what the hell is that smell?"

"Oh, that's Nuoc Mam. It's fermented fish sauce. We've nick-named it 'armpit sauce' because of the smell," he explained, laugh-ing. "The Vietnamese think it's a delicacy. They put it on everything they eat. Don't worry, you'll get used to the odor."

I seriously doubted I could.

We entered the restaurant through a bead-hung doorway. Rich led me to a small room with tables scattered around the edges. A Vietnamese girl dressed in black pajama pants, white gauze top and flat tong sandals was doing something on one side of the room.

It took me a moment to realize that she was performing a provocative, gyrating dance to Steppenwolf's "Born to be Wild." She had her back to us and didn't immediately realize we were there. When she finally spied us, she ran across the room shouting, "GI, GI! I love you!"

She was a little bit of a thing that couldn't have been more than fifteen years old. The slender child surprised me by jumping into my arms. Her voice didn't sound young at all as she said, "My name Sam. You finish lunch, I give you Number One massage and then we boom-boom. Only fi dollah, same price longtime short time, okay GI?"

I eased her back down onto the floor. "Nice meeting you, Sam. Let me eat first and then we'll see."

Leisure was already seated at the table reading the menu, oblivi-ous to my encounter. I pulled up the chair next to him and asked, "Hey, Rich, why didn't she jump on you when we came in?"

"I've been here eight months already, so they know me very well. But you're a cherry…fresh meat for the girls. They hope you'll be a longtime customer." He grinned mischievously at me.

"Longtime or short time, same fi dollah, right?" I picked up the menu and ignored his laughter. "So, what do you recommend to eat?"

"Water buffalo burger. It's thoroughly cooked and really tastes pretty good, at least compared to the mess hall."

I followed his advice. It was probably the safest thing on the menu. When it came out, I had second thoughts. The bun was tougher than French bread…which is probably what it was, consid-ering Vietnam had been a French colony for many years. Rich offered me a bottle of Nouc Mam when I asked him why the cook included rice with the burger. I didn't think it was very funny. The rotten fish smell was enough to make me gag.

We finished lunch, and I had to admit the burger wasn't bad. Sam arrived and I agreed to a massage. She led me to a small room in the back. Her method of massage—which she did by walking up and down my back with bare feet—had amazing results.

I skipped the boom-boom part. My upbringing had taught me that sleeping with a fifteen year old was statutory rape, no matter where I was. Besides, I could just imagine trying to explain it to Gretchen. I didn't think she would buy the "it was a bargain at five dollars, hon!" excuse.

About a week later, another plane landed on the dirt airstrip and the mortar man that Captain Torres had originally ordered finally appeared. I kept to my typing, and I thought about the places I could have been sent. It sure wasn't like the guys sitting on the beach sipping exotic drinks from a coconut, that's for sure. My life wasn't that cushy. On the other hand, I hadn't ended up at Phu Bai on the DMZ with Queen and Quinn, either.

I guess you could say I really did have a major bit of luck…and all because of one small typographical error. My typewriter and desk seemed to be in the eye of the storm of war. What I didn't know was that there was a change in the wind, and the unpredictable storm could move.

HELLO GOODBYE

Everyone who went to Vietnam has their own memories of what it felt like. I'm not referring to the fears and chaos of combat; those are emotions tied to specific events and places. No, I'm talking about standing outside, closing your eyes and just feeling the air around you. There was the heat and humidity, of course…and the monsoon season with its nightly torrential rains pounding like hail on the tin roof of the hooch. Mosquitoes carrying malaria were always a problem, and the Army-issued insect repellent wasn't much better. It's funny how the only plastic that bug juice wouldn't dissolve was the squeeze bottle it came in.

What I remember most is the dust. You couldn't get away from it. The heat and humidity decreased at night, the rains were seasonal, and the bugs were nocturnal. The dust, however, was a constant. Day or night, rain or shine…it was everywhere and on everything.

My new teammates already had a system in place to fight the dust by the time I moved into the hooch. Two Vietnamese girls from Phouc Vinh came every day except Sunday to clean the hooch and take care of our laundry. All of us contributed to pay these "hooch maids" for their service. That kept our barracks clean enough so we could at least sit on our bunks without raising a cloud of dust.

The other part of the anti-dust system was a shower. There's a funny thing about soldiers…wherever they go, they will always find some way of building their own shower facility. It doesn't matter if it's a bladder and tube dangling from a tree or a full-fledged hot water heater and showerhead; a soldier will always find a way to gain those precious moments of feeling clean.

Our shower was a rudimentary affair thrown together near the hooch. It consisted of a hodgepodge of salvaged and scavenged parts. Imagine a walk-in freezer with a bomb sitting on top, and you'll have a pretty good picture of what it looked like. If the screams from scalding water weren't enough to announce the shower was in use, one only needed to check whether the rickety, hinged tin door was propped closed. The three remaining walls consisted of tin sheets tacked into place, and were just wide enough to cover the lower extremities.

There was a serious lack of lumber in this contraption; the pallet on the floor had more wood in it than the walls and structural supports combined. On the very top of the shower was an old airplane fuel tank that always held several hundred gallons of water. That made showering into a religious experience. Every time you went in, you prayed "Please God, don't let that thing fall on me!"

We never failed to have hot water for our shower. The tank sat in the sun all day and that kind of exposure in Vietnam can turn water into steam. Unless you wanted to broil yourself, you either showered in the early morning or late at night.

I was in the shower early one morning, soaping myself down, when suddenly the ground began to shake. It didn't appear like the water tank was coming down on my head, so I didn't worry too much about it at first. The shaking started off fairly light, then grew more intense as the seconds passed. It got so bad that I found myself bouncing up, down, and sideways. I held onto the sides of the shower, feeling like a kid's stuffed bunny rabbit in a dryer.

It was like the drummer for The Stones was playing "I Can't Get No Satisfaction" on the tin walls of the shower. The metal rattled and vibrated to the strange beat as I managed to bounce over to the door. I grabbed my towel off the hook and wrapped it around myself, all the while thinking that this was either one hell of an earthquake or the VC had some really big weapons we didn't know about. The alert siren hadn't sounded, so I knew my bunkmates were still in the hooch instead of safely in the nearby bunkers. My only thought was that I had to warn them. I ran out of the shower and toward the hooch, which was about twenty yards away.

I flew into the hooch and skidded to a halt just inside the doorway. The rest of my bunkmates were sitting around, calmly playing cards or reading their newspapers. They were completely unfazed by the giant rumbling that still shook the floor under my bare feet.

"What the hell is that sound???" I asked, bewildered by their lack of concern.

Everyone in the hooch looked up at me and immediately broke up in wild laughter. I didn't understand it...here I was, trying to warn them to get under cover, and they were laughing at me. Spec 4 Andy Van Hoy explained. "Calm down, Moff. That's just a B-52 bomber raid. They're dropping a gift for Charlie a few miles from here. You'll get used to it, cherry."

I was mortified, and then my embarrassment slowly turned to anger. After several weeks working with the Battalion Morning Reports Group, I had been promoted to Spec 4...Van Hoy and I were the same rank. I actually had more field time than he did thanks to the RECON platoon assignment, and there he was laughing at me. Although I was standing there in nothing but a towel and Van Hoy was twice my size, I was ready to take him on. It's really not wise to laugh at a guy from Brooklyn.

Harry Melick, with his ability to read people, sensed the tension in the room. He broke out laughing. "It ain't nothin' Moff. You should've seen Andy, the first time he went in the shower."

"Yeah," joined in Spec 4 Jeb Bosselman. "We didn't tell him about the shower *or* the bombing runs. He thought a midday shower would cool him off. Talk about a shake'n'bake!"

I could just visualize it...Andy stood in the shower in the middle of the afternoon. He reached up for the cord to let the water fall from the fuel tank above him. Then, as the scalding water poured down, the whole shower shook from the bombs exploding miles away. It was hard enough for me to bounce to the door and escape the earthquake-tossed shower; at least I wasn't being steam-cleaned at the same time!

"Hold up, guys!" Andy waved his hands, attempting to quiet the laughter in the room. "That was all fun and games when I was the cherry, but you can't laugh about it no more. Moffett's the cherry now!"

"That's true, Pat," agreed Harry Melick. "Until a new guy shows up, you're it. Hope you've got thick skin."

I couldn't help it. The opportunity was too good to pass up. "Yeah, but at least I'm not a steamed cherry!"

We laughed about it, and even Van Hoy joined in. I understood that it was just part of being accepted into the section, and not something personal. That made everything okay between Andy and me. Over the next few weeks, the guys ribbed me about it quite often. I joined in the teasing just to let them know I could give as good as I got.

My hooch-mates stopped ribbing me after another guy, PFC Larry Speary, joined us and became the new "cherry." Larry was from Paxico, a small town in Kansas with a population of just under a hundred. Naturally, we gave him the normal ration of shit about being a farm boy. We nicknamed him "Oz" after the Judy Garland movie.

Oz was great, and we had a lot of fun with him while he was a cherry. Rarely a week would go by without one of us telling him to close his eyes, click his heels three times and say, "There's no place like home."

All of us outranked Oz, so he pulled the additional duties like KP—"kitchen police," the guys who peel potatoes at the mess hall—and cleaning the office. The rest of us pulled gate guard, roving patrol, and the other more responsible details that the company First Sergeant—commonly called "Top"—assigned to each section.

I was typing out a set of orders one day when Oz walked over to my desk with a perplexed look on his face. I asked, "What's up, Oz?"

"Top just told me I have latrine duty after lunch. What's that mean?"

The typing and conversation in the room came to a standstill as everyone listened. I leaned back in my chair and smiled. This was going to be fun. "It means you've got to clean the latrines. What's the problem, cherry?"

I already knew what the problem was. We used field latrines at Phouc Vinh, and they were completely different than the porcelain toilets and sinks normally found in a bathroom. For one thing, the base camp didn't have any plumbing. It most definitely didn't have working toilets.

Our latrines were basically wooden sheds divided into three or more stalls. Each stall had a flat plywood shelf about knee height, with a hole cut into the wood for the toilet seat. Below the hole was a catch-basin made of a fifty-five gallon barrel cut in half.

"Well, what does Top want me to do with it?" Oz asked. "It's an outhouse, right? Should I toss in some lime and a couple shovel-fulls of dirt, or what?"

That set the room to laughing. Captain Dowling stood in the doorway of his office, listening and shaking his head. I tried to keep a straight face. "Is that how you did it on the farm, Oz?"

"Yep," he said, nodding. "When the outhouse got too full, we'd just bury it and dig a new hole."

"Well, you ain't in Kansas anymore, Toto," I replied. "Here in 'Nam, we burn it."

The look on his face said that Oz didn't quite believe me. Andy Van Hoy jumped in to give me a hand. "It's true, farm boy. All you have to do is burn the honey pots."

"Honey pots?"

"The barrels under the shitters. That's what they're called, 'honey pots.' Add a little gasoline, toss in a match, and then stir." Andy pantomimed the motions of stirring a barrel with a stick.

"Just watch out, Oz. They're full of shit, piss and toilet paper, and they'll slosh if you aren't careful," added Harry Melick. "Don't even think about walking into the hooch if you get any on you."

"Thanks, guys." Oz still looked a little puzzled, but he trusted that we wouldn't mislead him. He headed off to take care of his new duty.

I checked on him twenty minutes later, just to make sure he wasn't having any problems. I wasn't really paying any attention to anything else and barely noticed the battalion Sergeant Major walking into the far door of the latrine. My newest teammate was barely visible on the other side of the wood building. He held a five-gallon gasoline can tilted at an angle.

"Hey, Oz!" I yelled as I stepped closer to the latrine. "I need to talk to you."

Oz waved. "Hold on. Let me get this started."

I really didn't want him to do that before we talked. The stench as a honey pot burned was horrible. It sank so deep into one's uniform that it took several washes to get rid of the odor. I'd had my share of latrine duty already and didn't want to smell that way ever again.

Before I could tell him to wait, Oz lit a match. I had just rounded the back side corner of the latrine when several things happened simultaneously.

Oz looked at me, his face proud as he waited for me to compliment him on a successful first attempt at latrine cleaning.

I saw that the honey pot was still under the toilet seat.

The match struck the gasoline.

Before I could even inhale, the gasoline exploded with a whump. A fireball rushed out of the space beneath the toilet, forcing Oz and me to jump out of the way. That's when we heard the bellow from inside the latrine. The voice sounded like a raging bull as it roared, "WHAT THE HELL! HEY!"

There was a mad stomping from within the latrine, followed by what sounded like hands slapping against bare skin. By the time that the door literally tore from its hinges, flames were already licking up the wooden latrine walls.

I had grabbed Oz and stood him up. "Get the fire extinguisher!" His reply was a blank, stunned look.

"That building. Get theirs. Now move!" I shoved him in the direction of the nearest building just as the battalion Sergeant Major rounded the corner.

"Moffett! You stupid sonuvabitch, what d'ya think you're doing!"

It's not a good sign when purple veins stand out on a Sergeant Major's forehead, or when his face is so red that it's almost blue. That's when the battalion's most senior NCO becomes a HEAT round…High Explosive Anti-Troop. The scorch marks on the tail of his fatigue shirt told me that he'd been a little too close—most likely on—the toilet when the honey pot went off.

At moments like this, it's always best to tell the truth. I stood at the position of attention and replied, "I am putting out a fire, Sergeant Major!"

It wasn't the response he expected. His eyes bulged and fingers flexed like they wanted to wrap themselves around someone's neck. "Did you do this on purpose?"

"No, Sergeant Major! I failed to properly instruct PFC Speary on the proper method of burning the honey pot. It won't happen again, Sergeant Major!"

Perhaps the crowd that appeared around us made him calmer, or maybe it was the fact that I took the blame for the junior guy in my section. Whatever the reason, the senior sergeant reined in his emotions.

His eyes still promised retribution as he slowly nodded. "That's for damn sure, Moffett. Now get this fire put out...and next time, ensure Private Speary knows to pull the honey pots out before he burns them!"

"Yes, Sergeant Major!" I don't know why I did it, but I grinned and said, "At least he didn't do it like he would at home."

The burly senior sergeant didn't look like he was in the mood, but morbid curiosity made him ask. "How's that, Moffett?"

"In Kansas, they just knock the shitters over and bury them."

The faint quiver on his lips could've almost been mistaken for the start of a smile. He recovered quickly and said sternly, "Put this fire out, Specialist. Then come see me. I have some pointers on remedial latrine duty that I want to give to you and Private Speary."

There was only one thing I could say. "Yes, Sergeant Major."

The door that the Sergeant Major ripped off the hinges was the only thing we saved from the latrine fire. Rich talked to the Sergeant Major and cleared the air with him, so Oz and I didn't have any serious repercussions from the incident. The guys from the hooch talked about changing Oz's nickname to "Pyro," but it never stuck. Besides, it was more fun to remind Oz that the wicked witch was killed by dropping a house on her...not by burning the outhouse with the Sergeant Major in it.

After that, life in Phouc Vinh continued on the quiet side for some time. If we hadn't had rocket attacks a few times a week, we might have forgotten there was a war going on. The rocket attacks were like postcards from Charlie. They were just his way of letting us know that he was still out there, and they were an invitation to come play. Of course, we always courteously replied with at least several roving patrols...and if Charlie was too shy to play with large groups of well-armed infantry soldiers, we would send a B-52 postcard of our own.

We always had adequate warning when Charlie attacked with rockets. The nearby airbase would sound its sirens, and the guys from the hooch would drop what we were doing and visit the reinforced bunkers for awhile. Then the sirens would sound the "all clear," and we would go back to our previous tasks.

It was the mortar attacks that caused the most problems...and in my case, they were a serious pain in the ass. The enemy only used mortars to announce that he wanted to cross the minefields and barbed wire to come into our camp and play.

I was relaxing in the hooch one evening, drinking a cold beer and playing cards, when the first mortar round hit near the edge of the camp. Everyone grabbed their helmets, flak jackets and rifles, and we headed for our section of the perimeter. Trip flares went off, illumination flares turned the night into gray daylight, and machineguns sent staccato bullets and tracers toward the far tree line.

The mortar rounds started getting a little too close. I hadn't reached my fighting position when several hit near me, so I did what every soldier is trained to do with incoming rounds. I threw myself onto the ground. The only problem was, the ground where I lay wasn't quite level. My head and feet were low, but the rest of me was basically sticking up in the air.

Another mortar round went off nearby, and something like an angry hornet bit me in the buttocks. It was just my luck to land near on a ground hornet's nest. I scrambled forward to my fighting position and stayed there, watching for any movement to my front...but Charlie decided he really didn't want to visit that night, and the mortar rounds stopped falling.

The section chief, Spec 5 Leisure, checked on everyone. He reached me and asked, "You okay, Moffett?"

"Yeah," I replied. "Something bit me in the ass, but I'm fine."

Rich shone his flashlight into my bunker-like fighting position, and then told me to turn around so he could see my backside. "There's not a lot of blood. I'll hold the fort here while you go see the doc and get it checked out."

"Come on, Rich, it's nothing."

"Then I won't be standing here long, will I? Now get your busted ass to the medic!"

There was no arguing with Leisure when he used that tone, so I climbed out of the fighting position and walked to the battalion aid station. My rear did start to hurt a little, but it really wasn't anything worth complaining about.

"Doc," the senior medic, had other ideas. It seems that standard operating procedures with medics is to toss the patient onto a stretcher and immediately cut away every stitch of fabric so they can see the wound. It would've been easier if he'd just told me to drop my pants and drawers so he could have a look.

"Yep, looks like a piece of shrapnel got you," Doc said. "The wound is clean, but I need to give you a couple shots so it doesn't get infected."

His "couple of shots" turned out to be sterile water to prevent infection…and they were injected directly into the wound. Up until that point, the injury didn't really hurt. Once he stuck the needle in my cheek, though, I yelped. The way I came straight up and off that table, I'd swear that I went up twenty feet and hit my head on the ceiling.

Doc slapped a gauze bandage over the injury and told me to keep off it. I rubbed my backside, promised the doc I wouldn't be back unless I was really dying, and started walking back to the hooch.

I passed several soldiers and wondered what they were laughing and joking about. There wasn't a full moon in the sky that night. I walked into the hooch and turned around to hang my weapon and gear on the hook near the door. Suddenly, the entire room burst out into laughter.

"Damn, Moff! That's a sight I don't want to see before going to sleep!" Andy Van Hoy teased.

"What're you talking about?" I didn't understand.

"Your ass, man! It's hanging out all over the place!"

I reached behind me, and that's when I realized what was wrong. The medic had cut my fatigue pants so they flopped down like a pair of Doctor Denton pajamas. My bare cheeks were completely exposed.

The special certificate that my teammates left on my desk the next morning was just the beginning of a week's worth of teasing. They gave me a purple butt instead of a purple heart. I could just imagine what my father would say when I got back home; he was a World War II veteran, and would most likely ask with a huge grin why I was running from the fight. It's strange, but I found myself wishing if I had to get hit by enemy fire…that it would've been anywhere else but my derriere.

The medics on base were the closest thing we had to a full-fledged doctor, and sometimes they were asked to do medical procedures that were out of their army-trained field of expertise. If you gave them enough time to research and rehearse, then the medics could do just about anything. It's not that I doubted their skills…but to me, it's like trusting a contractor who just read a "how to" book with the responsibility of building your million-dollar mansion. It would be very disconcerting to hear Doc say "oops" during surgery.

About a month after my minor injury, Captain Torres came into the Battalion Morning Reports Group where I worked. The Company Commander had always come across to me as a stern, hot-tempered, demanding and yet somehow fair officer. It came as a shock to everyone when he dropped his pants and underwear in the middle of the office.

"Okay, guys, what do you think?"

That was a loaded question, and one that no Drill Sergeant ever prepared us for in Basic Training. We all looked at each other in stunned silence and wondered if the officer had gone crazy. Was he asking us if he had the clap or some other type of venereal disease? Was he wanting our opinion on whether the hookers in Saigon or Bangkok would be pleased with mother nature's endowment of his male ability to please women?

Rich Leisure was the coolest about it as he replied, "Think about what, sir?"

"My vasectomy! Didn't Doc to a wonderful job?"

That word—vasectomy—caused two things to happen simultaneously. The first was an unconscious wince and protective closing of legs by every male in the room. Some things hurt just thinking about them, and someone taking a knife to a guy's private parts is excruciating mental torture. The second was that everyone turned their heads, but not before noticing the captain's mercurochrome-stained bald nuts. Seeing stitches where stitches don't belong caused some of the guys to place a protective hand in their laps.

Leisure was completely unfazed by it. He replied in a calm voice, "Looks good, sir."

That was one thing about Specialist Fifth Class Richard Leisure…he never came unglued or got ruffled by anything. Even though Specialists weren't technically noncommissioned officers, Rich had the duty of NCOIC—non-commissioned officer in charge—for the enlisted club on the base. That meant he had to handle rowdy soldiers when they were drunk.

Alcohol, soldiers, and war are a dangerous mix. A majority of the disciplinary problems in Vietnam can be traced back to this combination. Spec 5 Leisure ran into his greatest challenge from one of his own soldiers, and it almost ended in disaster.

Andy Van Hoy was at the enlisted club and he definitely had too much to drink. Rich calmly told him that he'd had enough, but Van Hoy was too drunk to listen. "I've had enough when I say I've had enough, and nobody is gonna tell me what to do!"

"You've had enough, soldier. Now go back to the hooch and sleep it off," Rich replied.

That just set Van Hoy into a destructive rampage. He broke chairs, threw drinks off tables, and made a total ass of himself. Rich simply wrapped him up in his arms and carried him to the door.

"Go home, Andy, before I have to call the MPs."

Van Hoy wouldn't listen. He kept trying to fight, so Rich dragged him into the yard and dumped him on the ground. "Last chance, soldier. Go back to the hooch."

By this time, half the bar had rushed outside to watch. Andy stood up, hands balled into fists. It was a serious mistake to fight in public, especially against a section chief. Hitting a Spec5, the equivalent to striking a sergeant, was a court martial offense. If he'd picked a fight at the hooch, the rest of us would've pulled them apart and calmed things down.

Rich was very calm as he asked, "What are you going to do, troop?"

"I'm gonna whip your ass," Van Hoy replied. "And then I'm gonna go back inside and finish my drink!"

There was only one thing Rich could do, and he did it calmly and confidently. He beat the tar out of Andy Van Hoy, and didn't stop until the soldier couldn't get off the ground. Harry Melick and I carried Andy back to the hooch and dumped on his bunk. After he sobered up the next day, Andy apologized to Rich for making an ass of himself.

That was the most exciting thing at Phouc Vinh for awhile. I kept my short-timer's calendar up to date, and could tell anyone who asked how many days I still had left in-country before I hit my DEROS…the date of estimated return from overseas. Life started to get into a routine, and then I had an incident with my laundry.

I came into the hooch after a hard day at the office and found my clean laundry folded, ready to be put away. There were some priorities to take care of first—I grabbed a cold beer from the fridge—and then I started putting away the laundry. That's when I noticed one of my fatigue shirts was missing.

This wasn't that unusual, really. The hooch maids all used the same giant tubs to wash the laundry, and sometimes shirts and pants wound up in the wrong hooch. Since our nametags were sown on the front of each shirt, they usually found their way to the right owner in a day or so.

I mentioned my missing shirt to Harry Melick when he came in, and I asked him to check his laundry. It wasn't there, and it wasn't in any of the other guys' laundry. I told everyone it wasn't a big deal and that my shirt would eventually show up.

That's when Harry told us, "We're gonna be missing something else tomorrow."

"What's that?" I asked.

"Tranh packed it in today. Her parents moved to Cu Chi a few months ago, and she decided to join them."

Tranh was our hooch maid. Her leaving without any notice caused a lively discussion verging on crisis with my bunkmates. We now had to find another maid to keep the dust down in the barracks and to take care of our laundry.

"Why didn't Tranh tell us earlier that she was leaving?"

"Don't ask me, man. She mentioned it to me when she came in this morning." Harry grinned and said, "Ya know, Moffett, she always had a crush on you. Maybe she took your fatigue shirt as a souvenir. Now she can use it as a pillow and weep for her poor, lost Moff-baby."

The smooching sounds he made led to a new line of conversation. The guys were more than happy to give me some pointers…like not sleeping with the hooch maid. They all knew that I wrote letters to Gretchen almost every night, and that I was faithful to my fiancé back home. It's all part of soldier humor, and I joined right in.

I didn't give the lost shirt any more thought until almost two days later. Around three in the morning, we were all sleeping in the hooch when the siren went off. That blasting noise from the airbase alerted everyone within miles that Charlie was sending his incoming rocket postcards again. We'd had quite a lot of practice responding by this time.

Normally, we rolled out of bed and into a sandbag bunker beneath our bunk. The all-clear would sound several minutes later, and then we'd climb back into bed and go back to sleep. It was easier than rushing to the nearby reinforced bunkers outside.

That morning, however, the berm was taking small arms fire from outside the perimeter. We grabbed our flak jackets, helmets and M-16s, and dashed to the perimeter in less than a minute. There was still small arms fire coming in as we dived into our bunkers.

RECON platoon happened to be in base camp that morning, and there was a definite change in the sound of the battle when they rolled up onto the berm and started firing. The rest of us felt like we were spectators to an incredible fireworks display as we watched the effects of RECON's heavy fifty-caliber machineguns, recoilless rifles and mortars on the far tree line. Within just a few minutes, both the rockets and the ground fire stopped completely.

Instead of attempting a pursuit at night, Captain Torres opted for shooting illumination flares over the berm until dawn. As the sun peeked over the horizon around 0630, I joined twenty other grunts in a patrol to go out and assess the damage. We climbed over the berm and moved outside the perimeter, looking for the remnants of last night's skirmish.

We fanned out with our M-16s locked and loaded. Caution was the watchword as we stepped over the wires leading to our Claymore mines, several of which had been detonated during the attack.

About a hundred yards out, I found a VC lying face down in the grass. He was clearly dead and missing various body parts. I couldn't tell if one of the recoilless rifles had nailed him, or if it had been a mortar round. Whatever had done the fatal damage also managed to mangle the VC's AK-47. Neither would ever fight again.

I moved slowly toward the body and looked closely to ensure it didn't have any sapper charges attached. That was one of the many tricks the VC did with their dead…they would place explosives beneath their dead that would blow up anyone foolish enough to flip the body over.

Apparently the enemy decided that it hadn't been worth facing RECON platoon's devastating firepower this time. The body was clean of booby traps. That's when I noticed the color of his shirt. It was olive drab. Army green. VC always wore black.

I flipped him over with the butt of my M-16 and couldn't believe my eyes. I yelled, "Over here, over here!"

"Hey, Moffett, what did you find?" called out one of the RECON platoon's Staff Sergeants as he ran toward me. The rest of the patrol was following closely behind him.

"My laundry."

"What?"

The entire patrol joined the sergeant and me. We all stared in amazement. The VC wore a US Army issue shirt with a nametag that read Moffett. My missing shirt had finally surfaced. Apparently our little hooch maid copped it and gave it to her VC boyfriend for good luck. I guess the plan backfired big time.

That was about as exciting as life got in Phouc Vinh for the next few months. Then the we received orders to jump the entire battalion—including the Battalion Morning Reports Group—into the field.

The 4th Infantry Division had taken heavy losses in various battles with the North Vietnamese Army and Main Force Viet Cong in the Central Highlands. The 101st Airborne Division received orders to move forward and support the 4th ID. My battalion, the 3rd of the 187th, was part of 3rd Brigade in the 101st, so we were just one of many units heading into the combat zone. We were also the support command for other units that got into trouble.

We loaded up and flew on C-130 aircraft to Dak To to support the 4th Infantry Division. Choppers took us to a firebase in Dak Pek where we set up the whole admin section. This was Montagnard native territory.

Everyone had heard of the Montagnards; most of us had seen the John Wayne movie, "The Green Berets." The Montagnards were a separate group of hill tribes unrelated to the Vietnamese. They disliked all Vietnamese, but especially hated the North Vietnamese Army soldiers and the Viet Cong.

The Montagnards were very friendly people to their friends, though. There were several Montagnard fighters at the base camp when we landed. They were like Indians out of a western, very carefree and trusting of the people they considered friends...but unforgiving to their enemies. I was very glad that they loved Americans; they idolized John Wayne and thought every American soldier was just like him. They gave tribal bracelets to everyone at the mountaintop base camp, welcoming us to their "tribe."

Most of the Montagnards worked with Army Special Forces—the Green Berets—as scouts. It was strange to see them at the base camp. The reason for their presence was that we were in the middle of Montagnard territory. Like courteous hosts, they were there to ensure we were comfortable. It was fascinating watching them move through the area like ghosts.

Ghosts were something the Montagnards believed in. They said that everything had a spirit, not just humans. The tribesmen loved all animals and believed that some of them were souls returning from the dead. It sounded like reincarnation mumbo-jumbo to me, but they assured us that even the mightiest of protectors—the tiger—would watch over us. Yeah, that's all I needed to hear. Some tribal savage thinking that man-eating tigers would protect us.

We set up a hasty perimeter at base camp, located on the military crest—the area just below the summit so you didn't skyline yourself—of a mountain top. Tents went up next, and soon we were generating all personnel records and administrative documents from the field.

We manned the perimeter with twenty-five percent strength that night. There were no reports of VC activity anywhere near our hill, and Captain Torres felt the risk was minimal. It also helped that we were well within range of a friendly artillery battery, and that the captain coordinated fire support already. If we needed them, the howitzers were only a phone call away.

I was Sergeant of the Guard in charge of the perimeter during my shift that night. We were stuck in the middle of the bush, surrounded by jungle, and everyone was nervous. Things were very quiet for most of the shift, until I heard something rustling in the bush.

Popping an illumination flare didn't seem wise…it would warn whoever was out there that they had been spotted, and it would tell everyone else that we were on the hill. Instead, I called the tactical operations center—the TOC—and reported the noise. I also requested the Starlight scope be brought forward to my position. The Starlight scope was a night vision device that would let me see into the dark jungle.

There was more rustling in the bush. Whoever was out there wasn't making any attempt to disguise their movement. I called the TOC and requested the Starlight scope again, and this time the night shift OIC must've believed my report. I had the scope in my hands several minutes later.

I fully expected to see a VC squad trampling through the brush. What I saw was actually far worse. It was striped, had huge paws, and seemed to be very upset with us. I think the tiger felt that we were camping on its turf, and it wasn't quite sure what to do about it. The giant feline was bending over small trees as it paced back and forth.

The TOC didn't believe my report, and soon I had almost every officer standing over my shoulder for his turn looking through the Starlight scope. Seeing is believing, and they were all believers as the group of officers headed back to the TOC. I could smell the coffee brewing from my position on the perimeter. I guess the officers decided that they would stay awake all night.

The Montagnards smiled knowingly, as if to say, "I told you so." They felt it was a good omen and that we would all sleep peacefully during the night. Sleeping was on the bottom list of my priorities, and I wasn't the only one who felt that way. Nobody got a lot of sleep that night. It wasn't because we expected to be attacked...even the VC weren't stupid enough to cross an angry tiger in the middle of the night. No, everyone stayed up because they were terrified of being eaten. The Montagnards just laughed and went to bed.

We broke camp the next morning and loaded everything back onto the choppers. It was a very pleasant ride back to Phuc Vinh, and there were many relieved soldiers when we were dismissed that evening. It was somehow very comforting to sleep under a roof in a base camp surrounded by barbed wire and minefields...without a large carnivore pacing less than a hundred yards away.

That was the first and last field exercise for the battalion staff, and it wasn't too much longer afterwards that I had to say my second set of farewells. Leaving my friends Queen and Quinn and getting shipped to Phuc Vinh while they headed north to Phu Bail...that all happened too abruptly for me to have time to get emotional about it.

The 3/187 came to Vietnam as a unit, and they were redeploying as a unit. I watched each day as my friends from the Battalion Morning Reports Group boxed their equipment and prepared to head home. I wasn't jealous. They served their time, and they deserved to go home. No, I'm afraid that I started to feel lonely. It's like watching your best friend who lives next door as his family starts loading the moving van.

Once again, the people I knew in Vietnam were leaving. I would be transferred to another unit for the remainder of my tour. Since my MOS was still 11-Bravo, there was really only one job that I was qualified for...and I fully expected to be shipped to an infantry unit. That thought really bummed me out.

It came as shock when Captain Torres called me to the front of the company formation just days before my friends were supposed to ship out. Specialist Fifth Class Rich Leisure stood beside him, grinning from ear to ear.

I reported to the commander with a snappy salute. "Attention to orders" is about all I heard as Rich started unpinning the Spec 4 rank from my collar. I didn't know what was going on, and even the captain's statement about being "promoted to the rank of Sergeant" didn't make much sense.

Then Captain Torres and Rich pinned sergeant stripes on my collar.

"You didn't think we'd leave you hanging, did you Moff?" Captain Torres asked. "The 101st Division has decided to centralize all of the battalion staff sections into one Division Morning Reports Group. You've done an outstanding job here, so that's where you're heading."

Rich finished pinning the new stripes on my collar. He nodded in satisfaction, then said, "You'd be the low man on the totem pole as a Specialist, and we can't have that. Now you're a Sergeant, and there ain't nobody going to fuck with you. Am I right?"

"Damn straight!" I replied, then snapped an even more impressive salute at the commander.

Another chapter in my military career closed and another group of friends moved on. That's just the way that the military works. I said my farewells to the guys in the hooch, bought the last round of beer at the enlisted club, and then packed my duffel bag.

I left Phuc Vinh just as I had arrived…by plane. We bounced across the single-lane dirt runway and were soon in the air. It wasn't too long afterwards that I stepped off the plane at Bien Hoa and reported for duty with the Division centralized reports group.

The Army has another saying, "No good deed goes unpunished." My sergeant stripes were still new on my collar when I discovered the truth to that statement.

CINDERELLA

I stepped off the plane at Bien Hoa and walked right into the middle of a mess. The first hint I had was the voice that yelled out from across the tarmac.

"Sergeant!"

There were several sergeants on the flight with me, so I assumed the soldier in fatigues was addressing one of them or someone on the airplane crew. The only thoughts on my mind were finding my new boss and then locating my new home. I figured the first task was to find Division Headquarters. They could direct me to the new consolidated Morning Reports Group where I'd be working. After that, I wanted to find my new hooch.

"Sergeant Moffett!"

I turned upon hearing my name. The same guy standing near the flight line waved again, and that's when I remembered. I was a sergeant now.

"Yeah! That's me!" I tossed the duffel bag over my shoulder and walked to the lanky soldier.

"Private First Class Wilmot, Sergeant...at your service. Captain Miller sent me to bring you over to the Morning Reports Group. He's really looking forward to meeting you." PFC Wilmot grinned as if he wasn't telling me everything, and then he reached for my duffel bag. "Let me carry that for you, Sergeant."

In my estimation, the PFC was too old to be a private. He should've known the unwritten rule that everyone carries their own load...or his infantry teammates would help him lighten it to the point he could carry it. I wondered what the soldier's story was as I pulled away from him. "I can carry it to the jeep."

The grin grew wider. "Sorry, Sergeant, but we ain't got no jeep. Tried to get one from the Air Force when I got here. They weren't having none of it."

"Then we'll walk. How far is it?"

The private pointed toward a group of buildings on the other side of the runway. I glared at him to make him understand I was in no mood for joking around. That erased the man's smile.

"Honest, Sergeant Moffett, I ain't yanking your chain. This is the Air Force side," Wilmot explained. "The Army side is over that-away. We've gotta walk 'round the runway to get there."

I waved to the crew chief of the C-47 cargo plane that brought me to Bien Hoa, and was surprised when he motioned me toward the aircraft.

"Hey, Moffett!" the chief yelled over the sound of the propellers. "Looks like we dropped you off on the wrong side!"

"Yeah," I yelled back. "So much for curbside service!"

"Well come on, we're taking off for Tay Ninh. We'll taxi around to the Army side and you can jump off there."

I wasn't about to argue as Wilmot and I scrambled aboard the plane. The look of respect on the private's face made me proud of myself. We had a Gooney Bird taxi instead of walking, all because I was a friendly person.

It never hurts to be friendly. My nonstop chat with the flight crew on the trip from Phuc Vinh paid off. The pilot was interested in World War II. He was fascinated when I told him that my father flew C-47's over the "Hump" through the Himalayas between India and China. The entire crew couldn't stop laughing when I told him my dad had overrun the runway in China one time, and how it took four thousand Chinese with ropes to pull the plane out of the mud. I probably exaggerated the number of coolies pulling on the ropes, but that's okay. It was a war story, after all.

"That's a Gooney Bird, alright," the pilot joked. "They're clumsy on the ground but graceful in the air!"

The pilot gave me one of his patches and made me promise to tell my father about the new breed of C-47. Unlike its sister aircraft, the new "Spooky" was an AC-47 gunship armed with three mini-guns. Each gun could fire six thousand rounds a minute. I'd heard of it, but not by that nickname…everyone in the 101st called it "Puff the Magic Dragon." Infantrymen felt a little safer when they knew "Puff" was nearby. The AC-47 gunship was the only fire support when patrols were out of artillery range…and "Puff" was just a radio call away.

I knew my dad would love "Puff." It didn't carry any troops, but the gunship had enough firepower to cover every inch of a football field in under five seconds. The mini-guns had a distinct sound; unlike machineguns which went rat-tat-tat, the mini-guns had a hum that sounded like a steady brrrrp.

We reached the Army side of the runway in about three minutes. I thanked the crew again for their help and renewed the promise to tell my father about them. There wasn't time to lower the stairs, so I tossed my duffel bag over the side and then Wilmot and I jumped from the open hatch.

I tossed a quick salute toward the cockpit and watched as the plane roared down the runway. The crew had done me a favor, and I wouldn't forget it. Just like I wouldn't forget how the Air Force guys wouldn't loan a jeep so that infantry grunts didn't need to walk two miles. My second cousin was an Air Force cop somewhere in Vietnam. I knew from our chats that the Air Force had a few vehicles to spare. Something would have to be done about the unbalanced state of vehicle affairs.

"We've got to go through there," Wilmot said, pointing toward a group of hooches about fifty feet from the runway. Waist-high elephant grass stood between us and the buildings. "Those are empty right now, just waiting for you guys to come in. We can drop off your duffel bag there if you want, then go see Captain Miller."

"Sounds good to me. Which one?"

"Doesn't matter. You're the sergeant, Sergeant. Just pick one."

"That one right there," I said, pointing to the hooch perpendicular to the runway. It wasn't much protection from the runway noise, but it was better than the others. Then I started wading through the sharp elephant grass. We made it to the other side of the grass with only a few loud curses. Wilmot led the way toward the hooch.

We heard thumping noises from inside the forty-foot wooden building. I wasn't certain what the strange sounds were at first, but Wilmot wasn't concerned about it. I followed him into the hooch.

A broom was the cause of the thumping. The straw broom was taller than the beautiful young Vietnamese girl who held it in her hands. She must've been no more than five feet tall. I guessed her age at around fifteen years old. She was dressed in the typical peasant outfit…long black pants, colorful gorse shirt, and sandals. A coolie hat sat on one of the lower bunks; I assumed it was hers.

Wilmot motioned for her. When she walked over, I was struck by the most incredible smile I'd ever seen. I wondered how she or any of the young Vietnamese girls I encountered could smile at all. The young ones had lived most of their lives in fear. Between the US military and the communists, their country was torn to shreds. They had little hope for a promising future.

Wilmot introduced us. "Mai, this is Trung Si Pat Moffett."

Her smile grew wider. "Hi, Sergeant Pat!"

"Mai is one of your hooch maids," Wilmot explained. "The other one, Sam, will be here in a couple days, when the barracks starts filling up."

I wasn't certain about Mai or any other hooch maid, not since I found my shirt on a dead VC in Phouc Vinh. Perhaps Wilmot sensed my hesitancy, or maybe he'd run into bias against Vietnamese before. Either way, he simply continued talking.

"Mai's father is ARVN, and she's very supportive of the US."

Knowing that her father was with the Army of the Republic of Vietnam made me more comfortable. If she and her family supported the South Vietnamese Army, then she was one of the good guys.

"Yes," Mai replied solemnly. Then, like a High School cheerleader, her face lit up as she raised her broom and declared, "VC number ten, GI number one!"

"Right, GI number one!" I grinned back at the wonderful young lady.

"Sorry to interrupt, Mai, but I have to take Sergeant Moffett to see Dai Uy Miller," Wilmot stated as he headed toward the door.

"Sokay. I clean, you go." Mai made a brushing motion with her hand, then with the broom.

I took the hint and tossed my duffel on the first bunk. Then I followed Wilmot out the door. We walked down the dirt street in silence until I asked, "So, Wilmot…what's your first name?"

"Jimmy, Sergeant."

"Nice to meet you, Jimmy. And quit calling me 'Sergeant,' okay? Call me Moff."

Wilmot kept a straight face as he mimicked Mai's greeting. "Hi, Trung Si Moff."

"Keep it up, kid. You're cruising for a knuckle sandwich." I thumbed back toward the hooch. "What did you mean when you told Mai that I was 'Trung Si,' and who is Dai Uy Miller?"

"Trung Si means buck sergeant. Dai Uy means Captain. Most of the hooch maids are very courteous, but many of them will call you by ARVN rank. You get used to it."

"And who is Captain Miller?"

"He's the CO of Admin Company. You'll meet him shortly when we reach HQ." Wilmot pointed toward a large single-story building. "That's where we're heading."

Since Wilmot was talkative, I pressed for more information about my new workplace. "And how's the new Morning Reports Group working?"

"It's FUBAR'd. The LT's green, so there's no HMFIC." He grinned. "Until now, that is."

I translated Wilmot's statement to mean the Morning Reports Group was messed up beyond all recognition, the lieutenant in charge was too new to know what he was doing, and there was no head honcho in charge. That's when it hit me…in the Army, no good deed goes unpunished. My guide just told me that I was in charge, and that didn't sound promising to me. It would be like the blind leading the blind. However, I couldn't let on that I was a brand new sergeant who didn't know what I was doing. It was time to redirect the conversation.

I stopped and looked at the young private. "Remind me never to tell you another acronym, Wilmot. You've been in the army too long. Your mother won't understand you when you get home."

Wilmot just grinned wider. "It's SNAFU, Sergeant. DEROS in twenty-five and a wake-up, then I'm CONUS-bound to the world on that freedom bird ASAP."

"There's a cure for acronym-itis," I teased. "Let me find a bar of soap."

He raised his hands in mock surrender. "It's cool, man. Relax, okay?"

I shook my head and started walking. There was no help for the kid, I could see that already. "You don't work in the Morning Reports Group, do you?"

"Nope."

"Good. Otherwise I'd have to arrange a little shower party for you."

"What's with you grunts and soap, anyway? First you want to brush my teeth with it, now you want to wash me up?" Wilmot shook his head as he walked beside me. "I think you've been humping in the bush too long. Couple of boom-boom trips with the Saigon girls and you'll calm right down, I'll bet."

I made an educated guess. "Is that where you lost your stripes, Wilmot?"

"Yep. Too many boom-boom girls and ba mui ba beers, came rolling in two days later. How'd you know?"

"You only have twenty-five days left in-country. That makes you a short-timer, and you should've made it to Spec 5 or sergeant by now."

"I can see the army has screwed up already," Wilmot stated. "Seems like they might've got the right guy in the right place at the right time. I'm glad I'm short, 'cause that's a scary thought!"

We both laughed, and I followed Wilmot into the admin building. He introduced me to Captain Miller and then headed for the exit. I never saw Private Wilmot after that. Rumor had it that he received another chance to get into Saigon, where he spent several extra days dallying with the girls again. I don't know if he made his freedom bird flight home, or if he ended up in LBJ…the acronym for Long Binh Jail.

Captain Miller shook my hand like he'd been liberated. He waved his arm to show me the empty office space full of desks, filing cabinets and typewriters. Then, with a relieved smile, he said, "I'm glad you're here, Sergeant Moffett. You're in charge."

A phone started ringing on one of the desks just as I turned to face him. I looked at the officer as if he was speaking in a foreign language. "In charge, sir? Of what?"

"You're in charge of the consolidated reports group, Sergeant. At least until the other team leaders arrive." He waited for the traditional "yessir." When it didn't arrive, he sighed heavily and explained. "Listen, it's like this. There are three teams; infantry, artillery and admin. You're the NCOIC of the infantry team after the other team leaders arrive. Until then, you're in charge of all the sections. Understood?"

I had no choice but to reply with, "Yes sir, but...."

"But what, Sergeant?"

From his irritated tone of voice, I knew that I wasn't going to receive any more information from him. The captain had issued his order, and it was up to me to figure out how to make it work. I nodded and gave a reply more confident than I really felt. "Nothing, sir. I can handle it."

"Good man." Captain Miller pointed toward the ringing telephone. "Then I'll leave you to it."

I waited until the officer left and then walked through the empty room. There were about forty desks in the office. The current layout was too chaotic. Each desk had a three-by-five card on it to show which unit's clerk would sit there.

The desks needed rearranging so that each team was in the same area. Several chalkboards and butcher block stands needed to be moved, and the phone lines rewired. I made mental notes of how I wanted the office to run, and then stopped at the desk with the ringing telephone. I picked it up.

"Reports group, Sergeant Moffett...." I spent the rest of the day answering phones to receive the daily reports from each subordinate unit, and I also rearranged the office. The tin roof made the room so hot around fifteen hundred—three o'clock—that I finally headed for the door. That's when I ran into my first subordinate who had walked from the airport.

"Who the hell are you?" My question was abrupt, but I was too hot to be cordial.

The young Specialist fumbled with a reply, and somewhere in there I heard what unit he was to work with. I pointed him toward his desk, explained how I wanted things to operate, and then sent him to his hooch to ground his gear. It was too hot to work, and I was in charge...and from that point on, the Morning Reports Group ceased operations at thirteen hundred.

That was the routine for the next few days. A new guy came in, one of the group would demand to know who they were, and then we'd put them to work. The system worked pretty well. Until DiOrio showed up, that is.

I was working at my desk one morning when the office door slammed. The entire room of soldiers fell silent, as if waiting for someone else to call out the traditional challenge and greeting. I looked up from my paperwork and stared at the most massive soldier I'd ever seen.

This guy was a soldier's soldier. He was six foot two, and at least two hundred twenty-five pounds of sheer muscle. His physique was pounded into a perfect "V" shaped body that Atlas would envy. He had the bearing and demeanor of a barely caged predator. It clearly said, "It doesn't pay to mess around with me."

Everybody else turned to look back at me, so I did the only thing I could. In a booming voice I asked, "Who the hell are you?"

"Mike DiOrio," he replied. "Who the hell are you?"

"Pat Moffett, you goumba. If you're infantry, then get your butt back here. I've got work for you."

DiOrio looked at me for a moment, then shrugged as if to say he wouldn't kill me today. He stomped toward me—not in an intimidating way, but because he had a very heavy stride—and stopped in front of my desk. "Yes, Sergeant?"

"Where you from, DiOrio?"

"Phu Bai, Sergeant."

I'd been expecting Spec 4 DiOrio. Rumor had it that he had a huge amount of combat experience in Phu Bai and supposedly killed numerous VC. His unit sent him to the rear to get him out of the fighting and give him a break. It was one of the army's unwritten rules, perhaps because having a hero in the unit was dangerous. Other soldiers might get themselves killed trying to emulate him, and morale would definitely plummet if the enemy finally managed to nail him.

Besides, DiOrio already had enough fruit salad. He received two bronze stars for valor, and two silver stars. It was even rumored that he came very close to being awarded the Congressional Medal of Honor as well. But another unwritten rule said don't ask about a soldier's experience fighting in the bush, so I didn't.

I doubted he would ever volunteer the details of his combat experience. All that mattered to me was that DiOrio could type. His unit sent him to the Morning Reports Group to get him out of harms way, and I needed him.

"That's your desk over there, Mike. This morning's report needs to be completed for your battalion, so jump on it. Ask if you have any questions." I grinned. "Do you have any questions?"

"No, Sergeant."

"Call me Moff. I'll show you around when you're done, and then we'll head to the hooch. It's just you and me for now, but the other grunts will arrive over the next few days."

DiOrio nodded and headed to his desk. Our primary task was to receive the morning reports that came in from the field. The clerks like DiOrio would type up the report for their units and send them to the other team leaders. I got all the infantry unit reports, and the other two team leaders took care of artillery and admin units.

I would verify the numbers for my team—no matter what the other team leaders said, infantrymen can count—and return any erroneous reports back to the clerk. Once everything was in order, I would consolidate the reports into one branch-specific roll-up report. Then the whole packet went to First Lieutenant Koneche for approval and signature.

After twelve hundred—noon—the group took care of secondary administrative tasks. Unless there was a critical task, everything was completed by three o'clock. There was no circulation in the building and the air in the office was stifling by mid afternoon. You could probably bake bread in the rafters from the sweltering heat under the scorching tin roof.

I released everyone to go back to their hooches where they could try to stay cool. I took DiOrio with me back to the hooch. Up to this point, I was the only inhabitant of the noisy barracks. It's not that I had anything against the other teams, but I wanted fellow grunts all in one place. It's easier on the military police that way.

Mai sat out in the sun, her wash tub and washboard beside her as we walked up to the hooch. After the laundry was dry, she would press it with an old iron. My laundry always came back pressed, and my boots were shined until they sparkled. It wasn't what I was used to, but the field grade officers and their general bosses required a "professional" appearance from their rear area soldiers.

The hooch maids worked for ten dollars a week doing one soldier's laundry for six days. Mai was there faithfully every day except for Sundays. Sam, the other maid, hadn't made her appearance yet. Between the two of them, they would be able to keep twelve guys looking sharp.

I introduced DiOrio to the petite teenager. "Mai, this is Spec 4 DiOrio. Take care of him like you're taking care of me, okay?"

She stood and smiled at the towering soldier. I could tell that she was a little frightened, and I didn't blame her. I wasn't five feet tall like Mai, and I was intimidated by the giant beside me.

"I do, Sergeant Pat," she said bravely. "I take care GI De-de…The Oreo."

It was amazing to see such a giant man be so gentle as DiOrio laughed. "Not 'The Oreo,' Mai. That's a cookie. I'm Mike DiOrio, okay?"

"Sokay." She appeared less afraid as she joked, "You too big. No cookie! I call you GI Mike, sokay?"

"That's fine, Mai."

I couldn't help but laugh. Her unexpected joke even eased my sense of intimidation…it's hard to be afraid of someone that a five foot tall girl called a cream-filled cookie. I led DiOrio to the hooch to show him our spartan living quarters. Then I closed the door and looked straight into his eyes so he knew I wasn't kidding.

"I only have one rule here, Mike. Nobody touches the hooch maids. If you want to get laid, do it somewhere else. Are we clear?"

DiOrio nodded. "Clear as rain, Moff. If you need any help enforcing that, just let me know. Mai's a sweetie. I'll make hamburger of anybody here who touches her."

I let out a sigh of relief. The last thing I wanted was to tackle a brute like DiOrio. It was a pleasant surprise that he also felt protective of Mai. "Thanks, Mike. Pick a bunk and ground your gear. I'm hitting the rack."

The hooch was basically a giant wood-framed building surrounded by metal screens. It let the breeze blow in; even the jet wash from the runway behind us was refreshing. Working in the office had baked all of the water out of me, and I was exhausted. I plopped down on my bunk and was almost asleep when I heard the spring on the door creak. A few seconds later, the door slammed. It wasn't surprising; the spring always made the door slam.

The refrigerator door at the far end of the hooch opened and closed. I debated rolling over to tell DiOrio that he could help himself to the beer I'd put in the fridge, then thought he'd figure it out for himself.

"Sergeant Pat," spoke a soft feminine voice beside my ear. "You sleep?"

I opened my eyes and wiped the sweat off my forehead. "No, Mai. I'm awake now. What do you need?"

"Not me, Sergeant Pat. You need cold beer." She raised a can of cold Budweiser in her hand. "This make you feel better."

I sat up on the bunk and took the beer. "Thanks, Mai. You're a godsend."

She graced me with one of her incredible smiles, then walked to DiOrio's bunk. "GI Mike, you sleep?"

That became one of Mai's traditions. She watched over the guys in the hooch and would bring cold beers to anyone who broke into a sweat. Of course, in Vietnam everyone broke into a sweat, so we ensured that the fridge was always well stocked. Having Mai around was like having a loving kid sister in the house, one who always looked out for her self-adopted older siblings. The young teenager was very active and enjoyed kidding around. She was the most open of all the hooch maids, and she took good care of "her GI's."

The next day dawned as every day in Vietnam seemed to…hot and humid, with a forecast of even more humid and hot throughout the day. I shrugged into my newly-pressed uniform and headed to breakfast and then work.

It was fifteen hundred when the Army receiving station called. Apparently the Air Force finally took pity on us grunts and were bussing soldiers to the Army side of the base. Another one of my guys arrived and waited at the receiving station for someone to pick him up. I told everyone to shut down the shop when they were finished and headed out the door.

It was a short walk to the station. At first, I didn't see any soldiers around. I assumed that the room's only inhabitant was a Vietnamese janitor because of his short stature. A layer of reddish-brown dust covered the man. It wasn't until he turned around that I could make out name tags on what must've been a uniform.

"Damn, soldier!" I walked toward him and shook my head. "Did you leave any dirt for the other grunts to play in?"

"Of course, Sergeant." Two red lines crossed his face under the dust as the man's lips broke into a smile. "There's plenty where I came from, enough to get into everybody's C-rats. You're not a red-leg unless there's grit in your chow."

"Artilleryman, huh?" I slapped him on the back, and immediately wished I hadn't. A giant dust cloud rose from the soldier's uniform. I started coughing from the fine powder and made a mental note not to do that again. There was still enough dust caked on him that Mai could plant flowers in her wash water after cleaning his uniform.

"All the way, Sergeant. I'm Herb Wise."

"Pat Moffett." I extended a hand toward the door. "The guys have already quit work for the day. We're heading to the bar, if you want to come."

"Sounds good to me. Do I get to shower first?"

"Sorry, no time for that. We can drop your stuff off at the hooch, though."

We were definitely an interesting sight when we walked into the Enlisted Men's Club, the Army's formal name for our on-base bar. My uniform was pressed and boots polished, while Herb's was barely recognizable as clothing. DiOrio made the same mistake I had by slapping Wise on the back; this time, I stood far enough away from the dust cloud that I didn't choke.

"Come on, Pig-Pen," DiOrio managed to cough out. "Grab a beer. You'll need it if your insides are as dry as your outside."

"Hey!" bellowed a voice from the other end of the bar. "We don't serve no gooks at the EM Club!"

Mike looked at me, slightly confused. Apparently Herb had heard similar insults in the past because he walked straight to the soldier across the room. I just shook my head and followed him. I could hear DiOrio's heavy stride right behind me.

Wise walked fast, I gave him that. He was in front of the PFC before DiOrio and I made it halfway across the bar.

Herb's head was barely level with the PFC's, who was still sitting down. That didn't stop him from getting right in the guys face and asking, "Who you calling a gook, shit for brains?"

The bar fell silent, as bars always do when the promise of blood tinges the air. The barstool scraped across the wooden floor as the young private stood. He was definitely taller and heavier than poor tiny Herb Wise.

DiOrio and I stepped behind Herb at that point. Mike spoke softly, which is always a dangerous sign. "Is there a problem here?"

It's times like these when I wanted to be one of the spectators. It must've looked incredible. Herb Wise was barely five foot and looked like he weight a hundred forty at the most. Behind him was me…and beside me was the colossal Mike DiOrio.

The PFC chose discretion over valor. He sat back down on his barstool and turned his head. "No problem, man. I made a mistake is all. Don't mean nuthin'."

We managed to survive the encounter without anymore insults. SP4 Wise nodded as if satisfied and walked back to our end of the bar. It soon became obvious that Herb was really cool, and so DiOrio dropped the Peanuts character nickname of Pig-Pen. Other guys from the Morning Reports Group showed up throughout the evening. Neither Mike nor I would warn them…and the other guys greeted Herb with a hearty slap on the back. We soon had that end of the bar to ourselves after the other patrons got tired of drinking a layer of dust on their beer.

Regrettably, we established a pattern that night. Herb Wise—who was barely tall enough to make it into the service because of his height—seemed to enjoy picking fights at bars. He would walk up to the biggest guys in the bar, and every one of them would tell him to get lost. Then Herb would get me and DiOrio. We'd walk back to the big guys and stand behind Wise as he asked, "is there a problem?" Oddly enough, nobody ever said yes to that question.

We found a better nickname for Herb the next day. I walked into the hooch and asked, "Where's Wise?"

DiOrio pointed toward the bunk. "He's crashed."

After that, it became a standing joke. "Where's Crash?"

That was always followed up with a finger pointing toward Herb's bunk and the question, "Where do you think?"

Sure enough, Herb "Crash" Wise was crashed out on his bunk. It wouldn't matter if he just came from chow, the office, or the bar…he always headed directly to his bunk and went to sleep.

Mai never felt threatened by Herb. I asked her about it once, and her reply said it all. "GI Herb okay. He my height!"

I debated ending the welcoming trip to the bar after the next soldier in our team arrived. The receiving station called me late the next afternoon; it was after work hours, yet they wanted me to pick up Spec 5 Brunetti. I wasn't too happy about it, as it interrupted the team's trip to the bar…but I wasn't going to let the guy sit there overnight. Especially not when he was technically my same rank.

The Army had two separate rank structures for senior enlisted. Sergeants had command authority and Specialists were technicians. Even though Brunetti and I were the same rank of E5, I held a command position while he held a technical position. The only real difference was that subordinates were required to follow a Sergeant's orders, especially when under fire.

As I walked to the receiving station, I was a little concerned about the possibility of conflict between this new Spec 5 and me. I was even more concerned when I saw him. Spec 5 Mike Brunetti was huge. He was six foot and at least two hundred and forty pounds. With an eighteen inch neck and huge thighs and calves, he had a body that any pro football middle linebacker would fight for.

I was pleasantly surprised that Brunetti wasn't interested in taking charge of the team. We went back to the hooch, where I told Mike to dump his stuff on a bunk and come with me to the bar. That was my first mistake.

Brunetti could definitely drink. If it wasn't for the fact that he drank faster than everyone else, he could've drunk all of us under the table. Herb Wise, Brunetti and I stayed at the club until closing time. Everyone else already went back to the hooch. That was my second mistake.

We started walking back to the hooch, Herb and I in the lead and Brunetti a few steps behind us. The street was a dirt road with drainage ditches on either side. There was standing water in the ditches, and perhaps that's what we heard. Or maybe it was the sudden silence behind us...whatever the reason, Herb and I turned almost simultaneously and looked back.

Mike Brunetti was gone. It took us several moments to backtrack, Herb searching one ditch while I looked at the other one. The splash of water over an obstacle led us to him. Brunetti lay facedown in the ditch as water rushed over his legs and buttocks.

I tried to pick him up but it was impossible; I could barely hold his head out of the water. It was almost comical. Tiny Herb Wise tried to help lift the unconscious burly giant and barely managed to get one arm out of the water. Brunetti's face was wet and his head kept sliding out of my hands. There was a splash as he hit the water, and then I'd have to haul his nose out of the muck.

Four or five guys were also heading back from the bar, and it took all of us to lug Brunetti's dead weight out of the ditch. One of the rescuers staggered off, mumbling something about getting a jeep; thankfully, he never made it to the motor pool. The rest of us managed to get Brunetti upright and then we half-carried, half-dragged him back to the hooch.

We teased Brunetti the next morning about trying to sleep on water. That's when Wise and I learned that his hands matched the rest of his bulk. A friendly pat on the back from Brunetti could be life-threatening. He didn't know his own strength. After we felt those affectionate and potentially rib-cracking swats, we urged him to consider another career. There was definitely a place with the Steelers waiting for him when he returned to the world and his hometown of Pittsburgh.

It would be awhile before that could happen, though. Spec 5 Brunetti was a new guy, fresh from the world. He got off the plane at Long Binh and then hopped a bus to the Morning Reports Group at Bien Hoa. Being regular army, he only had nine months in-country before his DEROS and the return flight home.

Brunetti earned the nickname of "Hulk" from the popular DC comic, "The Incredible Hulk." Even DiOrio agreed with it, even though they were both of the same build. For one thing, the Hulk was always a peaceful creature in his normal form. The comic book character only turned into a monster when angered. Mike was the same way.

Mai loved Brunetti, probably because he was very protective of her and treated her like a little sister. She always came every day with that smile…it was unbelievable that anyone could smile at all, and she always smiled. Yet the smile that she had for Brunetti was completely different. It wasn't love, at least not in any physical sense. It was just different.

Other guys arrived through the following weeks and soon every bunk in the hooch was occupied. One Sunday morning the guys and I were hanging out at our makeshift hooch bar. We were watching AFVN—Armed Forces Vietnam—on television and having our morning Budweiser.

It wasn't unusual to see local Vietnamese from Bien Hoa village at the base on Sunday. With proper worker ID's, the locals dressed in their Sunday finest were permitted to attend church services at the base chapel.

That morning, however, we noticed a particularly well dressed Vietnamese woman purposefully approach the front door of the hooch. She wore a turquoise Ao Dai dress with a matching umbrella, black tong, low-heeled sandals and black sunglasses. The shoulder length jet-black air was the perfect finishing touch.

As she stepped onto the pallet in front of the door, we realized there was something familiar about her. We waited in silent anticipation to see what she wanted. She opened the door and stepped into the hooch. The woman was a breathtaking beauty. Her umbrella closed softly and then she took off her sunglasses.

"Mai?" we all gasped in unison.

"Good morning, my GIs."

"Mai, you look really great in that dress!" I jumped off my barstool and offered her the seat.

"Thank you, Sergeant Pat," she cooed. In perfect English, as if she had rehearsed it many times, she said, "I just came to say hello before church service."

"Can we offer you something to drink?" Brunetti stammered. He looked around our makeshift bar and then realized there wasn't anything appropriate. However, he had offered and was gentleman enough to tell her the available options. "Um, we have Bud, soda, Jack Daniels."

"No, thank you. Mai must go or I be late for service," she demurred in her usual pidgin English. "I see you in morning."

Herb Wise stopped her with a question as she slid from the barstool and moved toward the door. "Hey, Mai! Say a prayer for us, will you?"

"I pray for GIs every day, not just Sunday," she replied. Then, flashing her incredible smile once more, she swept out the door and headed for church.

We were all grateful for that brief visit and—ever after—thought of her not as a hooch maid, but as our own Cinderella.

DEAR JOHN

Whoever said "absence makes the heart grow fonder" was never a soldier. If anything, every day spent away from home— away from "The World" as we called it—just made it easier to forget that there really was someplace other than Vietnam.

Our daily existence consisted of bland army chow for every meal, endless casualty and personnel reports, sweltering heat, and the rocket attacks on the nearby airbase that seemed like a nightly event. I soon regretted choosing a hooch near the airfield. The landing strip was the primary target of Viet Cong rockets and mortars, and the VC were anything but accurate. Missing something as large as a runway might seem an impossible task, but somehow the VC managed to do it consistently.

That was my life in Bien Hoa. There was no room in Vietnam for romance. Companionship could be found in Saigon for five bucks, but that was only sex. Even the hookers knew it when they called out, "Hey GI, I love you! You love me too, long time, short time, only five dollah!"

It was a cruder song than the one by The Doors which said, "Hello, I love you, won't you tell me your name?" The whores knew everyone as "GI," so that saved a lot of time cutting through the introductions. I envied the other guys in the hooch who took advantage of the prostitutes. Even when they ribbed me about it, though, I wasn't ready to jump into the bar scene of wild girls, booze and drugs. I still had someone waiting faithfully for me at home.

Surrounded by that bizarre atmosphere, The World took on a dreamlike aspect of its own. Stateside was a place of drive-in movies, chocolate malts, and cruising down the main drag with your favorite girl. I could almost remember doing those things, but after six months in a foreign land…home and The World didn't seem so real anymore.

There was only one thing that kept me anchored to what was going on in the States, and that was the daily mail call. I thoroughly enjoyed the letters and care packages from my mom, sure...but it was the letters from my fiancé that helped me through the nights. I sent my medals and awards to Gretchen for safekeeping before I left Phouc Vinh, confident that she would display them in a place of honor for everyone to see.

I carried a picture of Gretchen in my wallet. Sweat and Vietnam's humidity faded it over time to the point that I barely recognized her anymore. I kept all of her letters in my foot locker, secured with a rubber band and filed in chronological order. I would pull them out when the days started blurring into each other. Just reading them was enough to restore my faith that there was at least one certain thing in the world. My girl was at home, waiting patiently and faithfully for me to return so that we could get married.

Like The World, though, even that certainty began to fade. Eventually the perfume from her first letters, the ones she sent to me during my early months in-country, began to lose their scent. It wasn't long before they carried the same dry, musty odor of mildew that pervaded everything in Vietnam.

The other guys in the hooch gave me a hard time about faithfully responding to Gretchen's every letter. They noticed what I didn't... that the frequency of her correspondence and the undying promises of love grew less with each passing week.

I was too busy to notice. After DiOrio, Brunetti and Wise showed up, the Morning Reports Group started filling up quickly. The other two team leaders arrived and followed my lead by putting members of their own team into the same hooch.

It didn't take long for my section—the infantry part of the Morning Reports Group—to gain the reputation of being the "cool hooch." We were quite a motley crew, each with his own quirks and together blending into a section known for its strange personalities and hardcore partying.

There was one kid, Dannenberg, who was so squeaky clean that he just didn't fit in with the guys from the hooch. Dannenberg wanted to be a lawyer. He smoked a pipe, always had his nose in a book, and was so retentive about his appearance that the only thing missing was a British accent. Eventually the guys got so tired of him always complaining about their partying until two in the morning that they booted him out to another hooch.

Our other hooch maid, Sam, showed up that first week. It was obvious that she wouldn't be as considerate as Mai. Sam was older and the war had already taken its toll on her. She didn't smile or joke around. Cleaning the hooch was simply a job to do, one that put food on her family's table and nothing more. It wasn't a bad attitude...it was simply no more than most Vietnamese seemed to feel. They were indifferent to the war and so far in poverty that it didn't seem to matter to them who won. The most important thing in their lives was basic survival.

I admired their tenacity and stubborn will to endure any hardship...but there were times, when looking at the blank faces of Vietnamese peasants working the fields as we drove by on Highway 1-A, that I wondered if they had already lost something vital. It seemed as if they were automatons and no longer human.

Mai was the exception to this sense of hopelessness. Her quick smile and innocent joy for life was infectious, even when it caused trouble. She had only been working as our hooch maid for a few weeks when I caught the scent of something disgustingly familiar.

I had dropped by the hooch after breakfast to grab something from my locker when I smelled it. "Good lord, Mai, what is that godawful smell?"

She looked up from whatever she was doing to the refrigerator—I assumed she was cleaning it—and smiled that perfect smile of hers. As always, she was dressed in a gorse shirt and black pajama pants. "Good morning, Sergeant Pat!"

"Yeah, good morning." I walked past her and into the hooch, nose snorting as I tried to locate the source of the rancid odor. After making a circuit through the open bay, I ended up standing beside the young lady. That's when I noticed the small bread bag filled with black goo that sat on the refrigerator shelf.

I pointed toward the bag. "What's that, Mai?"

"This?" She pulled the bag from the fridge and held it up for inspection. "It Nuoc Mam, Sergeant Pat. Very tasty. You try?"

The smell reminded me of the first time I'd encountered the fermented fish sauce, back in Phouc Vinh with Rich Leisure. It had the same affect…I gagged and swallowed hard, trying to get away from the stench.

Mai opened the bag and extended it toward me. She was still smiling, as if it was a marvelous thing she tried to show me. "It my lunch, Sergeant Pat. Good with rice. Has fish head, see?"

One glassy fish eye peered through the plastic bread sack. That did it. I backpedaled toward the door, one hand over my mouth. "Get it out of here, Mai, please! No more Nuoc Mam in the fridge, okay?"

That's what I said, and I would swear to it. What Mai might've heard past the fingers that clamped my mouth and the retching sounds…well, that could've been something completely different entirely.

Nuoc Mam is worse than skunk musk. I knew some Marines near Da Nang who swore by the stuff. They proclaimed that there was never a need for a compass to get back to their base. It seems the Vietnamese had a Nuoc Mam factory near the base, and the Marines could just follow the scent back home. Why anyone would actually want to walk toward the stuff is beyond me. Then again, Marines are capable of doing lots of things that normal humans can't.

Mai seemed to have listened because I couldn't smell Nuoc Mam for several days. Then again, I wasn't smelling much of anything for several days. Everybody around me kept offering water because they thought I was dehydrated…they wouldn't believe that I had another reason for breathing only through my mouth. That's the only way I found to get rid of the scent and taste from my brief exposure to Mai's open bag of Nuoc Mam.

I was just getting my sense of smell back when SP4 Dave Corbus—a new guy that we nicknamed "Stymie," as he had the personality of the character from The Little Rascals show—asked one night, "What's that smell?"

"What smell?" I replied.

"You can't smell it?" Dave queried the other guys in the hooch.

"Yeah," said Herb Wise. "Smells like rotten fish."

I watched them circle through the hooch for awhile. It would've been funny if I didn't already have a strong suspicion what they were trying to find. They were like a pack of sniffing bloodhounds. I walked to the door and stepped outside before offering a suggestion over my shoulder. "You might try the fridge."

Dave Corbus was the unlucky victim who opened the refrigerator door. His reaction was immediate and predictable. "Shit, man! What is that stuff?"

Even standing outside, I wasn't immune from the sudden stench. I answered through clenched teeth, "Must be Mai's Nuoc Mam."

"Ah, man," declared Herb. "I've smelled it before, but it's never been this bad!"

Dave Corbus then reported the devastating news. "It spilled all over the beer, Moff. What're we gonna do?"

We had a case or so of domestic—as in American domestic, like Budweiser—beer in the refrigerator. I knew there was only one thing to do. "Drag it all out to the shower and wash it off. That should take care of it."

The guys and I carried all of the beer into our makeshift shower. There was no way that we could use the unit showers…they didn't have water hot enough to sterilize the beer. For another, they were several blocks away. As it was, my stomach steadily reminded me of roller coaster rides from childhood just from carrying the beer from the fridge to our shower around the corner.

The hooch shower had been one of my first projects. Just like in Phouc Vinh, it consisted of a rickety frame with an airplane fuel tank on top. Seems there was no shortage of spare airplane fuel tanks in Vietnam. All you had to do was ask the Air Force for one…as long as the asking occurred sometime in the wee hours of the morning when nobody was watching, that is.

The water was scalding, and we all waited until the tank was empty before examining the beer. It was no use. Even with several hundred gallons of steaming water, the stench of Nuoc Mam remained. You couldn't raise a beer to your lips without smelling it. Popping the top and holding the can away from your face while pouring didn't help either. Taste is mostly determined by scent, and we could definitely still smell the Nuoc Mam. Beer isn't supposed to taste like rancid fish. It just wasn't worth it.

We tried everything, but eventually we all reached the same conclusion. There simply was no other choice. With the ceremonial feel of a funeral, we carried the beer to the Air Force side of the runway and laid it to rest in the tall elephant grass. Perhaps the Nuoc Mam would've worn off by the time the flyboys found it…and if not, then the Air Force guys would learn that nothing in Vietnam was free. Not even domestic beer.

When Mai arrived for work the next day, she was greeted by everyone in the hooch. This time there was no miscommunication. We made it clear, while we loved her dearly, either she or the Nuoc Mam had to go. Our message must have got through because from that day on, Mai kept her dead fish sauce out of the hooch.

Peace reigned in the hooch as days turned into weeks, and then we picked up a mascot. It wasn't something that we planned to do but, like most adoptions in Vietnam, it just sort of happened. A mangy, floppy eared-looking thing simply arrived one day. It took a look at all the guys in the hooch, scratched itself with its remaining hind leg, and with a sharp bark announced that it was there to stay.

We called this three-legged dog "Tripod." He was a medium-sized dog—which made him an oddity in Vietnam, where a large dog meant more meat for dinner—so he fit right in with the rest of us oddballs in the hooch. From the looks of it, Tripod had lost his leg from an errant grenade or rocket attack. The missing leg didn't seem to slow him down at all, though. He was better at predicting rocket attacks than the Air Force guys across the runway from us, and would typically beat all of us in running to the safety of our protective bunker when the rockets started whistling in.

Tripod wasn't the only pet in the hooch, although he was the only one who managed to stay the entire time I was there. A cherry kid from the States bought a monkey from a local roadside vendor. He kept the thing in a cage near his bunk and thought it was the cutest thing. That was his first mistake…you should never have anything "cute" around a bunch of infantrymen. If you can't eat it, drink it or sleep with it, then it has no value to a grunt.

Brunetti hated that monkey. I think that was the first symptom that us 11-Bravo's were rubbing off on him. He claimed that there was no shutting the thing up. It screeched all the time, most likely because its young owner trained it to "sing" for its supper. I don't know where the monkey stored all of the bananas the kid fed it because it was always "singing." Even rocket attacks wouldn't stop the shrill screeching. I'll admit that after a few hours cramped in an underground bunker waiting out the attack, it was somehow disappointing to walk back into the hooch and find the screaming monkey still alive.

I don't think that monkey lasted a week. We woke up to the strangest sound one morning…the sound of silence. The young kid stood by the monkey cage, muttering something to himself in shock. It sounded like, "My monkey's dead." Didn't seem to matter that he kept repeating himself, as if disbelieving his own words.

Brunetti cleared it up for him, though. "Hey kid, looks like your monkey's dead."

That got his attention. He turned and looked blankly at Brunetti, then replied with an intelligent, "Huh?"

"Looks like he strung himself up by his leash." Mike pointed to the three-foot leash the kid used to walk the monkey. It was wrapped around the monkey's neck and the perch that the monkey used to sit on. "I guess he hung himself. Tough luck, wouldn't you say?"

The kid turned red in the face, as if wanting to say something alright. Discretion made him bite his tongue—or perhaps it was the fact that Brunetti outweighed him by a factor of three—and he did the only thing he could. He carried the cage outside and buried the monkey in the elephant grass beside the runway. We didn't have the heart to suggest that he just fling the tiny corpse into the grass. While it worked with our tainted beer, the kid probably wouldn't have appreciated how well elephant grass can hide things you don't want anymore.

After filling in the grave that he'd dug with an entrenching tool, the new guy walked back into the hooch. He packed his duffel bag and moved without saying another word into a nearby hooch. It was obvious from the glare he gave Brunetti that he thought the same thing the rest of us were guessing, but he never did confront Mike with it. Neither did we. Sometimes it's best to accept that freak accidents happen. Anything else is useless conjecture…it would be like playing guessing games about what could drive a monkey to commit suicide.

The empty bunk didn't stay empty for long. New guys were arriving every day for the Morning Reports Group and other sections at the headquarters. One of the new guys was SP4 David Motley. He was a self-proclaimed redneck with a huge southern drawl. Motley was always in trouble, and we were always having to bail him out of jail for starting barroom brawls. He loved messing around with people.

One of his favorite games was when anyone asked where he was from; he would reply, "Why, Cleveland, of course."

"Cleveland, Ohio? I've been there," was typically the response.

That's when Motley would lower the boom. "No, Cleveland, Mississippi, asshole! Where the fuck did you think?"

It wasn't that Motley was a bad kid. He considered all of us family. Based on the rules of how he was raised, in his mind that meant he had to take care of all of us. He called me "Patty," and was always protecting me at the club. Anytime I would strike up a conversation with other guys at the bar, Motley would come sauntering over and say, "Hey, Sah-gent Patty, ah dese guys botherin' you? If 'n theyah causin' you any trouble, you jes' let me know. Ah'll be sittin' in the cornah ovah heah, you jes' call me and ah'll be right theah."

His heart was in the right place, but he didn't seem to have the sense God gave a goose. He seemed to see things in black and white. Anyone who wasn't white, he saw as black. He nearly ended up suffering from friendly fire because of a stunt he pulled with Mai. I had warned all of the guys when they arrived at the hooch, "don't ever try sex stuff with Mai." I had Brunetti to back me up on this. Motley was the only one who ever pushed the issue.

Mai always did the laundry in a giant pot outside the hooch. I was crashed out on my bunk one day, counting pinhole leaks in my eyelids after a long day at work, when one of the guys yelled for me. "Sarge, you better wake up. It's Motley."

"He drunk again? What jail is he in now?" I swung my feet over the edge of the bunk and wiped the sweat from my face. There's nothing like trying to sleep in a broiler, which is what it felt like to take an afternoon nap in Vietnam.

"It's not that, Sarge. He's messing with Mai."

I was out the door in a heartbeat. Motley was standing behind Mai, but he wasn't roughing her up or doing anything physical. His words told me that I'd arrived in just the nick of time.

"Come heah lil' girl, ah'm your Big Dave," Motley said. "Ah got sumthin' special fo' ya."

By the time he reached out to grab her by the waist, I had him by the back of his neck. I was in a cold rage as I threw him against the wall. "What the hell do you think you're doing, you stupid sonuvabitch!"

"I wasn't doin' nothin', Sarge," Motley replied in a bewildered tone. "Just seein' if she was innerested in a little boom boom like the othah gooks aroun' heah. Wasn' nuthin', honest."

I was pissed. "Don't ever do that again! Find you a Saigon whore if you need to get your rocks off, but you leave Mai alone. Are we clear about that?!"

Motley nodded slowly, not quite understanding. "But damn, Sarge, she's jes' a gook."

"No, you stupid redneck, she's a woman and she works for us." It seemed that I needed to make things simple for Motley to understand. I thumped my forefinger hard against his chest. "I'll kill you if you ever touch her again! Got it?"

"Sorry, Patty." My words seemed to sink in as Motley looked at me like a kid whose feelings had been bruised. "I was jes' kiddin' aroun. It'll nevah happen agin."

I let him go and he found the fastest route out of my sight. Mai had been watching all this with wide eyes. It was obvious that she understood what could have happened, and she was terrified.

"You ever have a problem with any of the guys in the hooch," I told her, "you come to Sergeant Pat, or Sergeant Mike, or Herb."

Mai just stood there trembling and shaking, her head down and hands still wringing the shirt she had been washing. I touched her gently on the shoulder and asked, "You want me to make him bloody like VC?"

"Oh no, no." Mai raised her eyes to mine. Her generous heart could forgive even this as she shook her head and said, "No VC. It's sokay, GI Dave just kidding. No need no bloody like VC. It's sokay, Sergeant Pat."

It was a good thing for Motley that Mai was so generous and kindhearted. Brunetti heard about his stunt and it took some fancy talking to keep the giant linebacker-sized soldier from taking Motley around the back of the hooch and giving him an attitude adjustment.

That probably wouldn't have helped, though. Motley enjoyed a good fight and wasn't scared of anyone just because they were bigger than him. There was only one guy that Motley feared, and that was SP4 Chuck Johnson.

Johnson was a huge man who didn't say much. The guys in the section used to call him "Chief." He was stoned on marijuana all the time. It took us awhile to find out where Johnson was getting his stash, and the source was surprising. We had noticed that Johnson kept buying packs of cigarettes from Sam, the other hooch maid. It turns out that in Vietnam there were factories that packaged marijuana cigarette packs that were identical to name brands. There were twenty cigarettes in the pack, wrapped exactly like normal cigarette packs. Even CID—the Army's Criminal Investigation Division— would be hard pressed to tell one cigarette from the other.

"Chief" Johnson bought his joints from Sam and would take his lunch breaks to toke on a few factory wrapped marijuana cigarettes. It didn't seem to affect his job performance so nobody said anything to him about it.

Drugs weren't that uncommon in Vietnam. It didn't matter if you got it from a helpful full hooch maid or bought it from a vendor on the street corner of Saigon... a soldier could find marijuana just about anywhere. The thing that made Chief unique was that he didn't care whether anyone knew that he was using during duty hours.

It definitely affected his conversation ability, though. He was never one to talk much anyway, and after one conversation the guys from the hooch decided that maybe it was best to leave Johnson in silence.

We were talking outside of the hooch one day about a soldier's favorite topic, going home. I made the mistake of asking, "What are you going to do when you get home, Chief?"

Johnson looked at me with that blank stare of his and replied, "I still live with my mom so I'm going to go home. I'll say hello to her and drag my shit into the house and throw it on the bed. Then I'm going to grab my leather gear from the closet, jump on my Harley and leave."

We all looked at him, expecting to hear more. After several minutes passed with us staring at Johnson and him staring blankly back at us, it soon became obvious that there was no more to hear.

"Well, okay then, Chief." I looked at the other guys and their expressions were the same as mine. It seemed obvious that Johnson was about five cans short of a six-pack. "Sounds like a good idea, Chuck. Good luck with it."

That was probably the longest conversation we ever had with Chuck Johnson during the entire time I knew him in Vietnam. We never asked Johnson any other questions about where he was from or what he intended to do when he got back to The World. By unspoken consent, we all decided that we really didn't want to know.

It wasn't the fact that Chief was always stoned that terrified Motley. Unlike Brunetti, who would warn you that he was going to do you harm, Johnson would just burst into action. Motley was always running his mouth, but Johnson never said anything. Just goes to show you that it's the quiet guys you have to be worried about. They'll kill you.

Perhaps that's one reason why nobody ever messed with the "cool hooch." Most of us were infantry guys, and infantry soldiers played by a different set of rules. We did everything the hard way...we played hard, partied hard, and fought hard. Anytime there was a breach in the wire, everyone seemed to turn automatically and look at the infantry section of the Morning Reports Group. It wasn't by reputation only, either.

Shortly after the Morning Reports Group was up and running, a VC got into the compound. He interrupted everybody's lunch when he started shooting everything. Bullets were punching through the mess hall and people were ducking under the tables. DiOrio, Brunetti and I all had weapons so we went out to find him. It didn't matter that we weren't successful. What everyone else saw was that we were the only three guys who got up and chased after the intruder.

Even our boss, Lieutenant Koneche, wanted to be surrounded by infantry guys after that. The section was ordered to take its position on the defensive berm. On the berm, the LT walked up to me as the senior sergeant and asked in an embarrassed voice what he should do.

I told him, "Stay near me...because I'm staying near DiOrio, and Brunetti won't be far away."

Forty clerks holding M16s was a truly frightening sight. I wasn't certain who was more dangerous, the other guys manning the wall nearby or the VC roaming the base. The only barrels I saw pointed my direction were held by friendly hands, so I tended to be more concerned about fratricide. That was a story I didn't want to explain when I got back to The World.

"Well, Dad, it's like this...I was watching the woods in front of me when some kid from Finance discovered his M16 had a trigger. Normally that's not important because they aren't trained on how to take the weapon off safety, but this time the kid figured that one out. No safety, pull trigger, gun go bang...easy thing to figure out, even for a REMF number cruncher like a Finance guy. Next thing I knew, I was waking up in a hospital on Okinawa with my ass looking like Swiss cheese." Nope, that's definitely not the kind of war story I wanted to tell.

Miraculously, though, nobody was shot by friendly fire. The enemy attack wasn't very coordinated either. It seems that the VC had dug tunnels into a church located between Highway 1A and the army base. After their initial attack failed, they all ran back into the tunnels and were hiding in the church again. We were told to just man our positions and that the Air Force would take care of it.

What happened next was an incredible sight to watch. The church was in our sector of the perimeter. I watched a jet fighter roll in and fly straight for the church. A bomb fell away from the aircraft and dropped right through the steeple. Either it was a lucky shot or that pilot was very talented. Either way, we all cheered as we watched the building turn into a fireball. There was nothing left but charred boards and a ton of toothpicks.

The next morning, LT Koneche—our administrative lieutenant—was feeling his oats. There were probably ten guys around him laughing and joking as the lieutenant concocted a war story about his heroism during the attack. Just because the "all clear" siren sounded wasn't a guarantee that all of the VC had been captured or killed, so I did what any responsible NCO would do...I told the LT that he provided the enemy with a wonderful target of opportunity. He seemed to take exception to my statement that while the war might not miss him, it would definitely miss the other nine guys. They had work to do, and it would be best if he broke up the clusterfuck before some VC straggler decided the group was worth a few sniper bullets.

He didn't hold it against me, though. From that point, the Lieutenant made certain during an attack that he was surrounded by guys from the infantry section of the Morning Reports Group...typically, DiOrio, Brunetti and myself. It's easy to look cool under fire when you're surrounded by soldiers who know what they're doing.

That didn't mean the Lieutenant trusted us completely. He had a young private by the name of Billy Dobler as his snitch. We didn't hold it against the officer; after all, it was part of his job to keep tabs on his subordinates.

No, the one we had a major case of the ass about was Private Dobler. The kid was from Baltimore originally, and his version of street-smarts went against my Brooklyn-raised grain. I was raised to stand your ground and fight for what you believe in...Dobler used whatever he could dig up to drop dime on his buddies. He was a regular army clerk from the States who constantly whined about being shipped by mistake to Vietnam after he'd been promised a cushy job in Germany by his recruiter.

That was his first mistake...he believed a recruiter. His second mistake is that he traded information for favors. He was a snitch, and that didn't agree with us in the cool hooch. Anytime somebody in the Morning Reports Group stepped out of line—came in past curfew from Saigon, tied one too many on at the club, or traded MPCs on the local economy—Dobler would snitch to Lieutenant Koneche.

Luckily for Dobler, the Lieutenant never acted on the information that the stoolie provided. Koneche was an okay officer in that he knew what everybody was doing, yet also knew when to turn a blind eye. He wasn't the type of officer that an 11-Bravo would want leading them into combat, but that was okay. Infantry wasn't his branch. The LT was part of the Adjutant General corps. We had no problems following him to the office. That was the battleground he was trained for, and he ran his operations very well.

I expected Lieutenant Koneche to interfere when Staff Sergeant Williams, the new Admin Sergeant, arrived from Stateside. Williams was technically the supervisor over each team chief. He wanted to jump right in and make operations "improvements" on his first day, and he turned to the LT for support in implementing his ideas.

Lieutenant Koneche simply pointed my direction and said, "Talk to Sergeant Moffett. He put this whole operation together. I'm very pleased with how it's running."

The Morning Reports Group was normally a very noisy place in the morning. Typewriter keys would clack quickly against ribbon and paper, and the ringing of carriage returns made it sound like a bicycle race. The typical noise level gradually decreased as SSG Williams walked past each desk. Everyone slowed their typing pace to listen.

"Sergeant Moffett."

I looked up from my typewriter at the large NCO in front of me. The first thing I noticed was that he was a soft-spoken fellow. The question about his masculinity crossed my mind, but I stowed it away for later consideration. There was enough potential trouble without wondering if my new boss was gay.

"Yes, Sergeant Williams?" I replied.

"You've done some fine work here, Sergeant, but I think it's time for a few changes."

I held his gaze for a moment and then slowly scanned the room with my eyes. To tell the truth, I was silently begging my teammates for some assistance. It didn't work that way. Brunetti told me later that the look on my face promised dire consequences—seventh level of hell type punishment—if everyone didn't get back to work. Just goes to show that reading someone's facial expression can be very difficult. Or perhaps I had unconsciously learned the "gonna rip your head off" look that other sergeants seemed to have down as an art.

Either way, the room suddenly exploded with noise. Everyone seemed determined to type faster than ever, and nobody would raise their head to meet my gaze. I decided that I didn't want to be chewed out by a senior sergeant in front of my guys, so with a heavy sigh, I looked back up at SSG Williams.

"Why don't we discuss this outside, Sergeant," I said. It was meant to be a question, but it came out as a challenge. "There's a morning report to get out. We don't need to disrupt that process."

I didn't wait for Williams to respond as I stood up and walked away from my desk. Footsteps behind me told me that my new boss was following. I walked through the door and stepped outside.

"Now Sergeant Moffett —" the new Admin Sergeant began.

I didn't let him finish. "There's nothing wrong with how we do the morning report, Sergeant Williams. We've had compliments from Corps and higher that this division is always the first to report in. So what's the problem?"

"I just have a —"

"Few suggestions, yeah, I heard. So here's the deal, Sergeant. If it ain't broke, don't fix it." By this point, I was surprised to find that I really was angry. I looked him straight in the eye and made the challenge official. "I'd suggest that instead of trying to take charge, you should try to join us first. Later, if you still have suggestions, then bring them up to me and the other two team leaders. Sound fair?"

Williams was quiet for a moment. Then he nodded. "Sounds fair, Sergeant."

"I'm glad that's settled then." I motioned toward the door behind him. "Shall we go back in and see how they're doing on this morning's report?"

That was the only conflict I had with the new Admin Sergeant. He basically stayed out of my way and became the buffer between the team leaders and the officers. Lieutenant Koneche wasn't the only Adjutant officer for the Morning Reports Group; we also had Captain Fitzgerald and Lieutenant Collins. There's one of those unwritten army rules which says if a unit can actually accomplish its mission on time that it isn't performing at its full potential. Instead of rewarding success, the system piles on more work until everyone can barely get anything done.

Staff Sergeant Williams knew how to handle officers, and he did a terrific job in keeping additional tasks from getting dumped on our desks. I never could've done it. Politics never interested me—I was a grunt and trained that the easiest solution to a problem was to shoot it—and so Williams actually performed a critical duty. He kept the brass off our backs so we could accomplish our primary mission. It isn't every day that occurs in the army.

It turns out that my two initial concerns about SSG Williams never erupted. I was colorblind in an era where race was a dividing line with many people, so I fully expected problems from SSG Williams because he was black. Skin color never mattered to me and the only color I saw in the army was olive drab. It turns out that Williams felt the same way, so there weren't any race conflicts in the Morning Reports Group. The second concern, that Williams was a homosexual…well, it wasn't until he showed up to a reunion many years after the war with a drop-dead gorgeous blonde on his arm that we knew for certain he was straight.

This was one of the best times in my military tour. I was de facto in charge of the Morning Reports Group, well respected by the guys in the hooch, and surviving the almost nightly rocket attacks. There were too many things going on for me to notice that The World had stopped sending me mail.

The guys in the hooch noticed, though. They kept trying to get me to go to Saigon each weekend. The trips weren't scheduled R&R—Rest and Recreation—but simply a benefit of being near the capitol city. All we had to do was thumb a ride from a passing military vehicle and we were soon striding down the brightly lit streets of an incredible party town. I could've had any girl who approached me. Granted they were hookers, but that wasn't the point. I turned them down because someone special was waiting for me at home.

Then the letter from my mother arrived. It started off strange because it mentioned my father. That was odd because my parents were separated. My father, Joe Moffett, was quite the character…too much character for my mother's taste, and so after too many years of marriage they decided to go their own way.

My father got an apartment in Jackson Heights. He was a huge guy who worked in construction, but he wasn't a physical fellow. Any time I got in trouble as a kid, he would sit me down and talk to me instead of pulling out the strap like other kids' dads. There were times I wished for the strap; he had eyes that could cut right through you and warn you never to pull a stupid stunt like that again.

Mom was your typical Rosie the Riveter woman; she worked in the factories while my father was a navigator in C-47s during WWII. Saying that she wasn't thrilled with my taste in women— Gretchen in particular—would be an understatement. Mom didn't trust her any farther than she could throw her.

It turns out that she was right. In her own no-nonsense but loving way, she spelled out in her letter what happened. It seems that my father, who was always "the guy" to go with to party at the bars—had been taking Gretchen and her best friend Lorraine to the local joints. Some people might consider it chaperoning, but they didn't know my father. He was simply taking two attractive ladies out to show them a good time. Then he would escort them home safely.

During the last such trip as described in my mother's letter, my dad and the girls ended up in another bar. Gretchen apparently started drinking too much and was getting a little amorous from the alcohol.

My mother was sugarcoating that part. I knew that Gretchen could put away her share of cocktails without getting buzzed; I had learned early on never to play drinking games with her. However, my mother didn't know that—it would've been added to her shopping list of everything wrong with Gretchen if she had—and so she almost excused Gretchen's conduct at this point.

The woman who wore my engagement ring, who had promised to wait faithfully for my return from Vietnam…started hitting on a draft-dodging college guy at the bar. They talked about how the war was wrong and how anyone over in Vietnam was a baby killer. Oh, and of course, they also talked about whose bedsprings they were going to wear out over the course of the night.

That's when my dad stepped in and asked, "What are you doing, Gretchen? My son's in Vietnam!"

Whether it was because my father admitted to having a boy in the war, or because the college boy didn't want anyone interrupting his seduction of a betrothed woman…either reason was sufficient for what happened next. The punk upended his beer and conked Joe Moffett on the side of the head with it. That was enough to lay my dad out on the bar.

One would expect a faithful fiancé to come to her promised father-in-law's aid at that point. Gretchen didn't. She went home with the college boy. The bartender called the cops and an ambulance. My mother heard the story from a policeman and later, after he awoke, from my father.

I finished the letter once, then read it again, and finally a third time. It was nighttime and sirens went off from the airbase nearby, but I couldn't hear them. Never heard the all-clear sirens either. Sometime during the night, someone put a cold can of beer in my hand, and then another when that one was empty.

The first sound I heard was Mike DiOrio. He laughed. It was a hearty belly-laugh that somehow seemed so out of place with where my mind had been. I looked up at the crazy goumba and saw him grinning down at me.

Mike sat on the bunk beside me and gently pulled the letter from my hands. He skimmed it for a few seconds, then slapped me on the back. That was enough to get my attention. It—or what felt like several bruised ribs—shocked me back to reality. I was in Vietnam, not back in The World.

"So, Moff," DiOrio said loud enough to announce it to the entire hooch. "Looks like you're going with us to Saigon this weekend, huh?"

For some reason, that really sounded good to me. I had a few things to take care of over the next few days…like a letter to write to my mom, asking her to retrieve my medals from Gretchen's place. I wouldn't be surprised to hear that Mom was handed them in a cardboard box.

Oh, and there was another letter I had to write. It would be strictly a formality, really. The standard "you bitch, the engagement is over and I hope you burn in hell" sort of thing. Nothing personal, of course.

Gretchen's response would be just as formal. It was actually a time-honored tradition. Soldiers throughout the wars referred to it as a "Dear John" letter. It's the one where the girl announces that she's found someone new back in The World, so sorry but I'm moving on with my life and it isn't with you.

That was fine by me. There were simply too many beautiful Vietnamese women in Saigon for me to feel too broken up about it.

"Yeah," I said to DiOrio, grinning. "I'm going with you this weekend. I've got months of getting laid to make up for, and it's time I got on with it."

Mike's response spoke for everyone in the hooch. "That's what we've been waiting to hear."

HOUSE OF THE RISING SUN

I wasn't surprised at how quickly my heart seemed to have healed from Gretchen's betrayal. Part of it was because, except for the sex, things hadn't been going all that well between us before I'd left Stateside. The army training had focused my attention on one thing—simple survival—and I didn't seem to care anymore about the trivial "who's dating whom" nonsense that filled Gretchen's world. The sex was good, though. Thinking back on it, perhaps that's the most important thing I'd been concerned about…getting home and getting laid.

Being faithful and waiting until my return trip home to have a good time was the honorable thing to do. It was also kind of stupid. While Gretchen was having a grand time at the bars back in The World, I was sitting around the barracks every weekend. Sure, she was being chaperoned to an extent by my dad, but at least she was having fun. I was left to stare at four blank walls instead of heading south with the guys. Saigon was one of the party places of the world and I was purposely denying it.

I was free of my engagement promises now. It was actually quite liberating. I had a lot of time to make up for, and the guys gave me plenty of hints about what we were going to do.

There were plenty of girls in Saigon. The guys from the hooch let me know about it every time they got back. They had been going to the city long enough that each of them had a steady bar girl.

Someone from the States would probably label the bar girls as prostitutes. It wasn't really any different than a date with a girl back home, though…except the bar girls were a lot easier on the wallet. From what the guys told me, you didn't have to worry about false compliments or the typical dating game to get them into bed. All you needed was to buy them a few drinks, hand over a few bucks and then get down on it. Same thing as the American girls I'd known, but you didn't have to take them to dinner and a movie first.

Sex was very important to soldiers, especially those who'd been out in the bush. It was a physical gratification, sure…but it was also a pleasurable reminder that the soldier was still alive. Some might suggest that there was a link between sex and violence, but I never thought that was the case. If anything, the link was between sex and fear…the fear of dying. Being with a woman helped ease that fear, even if only for a short time. It made you feel alive.

The week following Gretchen's letter passed quickly. Before I knew it, it was gone. Friday night came and I had to pay a short visit to the base PX. Even though I had not ventured to Saigon with the guys from the hooch, I already knew of the some of the things that went on. It wouldn't do for me to arrive unprepared.

The PX at Bien Hoa was fairly large. Not as big as those on the stateside bases, but it carried most everything a soldier would need. Most of it was stuff the Army provided in care packages. However, there was something about buying amenities that weren't olive drab green. Foot powder, deodorant, candy bars, cartons of cigarettes, even local knickknacks that a soldier could mail home to his wife and kids. Vietnam was mostly a Buddhist country and so you could even find small brass statues of Buddha. It didn't mean anything to those of us in-country, but they made for pretty trinkets to let the kids back home know "Daddy was thinking of you."

The item I was looking for would place me on the opposite end of the "daddy" spectrum. I found it on one of the dusty wooden shelves beside packages of small rubber bands. I picked up a box of Trojan condoms and headed for the front counter.

Vietnam had its fair share of venereal diseases like syphilis and gonorrhea. It didn't pay to play around with sex that at the very least could leave you with a constant drip, drip, drip. The only way to ensure that a hooker was clean was to keep yourself protected. My mother didn't raise a fool. I figured a box of Trojans would keep me safe for the weekend.

Soldiers had discovered another use for condoms. If you unrolled a condom over the barrel of your M-16 and secured it with a rubber band, you didn't have to worry about water clogging the barrel. There had been a few incidents with the earlier version of the M-16 rifle. Vietnam seemed to be half-covered with rice paddies. There was water everywhere you went. A soldier's rifle invariably ended up underwater as he slugged his way through the rice paddies. When the soldier fired the weapon later, it could blow up in his face. Soldiers being soldiers—there's nothing like innovation in combat, after all—came up with a practical solution. A condom provided another type of protection because it kept the water out. The rubber was also thin enough that, when the weapon was fired, the bullet would pass right through it.

Herb Wise was at the cashiers buying a case of Budweiser for the evening libations. He grinned as he saw the single item in my hand and said, "Damn, Moff, you ain't that handsome. What do you expect to do with all those?"

I laughed. "With all of the backlog I've been building up, I thought it would be safest to double up. Don't want to get into trouble because I blew the head off the rubber, now do I?"

"Yeah, well, I'd take a lot of cash if I were you." Herb slugged me in the arm in jest. "With enough money, maybe even one of those Saigon hookers might consider doing you once. Just try to find one that isn't too wrinkled and has some teeth left, will you?"

"If I need one like that, I'll know who to ask." I slugged him back and grinned. "Just let me know if she's your girlfriend, okay?"

"Ah, Moff, that was low. Speaking of low, I think you made a mistake." Herb exaggerated looking really close at the box in my hand, then turned to the young SP4 at the register. "He has the wrong box, doesn't he? Do you have any of these in mini size?"

The specialist just shook his head, slightly bored with the banter. "Nope, that's the only size we carry. If either of you need to make it smaller, just tie a knot in it."

Getting razzed by one of the guys from the hooch was one thing, but I couldn't let a bored PX cashier get away with a jibe like that. I replied, "Sounds like the voice of experience to me."

The specialist glanced at the stripes on my sleeves and cautiously shook his head. "Working here is like being a bartender, Sergeant. Some of the guys come back all embarrassed, wanting advice and a refund because it slipped off. I tell them to tie a knot in it. Never had anyone come back a second time."

There wasn't much to say to that, so I paid for my purchase with MPCs. I hated those things. Carrying around a wad of cash would normally make you feel rich, but not when half of them are nickel and quarter bills. I laid the exact amount on the counter, took my small brown paper bag, and headed back to the hooch.

We woke early on Saturday morning. The air was full of energy as we headed toward the battalion CQ to sign out for our weekend pass. Several of the married guys discussed going shopping to find clothes and stuff for the wife and kids. They received quite a bit of ribbing about that. The rest of us single guys talked about all the clubs that we intended to hit.

Signing out for pass was not a big thing. The battalion CQ maintained a sign-out roster. I filled out my name, unit, destination, and the time I was leaving the compound. Then I handed the clipboard back to the CQ and joined the rest of the guys outside.

We were a motley crew as we headed toward the main gate. All of us were still in uniform. The guys who had civilian clothes—or "civvies" as we called them—would change as soon as we got to the hotel in Saigon. Several of the guys carried their civvies in green nylon bags, the type used by Air Force pilots to carry their helmets. Everyone else carried the off-duty clothes in backpacks, suitcases, or the standard Army-issue green cloth laundry bags. With the hodge-podge of luggage and bags dangling over our shoulders, we looked like a ragtag bunch of hobos.

A soldier in the guard tower lifted one hand off his M-60 machine gun to give us a good luck wave. A jeep blocked the checkpoint. We waited for the gate guard to finish checking military identification cards of each passenger in the jeep. It didn't take long. He'd been doing gate duty long enough that he seemed to recognize the faces of everyone going through. He lifted the bar on the gate and waved them in to the base, then turned to us.

"Good morning, Mike," said the guard. "Off for another wild ride in Saigon?"

Mike DiOrio nodded. "Yeah, Jack. Anything we can pick up for you?"

"Nah, I went the other day." The young soldier waved us through. "The road is clear, at least for the next mile or so. After that, you're on your own. I'm not expecting any convoy or vehicles out of here for the next hour, or I'd see if you couldn't catch a ride."

"That's alright, buddy," DiOrio replied. "We know the deal. Make it to Highway 1A, then we'll be clear to hitchhike a ride to Saigon. If you hear gunshots and screams, though, you might send someone to our rescue."

The gate guard chuckled. "Well, you ain't armed so it won't be you shooting yourselves in the foot. Other than that, there's little chance of getting hit. Have a great time, guys."

I followed the guys through the gate and onto the reddish clay road. Nobody else seemed worried, but I didn't have a warm and fuzzy feeling about walking weaponless through several miles of open road. The VC were consistent about shelling the airfield; a group of unarmed US soldiers in the open seem like a grand target of opportunity.

"Umm, Mike," I began in a stage whisper to DiOrio. "Are you sure this is safe?"

"Hell no, Moff, but that hasn't kept us from doing it every weekend for months now."

I kept looking at the stunted trees that popped up occasionally on the side of the road. There wasn't much cover to hide under. On either side was nothing but miles of short grass or fields. Anyone with a decent pair of binoculars—or a sniper scope—could've seen us from a mile or two away.

This was going to be a hair-raising hike for me. I kept waiting for the crack of a rifle. It was still early enough in the morning that the air was almost cool, so the typical Vietnamese humidity wasn't solely responsible for the sweat running down my back.

"Relax, Moff," said Herb Wise. "Charlie sleeps during the day so he can attack us at night. There's nothing to worry about."

"Yeah, well hopefully those aren't going to be famous last words." In times like these, there is only one way to relieve the tension. I laughed. "I'd feel a lot better if we had some wheels."

"Wouldn't we all," commented Herb Wise. "Hey Brunetti, got some in that laundry bag of yours?"

"Yeah right, Crash," scoffed the burly giant. "With your nickname, you think I'd loan you a set of wheels?"

"Training wheels, maybe," DiOrio interjected.

Corbus jumped in as well. "Bet he couldn't wreck one of those Saigon tripeds."

That's how we made it safely down the two or three mile stretch to Highway 1A. The guys succeeded in keeping my mind off any VC shadows hiding in the grass by bantering back and forth. It's hard to feel threatened when you're laughing.

Highway 1A was a main supply route. It didn't take long before a deuce pulled onto the shoulder. I suspected that one didn't pull rank when hitchhiking. By army regulation, the highest ranking person is supposed to sit in the passenger seat of the vehicle. I didn't push the issue; figured if the driver offered then I'd accept. Otherwise I was just another tourist on his way to paradise city.

The driver didn't offer. He glanced at my stripes and asked if we needed a lift, then waited to see what I would do.

I said, "Thanks, man, that's great!" Then I climbed into the back of the truck.

Brunetti climbed in beside me and then the others scrambled over the tailgate. Lucky for us, the deuce was open to the air and didn't have its tarp over the cargo area. It was like riding in a convertible.

The sun was well over the horizon by this time. The heat and humidity had reached their typical morning sauna level. After the truck began moving, the wind blowing over us was a godsend. It seemed to drop the temperature by ten degrees. Undoubtedly the local Vietnamese thought we were heading to the psychiatric ward. We stuck our heads into the wind like dogs with their heads out the car window, tongues wagging.

This was only the second time I'd really managed to see the countryside. The first was during my ride into Phouc Vinh that I mistakenly thought was a parade in my honor. My other trips had all been by plane.

Riding along Highway 1A showed me a different view of Vietnam. There were miles of rice paddies. Hundreds of tiny figures stood ankle-deep in the flooded fields, stooping over and doing something. I couldn't tell if they were planting, weeding or harvesting. The picture would be the same during my other trips to and from Saigon.

Vietnam was in a tropical climate so there weren't any real seasons. It seemed like a hell of a way to live one's life, wading through the same muck every day. From the simple clothes and hand-woven coolie hats, I couldn't see where the people were making any profit from it. It seemed like they hadn't climbed any higher than basic subsistence level. Compared to what I'd grown accustomed to in the States, it seemed really sad.

We passed through several villages with their dirt side streets and wooden sidewalks. The drive was a transition forward through time and civilization. Medieval-like shoeless peasants working in the fields were replaced by car-driving businessmen. Thatched roofs gradually changed to tin roofs; wood-frame structures became actual concrete buildings.

Then we reached the outskirts of Saigon. We passed through what in any other city would be considered slums. Yet, in Vietnam, the ramshackle houses were still better quality than those in rural villages. The place seemed more animated, as if the city ran at a faster pace.

We drove deeper into the capital. Traffic was a chaotic mess. I could understand why most people seemed to prefer using bicycles over cars. The heat and humidity caught up with us as we lurched through the clogged streets.

Brunetti finally had enough of it. "Let's just walk. The hotel's not too far from here."

"You guys already got a hotel? What, you called and made reservations?" I was impressed.

"Standing reservations, Moff," Herb replied. "We're regulars. If they're running short on rooms—which only happened once—the hotel will bump other GIs waiting in line when we show up."

I thanked the deuce driver for the lift and then bailed out of the back. Turning to Brunetti, I asked, "So you know the lay of the land, right?"

"You bet. The Mai Loan Hotel is a few blocks that way." Mike grinned mischievously. "Just keep one hand on your wallet."

"Thieves?" I asked, looking at the crowded sidewalk. "Pickpockets?"

"A few of those," Herb replied. "Not many, though. Street urchins and beggars, mostly."

DiOrio joined in the teasing by pointing. "What your really have to watch out for is one of those."

I followed his finger and gazed at a strikingly beautiful young woman on the opposite street. She was dressed in a form-fitting red Ao Dai dress. Her form fit very well in the tight cloth. "Holy shit. I think I've died and gone to heaven!"

"Not yet, man," Herb said, laughing. "But you will!"

"Just watch out for those types over there," Brunetti warned. "See the one in white? She's a lady and won't talk to you. Same goes with a girl in black. They're normally chaperoned so it's easier to tell them apart from the street girls."

I followed Brunetti's finger to see a petite young woman dressed in a white Ao Dai. "Lady, huh? What makes them so special?"

Herb laughed and slapped me on the back. "Just like the debutantes back home, Moff. They have the cultured background and sometimes even the money to go with it. Best to just leave them alone."

"Not a problem," I replied. "I'm not looking for a gal that I have to chase into bed. Especially if what you guys have been saying is true!"

My companions laughed as if relieved I wasn't going to make a play for forbidden fruit. I'd heard about the "ladies" in Vietnam already. It wouldn't be wise to cause an international incident by insulting our host nation's culture.

The girls were strictly off-limits, not only to US soldiers but to their own male peers. As in many cultures, the girls followed strict and formal values. Getting a date with one would involve asking her father first, who would run a background check on your family to see if it was socially acceptable. If you made it past that hurdle then all dates would be chaperoned by members of her family. The first time you'd ever get to go alone with the young lady was on the wedding night.

I wasn't interested in that kind of game. Gretchen was out of my life, and I was only interested in having a good time. Nothing serious…the last thing I wanted was a Vietnamese wife. Matter of fact, I didn't want a wife at all. I just wanted a woman's company at the bar and perhaps for the evening. No promises, no commitments.

We continued down the street, occasionally having to squeeze through crowds of people. Unlike walking the streets in Brooklyn, the Vietnamese were too small to cause a real problem. I could see over their heads and plan how to get through the throng of people.

That gave me a chance to actually look around the city instead of focusing on not getting run over by another pedestrian. Saigon was an old city, and the architecture reflected a blend of oriental and French colonial structures.

The buildings were a collage of colors. Some were simply white-washed, others a mixture of yellow, blue, white, and any combination of colors imaginable. There was an air of decay about it all. Little care seemed to be taken on maintaining the structures.

Streets were narrow and crammed with street peddlers and shops. Even the thin alleys branching off the main streets were packed with open-air markets. Two people would've found it difficult to walk abreast through the claustrophobic alleys.

In contrast, the main boulevards downtown were wide, open thoroughfares designed to showcase the magnificent French-style buildings. Fountains and flower gardens decorated the parks between the streets. One could sit outside the corner cafes under an umbrella-shaded table to watch the world go by, just as if the person was in Paris.

I learned quickly that Saigon was a schizophrenic city. Like the white-clad ladies in their Ao Dai dresses versus the street prostitutes in their red Ao Dai's, the city was a warped blend of clashing cultures. It seemed to be at constant war with itself over its past and future…with the result that the people only lived in the here and now.

It was obvious in their buildings. The city had suffered under the Tet Offensive in 1968. Buildings that stood during the previous year had been destroyed by the conflict; that was the past. There were no plans to clean up the rubble and rebuild; that would've been the future. Instead, fish and rice sellers set up their carts beside burned-out buildings or directly on the shattered stone. That was now, and the people were perfectly comfortable with it.

My feet started hurting after the first hour of walking. We had already passed several hotels that looked promising to me. Since I didn't know where we were going or how much longer it would take to get there, I nudged DiOrio. "Hey, Mike. How about that one over there?"

He followed my finger, then shook his head. "What one? There a girl you're looking at, Moff?"

"No, goumba, the hotel! My feet are killing me, man. Can't we just find a place and be done with it?"

"Sorry, Moff. I forgot that you haven't been here before." He jutted his jaw toward the hotel I was suggesting. "That one right there will cost you a month's pay to stay the night. The one around the corner, you can get a room for three bucks a night…but you won't wake up with a wallet in the morning. You gotta be careful around here, man."

"So where are we heading?" I asked, dodging another short pedestrian.

"The Mai Loan Hotel," DiOrio replied. "It's about another five minutes walk. Think you'll make it?"

"Yeah, if it's only five minutes."

It turned out to be closer to fifteen minutes, but I didn't mind. We walked into the four-story stone building and it was like stepping back in time. Wide-bladed ceiling fans slowly stirred the cooler air. The white marble floor, stained from many years of use, led to the dark stained and varnished wooden front desk. Broad-leafed plants were everywhere, providing little pockets of seclusion for people to read their papers or have private conversations. The brass rails on the winding staircase to the side were deeply tarnished, but it still carried its old-world charm.

We stepped up to the front desk and Herb rang the bell. The manager, a distinguished Vietnamese gentleman in a dark blue double-breasted suit, stepped forward to the desk. "Good morning, gentlemen. Welcome back to the Mai Loan Hotel. Would you care for a room?"

"Good morning, Mister Tinh," Herb replied. "Yes, rooms for all, please."

I was impressed. The manager treated us as if he ran a five-star hotel and we were rich patrons. A bellboy arrived, dressed in his white jacket and hat, to take our luggage up to the rooms. It felt silly to give him my laundry bag, yet he carried it with professional pride to the room. He was even subtle about waiting for the tip.

"Take a shower and change into some civvies," Brunetti suggested. "We'll pound on your door in an hour, so you'd better be ready."

"Sure," I replied. "Where we heading?"

"The Tiger Bar upstairs. If you aren't impressed with what's there then we'll hit the streets for the evening."

"Sounds great," I said, stepping into my room. "I'll see you in a bit."

The room wasn't anything to write home about, yet it was far better than some American hotels I'd stayed in. The wooden furniture was old, the bed squeaked, and the faucets bore decades of rust stains. Yet the wood paneled walls were worth a fortune and the eight-foot tall bay windows were magnificent.

I showered quickly and dressed in khaki slacks and a short-sleeve cotton shirt. It didn't take long before I heard the door try to jump off its hinges as Brunetti gently knocked on the wood.

"You ready to go, Moff?" my giant friend asked after I'd opened the door.

"Ready and willing," I replied.

We headed up the stairs to the Tiger Bar. It was lunchtime and the guys reassured me that the bar served some food. I was looking forward to eating something that didn't have USDA stamped on it.

I didn't expect the bar to be hopping so early in the day, but it was. We heard music blaring through the strings of beads that served as the door to the room. DiOrio held the beads to the side and motioned for me to enter.

"After you, Moff," he said.

I didn't trust the grin on his face but I stepped through the arched doorway. The bar was larger than I expected. Sometime during its early life, it probably also doubled as the hotel's restaurant.

"Hello, GI," called a very pleasant female voice from the barstools. "Buy me Saigon tea, we party!"

I waved at the bar girl and stepped aside for my buddies. There was a squeal from the bar and then a lovely young creature flashed past me and slammed into DiOrio. "GI Mike, you come back!" the girl giggled.

"Yeah, Suzy, I'm back. Now be a good girl and bring us some beer, okay?"

We found a table next to one of the open windows. Suzy returned with a pitcher of beer and glasses…and a small thimble of Saigon Tea. It was every bar girl's drink of choice. More precisely, it was the drink that the local mamasan who ran the girls required the girls to order.

Selling Saigon Tea was a lucrative business. It added roughly two dollars on the tab per "tea," was mint or some other non-alcoholic mix, and kept the girls sober while their guests got plastered. Of course, the girls made more money later in the evening and split part of that with their mamasan as well. The tea was just in case the guy was too drunk to perform. At least that way, the girl got something for entertaining the man throughout the evening.

"Just one tea," DiOrio commanded as Suzy slipped onto his lap. "We'll make up the rest this afternoon. If you're a good girl, maybe we'll have dinner and then something else this evening."

Suzy giggled again as she ran her hands over his chest. She kissed him firmly on the lips. When they separated, both sighed heavily.

"Slow down, Mike," Herb Wise suggested. "Or at least take it to your room!"

"Later, Herb," DiOrio replied before diving in for another kiss.

"Is it always like this?" I asked Wise as I poured the drinks.

Herb nodded in mock disgust. "Yeah, they can't keep their hands off each other."

They didn't, either. For the next hour, the two lovebirds smooched and pecked on each other. The only time DiOrio came up for air was to chug down some of his beer. Then Brunetti showed up with his bar girl and commenced to swap spit with her in front of us as well.

I started to feel uncomfortable about it for several reasons. Although Herb and I tried, it was extremely difficult to hold a conversation at the table with the two couples making out right beside us. Also, it had been eight months or so since I'd been with Gretchen. The sounds and seductive motions going on in front of me reminded me of a few pleasurable moments of my own. Suffice it to say that I couldn't have stood up from the table without embarrassing myself.

"Well," I started, and then coughed in shock. DiOrio had his hand halfway up the girl's skirt. I fully expected the morality police to appear at any moment and cart us all away. "I'm glad to see someone is getting some, but this is ridiculous. Aren't there laws against this kind of publicly displayed affection?"

"Nope," Herb replied. "It's good for the economy. Lots of US soldiers spending lots of bucks on a few girls. Most of these gals make more in a year than the government officials."

"So this is what you guys do every weekend. Why isn't there a babe in your lap?"

Herb looked slightly uncomfortable at the question. "My chick's at one of the other bars. I'll pick her up later."

"Aw, come on, Herb," I began, fully intending to grill him. At that point, I truly didn't believe he had a girl waiting for him. "You can admit it. You really—"

Herb didn't say anything to interrupt me. He just raised his glass and tipped it toward the doorway behind me. Then he grinned.

I turned and my heart stopped. Standing in the doorway was the most beautiful woman I'd ever seen in my life. She was stunning. Deep brown eyes looked my direction and then sultry lips parted in a smile. She flipped her lustrous long black hair over her shoulder and started walking toward me.

"You can breathe now, Moff," someone said near me. I think it was Herb Wise, but I couldn't swear to it. My eyes were solely for the petite woman striding toward me. It seemed like I could hear the swish of her Ao Dai skirt-jacket brushing against the silk pantaloons.

She reached the table and leaned toward me. "Hello, GI. What's your name?"

"Pat," I stammered. I felt silk slide over my khaki pants as she slipped into my lap.

"Buy me Saigon Tea, GI Pat?"

I'm normally very confident around women. This wasn't like me at all. It didn't help that the obstruction which would've embarrassed me earlier was now pressed against the firmest derriere I'd ever…well anyway, this situation simply wouldn't do. I cleared my throat and attempted to regain control over the situation. "Jack," I said, indicating that I'd buy her the beverage that I'd been drinking. It was a Jack and Coke.

"Jack?" she asked, smiling sweetly. "You name not Pat?"

"Yes, it's Pat," I said, flustered. "I'm just saying that you can have a Jack—"

"No need, Pat Jack," she replied. "I love you both names, long time."

What's a guy supposed to say to something like that? I heard a choking sound from across the table and peered around the girl in my lap. Herb Wise was beet-faced and doing his best to keep from exploding. I glared, which didn't help him any at all. He burst out laughing. That caught the attention of my other two hooch mates. They came up for air to see what was going on.

"Well, just look at you, Moff!" Brunetti exclaimed, elbowing me in the ribs. "That didn't take you long at all."

The girl had taken me by surprise, but I wasn't going to be let it make me timid. I wrapped my hand around her waist and looked up into her dark brown eyes. "So tell me, sweet thing, what's your name?"

"Luan Dinh," she replied.

"And he's Pat Jack," Herb added, still laughing.

"It's just Pat!" I corrected. It didn't help.

"Okay, Just Pat Jack," Luan teased. "You buy me Saigon Tea now?"

That was the first of many Saigon Teas that I bought for Luan. We stayed at the table for another hour before I could find a suitable excuse to take her back to my room. That excuse was simply that I didn't want to make Herb uncomfortable. DiOrio and Brunetti had already made their excuses a few minutes earlier.

Luan and I went back to the hotel room. I was raised to never tell tales about a lady. While Luan's occupation didn't exactly put her in the lady category, she was a special woman during a frightening time in my life. She helped remind me that I was alive, whole, very young and very male. I consider her a special lady for that, and so I'll leave what happened behind closed doors as our secret.

We spent the afternoon in my room and then joined up with the others downstairs in the lobby. That Friday evening was spent carousing the town. We had dinner at a nice family restaurant—each couple behaved accordingly—and then hit the bars.

Nightlife in Saigon was incredible. The city by daylight was dirty and crowded, but by night it was a spectacle of lights and sound. It seemed like Christmas with all of the different colored lights flashing. The streets hummed with a different type of energy as loud rock and roll music blared through open bar doors.

DiOrio cautioned me at one point, after the girls had left to powder their noses. "Just a bit of advice, Moff. Don't swap girls from the same bar."

"What do you mean?"

"They're very possessive of their men. I know," he said, shrugging his shoulders, "it doesn't make a lot of sense. Yet the girls will treat their men as the most special thing in the world. Like all women, they get their feelings bruised if you don't show them the same respect."

I was confused. "What, do you mean to tell me that Luan will get jealous if I hit on Suzy?"

"More than jealous," Mike replied. "She'll try to gouge Suzy's eyes out for stepping on her turf."

"Anything else I need to know?" I asked.

"Just this. Don't ever put a girl up in an apartment. That means you're serious about her. It's more binding to a bar girl than a wedding ring. You'll never get rid of her."

Whether he knew it or not, DiOrio had told me probably the only thing that would've made me step back and be cautious. I wasn't in love with Luan, but I could definitely see spending a lot of time with her. I'm also not the type who enjoys sharing; the thought had already crossed my mind of putting her up in a place so that she was exclusively mine.

After the games with Gretchen, anything remotely approaching marriage was enough to cool my jets. I reminded myself that this was a business arrangement. No strings attached, no commitments or promises made.

Luan and I spent the rest of the night back in my room. She was still there in the morning, as if waiting for something. That's when I remembered. The girl wanted to be paid for her services. She didn't turn suddenly cold and business-like; instead, she maintained the same sweet affection she'd shown me all night. We kissed, she took the cash and said she'd wait for "her Pat Jack" at the bar if I wanted to buy her more Saigon Teas, and then she left.

The guys and I spent the day sightseeing around Saigon. My first impression of the city didn't change. It was beautiful in places—the pagodas were fantastic—yet it was still a hodge-podge of cultures. I went back to the hotel wondering if the Vietnamese people would ever learn to live for tomorrow instead of simply surviving today.

Luan was with a guy when we walked into the bar that evening, but she jumped right up and came to sit on my lap. I wondered what the lines were that I shouldn't cross…whether there were some taboo topics that were best left alone. Yet I wondered how she could drop a potential customer just to be with me.

"He no buy Saigon Tea," was her reply when I asked her later. "You Number One GI, Sergeant Pat Jack. He Number Ten!"

"A cheapskate, huh?"

"Very cheap," she replied firmly. "Number Ten GI!"

The night's festivities were guaranteed for me, then. We went out as a group and hit the town, then returned to the privacy of our rooms. A similar scene occurred the next morning as she accepted my money.

"You come back, Sergeant Pat Jack," she said, then kissed me. "You ask for Luan, I come. Love you long time, you so sweet."

We kissed goodbye one last time and then I got ready for the trip back to the base. There was no telling how successful we'd be in hitching a single ride back to Bien Hoa. From what the guys had told me, we could spend half the day walking and hitchhiking before we reached the gates. It didn't matter as long as we made it back before nightfall.

The guys were waiting for me downstairs. I returned the key and paid for my room, then tossed the laundry bag over my shoulder. It was a little heavier with clothes and bargains that I'd bought the day before.

"Ready to head back to the house, Moff?" asked Brunetti.

"Yeah," I replied. "Not looking forward to the walking, though."

Herb Wise laughed and clapped me on the back. "The way that bedroom door of yours was bouncing, I'm surprised you can walk at all!"

"Don't let him get you down, man," DiOrio replied as we headed for the door. "He's just jealous 'cause his girl never showed. I'm starting to wonder if she's real or not. Never seen him with a girl the whole time we've been coming here."

I could handle the ribbing from Hulk and DiOrio, but I wasn't so sure whether how Herb would take it. Slapping Wise on the back in return, I said, "Well, from the annoying thumps I heard from his side of the wall, I'd say he did okay last night."

"Really," DiOrio said, looking sideways at our smaller comrade. "And here I thought he spent all his time in the library."

"What's wrong with that?" asked Herb. "You'd be amazed at the type of girls who frequent the library."

"Doesn't matter," Brunetti interrupted before Wise could dig himself into an embarrassing hole. "I have to give it to Moff. He's nabbed the best catch of all of us."

"What?!" DiOrio yelled in mock anger. "There ain't no way...."

I sighed heavily to myself. It was going to be a long trip back and probably an ever longer week full of machismo, chest thumping and bragging until we had the chance to return. It didn't matter to me, though. I knew who'd had the most beautiful girl in Saigon. With that certainty settled firmly in my mind, I could let DiOrio ramble as much as he wanted.

(UN)FAIR TRADE

Life was extremely pleasant for me over the next few weeks. It followed the same pattern during the work day that had become an established routine. Begin work at oh-dark early in the morning, get the morning report done, resolve any issues with the brass, and then go sweat in the hooch until sundown. It wasn't a bad life.

Even the weeknights were cool...as in kinda cool and pretty neat, not in regards to the constant humidity. The guys in the hooch and I formed a do-wop group just to pass the time. Since I had the reel-to-reel, we'd pass the hours with a few cold beers as we caterwauled into the microphone.

It wasn't anything that would get a record producer's attention. Matter of fact, when we listened to it sober, it sounded like a bunch of guys having a good time. We weren't serious about the music. Nobody really wanted to take the lead and institute formal sessions.

We didn't have sheet music; all of the songs were done from memory. Even "Stranded in the Jungle," an old classic by The Cadets, ended up with new lyrics after we were through with it. That was okay, though. We weren't singing to win any contests. It was for fun and camaraderie. The music and the partying brought all of us closer together and made us into a family. It was a warped family, true...but that's only to be expected when you cram a group of guys together for months on end and force them to live peacefully together.

The only time that I truly had to call my own was the weekend in Saigon. If I wanted to spend every minute with Luan, I could. It helped me separate myself from the war for a time. Reporting unit casualties and replacements can become depressing after awhile; you become cold to it. People become numbers. A name becomes another figure to place into the proper column. It was war by accounting, and it was getting to me.

The trips to Saigon helped restore my perspective. With Luan, I could remember what life as a civilian felt like. More to the point, I remembered what *life* felt like. It was full of tastes, sensations, scents. Luan helped remind me that there was more than just the war. There were people, each with their own hopes and dreams.

I noticed that this new perspective slowly affected my work. The names on casualty lists weren't just numbers anymore. They were people. The casualty card that listed a kid with a GSW—gunshot wound—became a person to me again. He would head to a hospital in Okinawa or Hawaii where he'd be patched up and then sent home. It wasn't a loss like we stated on our morning report. Granted, the unit didn't have that soldier anymore…but the kid was alive. It somehow made a difference to me, knowing that.

Everyone found their own way to cope with their job. Some of us found our pressure release in Saigon, others found it in the strangest places. Officers came and went through the headquarters; one of the oddest coping mechanisms I ever witnessed came from our new colonel.

I was sitting in the hooch before breakfast one morning, thinking about what the day would bring as the guys around me got ready for the work day. The screen door flew open and a young PFC dashed through the door. He was huffing and puffing like he had just run a marathon.

"Sergeant Moffett!" he yelled. "Is Sergeant Moffett in here?"

"Yeah," I said, wondering what was going on. I shrugged into my uniform blouse and started buttoning the shirt. "I'm over here."

The young troop ran to my bunk. That was an amazing feat in itself, as I was only four feet from the door. He could've jumped and made it faster. As it was, he had to grab the metal rail of the top bunk to stop himself from slamming into me.

"Sergeant Moffett! Colonel Lowery sent me to come and get you! He wants you right away!"

I had to give the boy credit. He had a phenomenal parade-ground voice that could be heard for miles. The only problem was that he did it in a very small enclosed space. Anyone who hadn't already woke up had definitely received their wake-up call this morning.

"Slow down, soldier," I advised him calmly. "Catch your breath."

"Yes, Sergeant!" he bellowed, then gasped for air.

There's something to be said for motivation. I hadn't seen the soldier around before so I assumed that he was a newbie. After considering whether to tell him to slow down, I decided that I'd be wasting my breath. The young pup would soon learn that moving a hundred miles an hour was hazardous in Vietnam. The heat and humidity demanded a much slower pace.

I finished buttoning my shirt and grabbed my hat. "By any chance, did the Colonel say why he wanted to see me?"

"No, Sergeant...just that it was important!"

Man, the kid had a lot to learn. There was a wide spectrum of "important" in the Army. Every officer thought their task was critically important. That's why the Army had NCOs...to actually prioritize the workload. Otherwise every soldier would be out of breath like this young man in their attempt to satisfy the officer's "important" task.

"Okay, Private," I smiled and clapped him on the shoulder for successfully completing his mission. "Tell the Colonel I'm on my way."

"Yes, Sergeant!" the enthusiastic troop replied. He raced toward the door.

"Private!"

He managed to skid to a halt without punching through the screen door. "Yes, Sergeant?"

"Walk, son." I pointed toward the door. "You're going to have a hit-and-run and hurt somebody, you keep moving like that."

The kid turned a pale shade of red. "Yes, Sergeant. I'm sorry, Sergeant."

The screen door swung open and Mike Brunetti stepped into the hooch. He was buck naked except for a towel wrapped around his waist. Hulk squeezed past the soldier barring his way—which is a delicate way of saying that he squished the kid against the wall—and stepped into the room.

"Or you could run into a brick wall," I told the young private, pointing to Brunetti. "So shift to a lower gear and walk back to the colonel's hooch, okay?"

"Yes, Sergeant," he replied as he stepped through the open door.

"What's that all about?" Brunetti asked after the kid left.

"Dunno. The Old Man wants to see me."

The other guys had gathered around at this point, curious to know what was going on. Herb Wise asked, "You don't think he knows about our trips to Saigon, do you?"

"Nah," I said confidently, securing the green baseball cap on my head. "If he'd wanted to chew me about that, he would've called me into the office."

My response was off the cuff. I hadn't had the chance to wonder why the colonel wanted to see me. Herb's question started me wondering, though. Could the Old Man have heard about the Saigon excursions? While they weren't exactly against regulations, they weren't specifically allowed, either.

I walked to the door, turned to the guys and grinned. "It's nothing to worry about. I'll let you know what he wanted when I get back."

It was still dark and quiet outside as I walked through the cluster of hooches. I made my way up the small dirt path that lead to the Colonel Lowery's trailer. While enlisted guys got wooden huts to live in, the officers rated air-conditioned trailers. Rank truly had its privileges.

I knocked on the door and was surprised when it immediately opened. It wasn't a good sign that he didn't just yell "Enter!" and let me open the door. The Colonel had actually been expecting me. At that point, I truly expected that I was going to have my head handed to me on a platter for something. Finding out the "something" was going to be the trick.

"Thanks for getting here so quickly, Sergeant," the Old Man said, waving me into the trailer. "Come on in."

He waited until I'd walked into the trailer and had closed the door behind me before speaking again. "I have a special mission I want you to handle, Sergeant. It's a one-man job, and it's going to take someone who understands discretion. You are discreet, aren't you, Sergeant?"

"Yes sir! Absolutely!" I replied. At that point, I was completely lost as to what was going on. A special mission? Discretion required? It reminded me of the strange coincidences when I'd flown into Phouc Vinh. That situation had seemed like cloak-and-dagger stuff, too. Was this going to be something similar, or was it really a secret mission?

"Good man!" The colonel plopped down onto his couch. "The rumor mills were correct. I knew that I could trust you."

"Sir?" I asked, uncertain where this was heading.

The Colonel simply smiled. "You've been very discrete about your trips to Saigon, Sergeant Moffett. Good thing, too, or else we'd have half the base down there every weekend. Then I'd have to write up a policy forbidding it. That wouldn't be good, now would it, Sergeant?"

I slowly shook my head. "I'm not sure that I know what you mean, sir."

He broke into sharp laughter. "See what I mean? Very discrete! I like that. So, here's what I need you to do, Sergeant. You know where my mess hall is?"

"Yessir." I knew that the higher-ranking officers—full colonel and above—had a special mess hall. I'd never heard it referred to as the Colonel's mess hall, though.

"The General's cook is going to give you a box. Under no circumstances are you to look inside. Is that clear?"

"Yessir."

"Good. There's a Loach outside the mess hall that will take you to ARVN Regional Headquarters in the village of Phan Rang. You following all this, Sergeant?"

"Yes sir. Get the box, get on the Loach, go to Phan Rang."

"Very good. Now, once you're there, you will be met by an ARVN soldier. He'll be carrying a box. All you have to do is exchange boxes and come back. Is that clear, Sergeant?"

"Yessir. Crystal clear."

"Very good. Then get on your way, Sergeant. And remember, discretion is the code word here."

Confused and curious, I snapped a sharp salute and left the trailer. It was still dark outside, which added to the mystery. What was going on? He obviously knew about our trips to Saigon and made their continuation a condition of this mission. Was he asking me to do something illegal? Or was it a classified mission, very hush-hush? No matter how I tried, I couldn't come up with a reason for the early morning secret mission.

I made my way to the Colonel's mess. That was another strange thing. A mission that began in the kitchen? How strange, I thought, but it was his call. What better way to disguise a classified—or illegal—mission from VC spies or other prying eyes. Nobody ever suspected a cook.

Even though I was getting more mystified with all the questions, I managed to take a good look around the kitchen. It was very impressive. Having served my time with KP and DRO—kitchen police and Dining Room Orderly—during Basic Training, I knew what the kitchen side of the Army's mess hall was supposed to look like. This layout was a better set-up with higher quality utensils than one would expect to find in even the top Stateside franchise restaurants. It was quite obvious that the upper grade officers dined very well indeed.

A man in a chef's hat and white jacket—not the typical apron that Army cooks wore—waved me toward him. There was nobody else in the kitchen. I assumed that he was the general's cook. From the thick beard and moustache, I also wondered if he was a civilian contractor or a member of the Army. If he was a soldier, he must be a fabulous chef to break regulations with that beard.

"I'm Sergeant—"

"No time, Sergeant," the chef said, anxiously waving me toward him again. "Glad you're here and all, but we've got to move. This is what you're taking."

He opened a large freezer door and pulled out a suitcase-sized box. There were no markings to tell what might be concealed beneath the wax paper wrapped box. I accepted the box from his waiting hands. It was about twenty-five pounds, I guessed.

"The pilot already knows the way," the chef explained quickly. "Once there, give them this box and bring back the one they give you."

I opened my mouth to ask what was in it. Before the words came out, I heard the start-up whine of a helicopter from outside the kitchen. Someone with a lot of clout wanted this box delivered right away. The mission was not only very secretive and mysterious, it apparently also had some heavy-duty firepower behind it. There weren't too many people who could authorize a helicopter just to deliver a frozen package of who-knows-what.

"Go, go!" the chef ordered, pushing me toward the door. "We don't have much time!"

The helicopter—an OH6 Aero Scout Light Observation Helicopter, commonly referred to as a "Loach" from it's acronym of LOH—was ready for liftoff when I scrambled into the back of the Loach.

"Hold on, Moffett," the pilot announced as he pulled back on the stick.

We were airborne in seconds. I recognized George; he was a good man to have beside you in case trouble came our way. I carefully stowed the package between my feet and placed my arm around the mini-gun which hung out the left side of the helicopter.

"Hey, George," I shouted as the Loach lifted off. "What do you know about this operation?"

"Not much," he shouted back. "Just that we're supposed to get there and back ASAP."

As we headed east, I realized that there were quite a few things that I didn't know. How far were we going? How long would it take us, and what kind of trouble could we be facing? I did know that reaching Phan Rang required flying over several hot zones. What happened if we went down? The mini-gun beside me could dish out some major damage, but it required power to operate. Crashing would deprive us of our primary weapon. I was glad that I'd taken my M-16 with me when I reported to the Colonel's trailer. Of course, the thirty-round magazine wasn't going to last very long if we ran into trouble.

There's an interesting thing about flying. Everything seems so peaceful from the air. I watched the sun cross over the horizon, a crimson ball that slowly changed to white. The fresh air and vibrantly colored view was exhilarating. Green vegetation, blue rivers and thatched homes passed by below us. It was beautiful down there; no sign that a war was going on.

Our route took us directly east. We paused briefly at Phan Thiet for refueling before heading north, hugging the beach on a direct line to Phan Rang.

"Not too much longer," George informed me. "But when we get in the neighborhood, I'll need your help to look for the ARVN headquarters. That's where we're supposed to be going."

"Got it," I replied. ARVN, of course, stood for Army of the Republic of Vietnam; they were the good guys that the US forces had come to assist against North Vietnam.

Refueling didn't take long, and then we were in the air again. Eventually we sighted a large structure. The only indication that it was ARVN headquarters was the large flag flying from a pole in the courtyard. Otherwise it would've been easy to mistake the walled residence as simply some rich Vietnamese official's country home.

It was massive. In its early days, the mansion had probably been the home of a prosperous French colonial plantation owner. The structure definitely followed the French Colonial era architecture, full of graceful arches and gables.

"Must be it," George shouted over the noise of the helicopter blades overhead. He circled several times to be certain. "It's got all the signs."

I didn't say anything because I really didn't know what we were looking for. The place had an ARVN flag, but beyond that there was nothing to give any indication about its purpose.

As we descended, an ARVN soldier hurried out of the ornate stone building. He positioned himself in the center of the open field in front of the house. The entire place was surrounded by a ten foot high block wall; now that we were closer to the ground, we could see guards patrolling the walls.

George landed with practiced ease. I didn't even feel us touch the ground. He kept the rotors turning as I looked out the door. The ARVN soldier was just beyond the reach of the spinning blades. I could clearly see his face; he wasn't excited about the chopper landing so close to him. Not that I blamed him; at my height, I would've been concerned about losing my head. The guard was too short for that worry, though.

I pulled the strange package from underneath the seat and opened the door. The blades of the Loach were still turning at high RPM as I ran, crouching as low as I could, toward the ARVN soldier. My M-16 kept trying to slip off my shoulder and trip me as I carried the valuable box with both hands.

Moving quickly out of the propeller wash, I rushed past the ARVN soldier to what I felt was a safe distance from the whirling chopper blades. I placed my box on the ground while I was still bent over, then stood up to my full height. I'd guessed correctly. The blades were a good ten feet away, a safe distance from my neck.

The soldier joined me. He was carrying a container about the size of a banana box. I didn't speak more than pidgin Vietnamese, so I pointed toward the box on the ground and smiled.

"Tom!" the Vietnamese said, smiling. "Tom!"

"Pat," I replied, assuming that he was giving his name and wanted mine in return.

He shook his head, confused. Then he repeated his word, "Tom!"

I thought back over everything the Colonel had told me. Was this a password? If so, what was the countersign? That's when I remembered the Colonel's code word. Smiling, I replied, "Discretion."

The ARVN still looked confused, but he extended the box in his arms toward me. "Con ga! Con ga!"

One of these days, I promised myself, I really should learn to speak Vietnamese. It was embarrassing to have no clue what the man had just said. It could've been anything from "take this, it's heavy" to "be careful, dangerous explosives inside." There was one thing for certain, though. Using two soldiers who couldn't speak a common language would definitely keep the secret mission secret. If ever asked, all I'd be able to say was that I delivered a box and took one back with me to Bien Hoa.

I accepted the heavy box. It was heavier than the other, and it seemed to have an odd center of balance that kept shifting. I wondered if it contained liquid…and then quickly set that thought aside. The last thing I wanted on my mind during the trip back was the thought that I might have a liquid explosive like nitroglycerin at my feet.

With the exchange complete, the Vietnamese soldier picked up his box and returned to the building. I crouched low and walked quickly back to the Loach. It was difficult trying to open the door while keeping the box steady and my M-16 from falling off my shoulder. I wasn't taking any chances with the contents of the box. It received the same gentle treatment I'd give carrying a dozen loose eggs in my hands.

"Well, what is it?" George yelled from the pilot's seat as I climbed into the chopper.

"Your guess is as good as mine!" I yelled back.

"Did he say anything?"

"Nope, just his name and something like 'conga.' I didn't think he was asking me to dance, though."

"I hope not," George replied as he pulled back on the stick. We were airborne as he finished his jibe. "I've seen you dance at the NCO Club."

"What's that supposed to mean?" I demanded.

"Can't talk," he said, laughing as the chopper cleared the block wall. "I've gotta pay attention to flying right now."

I jabbed back. "If you fly as well as I can dance, we won't have any problems."

"Then this will be a short trip," he retorted.

The flight back continued in the vein. There's something about putting soldiers from different walks of life together. No matter what their differences, they'll have one thing in common…verbal repartee.

We flew low and hugged the beach, refueled again at Phan Thiet, and then hurried back to Bien Hoa. George put the chopper down beside the Colonel's mess. I cautiously lifted the strange box from the chopper and carried it gently toward the kitchen. The Loach lifted off quickly from behind me and headed toward its landing pad and refueling point. All in all, the mission had taken five dangerous hours.

I still didn't know what the mission was about, though. The bearded chef was waiting for me when I entered the kitchen. The enthusiastic look on his face made me proud; whatever was in the box that I'd picked up at Phan Rang was very important to him. I set it down on the stainless steel countertop and turned to face the man. This time, I was going to get some answers.

"Thank you, Sergeant," the chef said, still eyeballing the box.

I crossed my arms and stood my ground. "So, what's in it?"

The man would make a fabulous poker player. His face was expressionless as he asked, "Didn't the Colonel tell you?"

"No," I replied.

"Then I'm afraid I'm not at liberty to say."

"Aw come on! I just risked my life for you guys and you can't tell me what it's all about?"

"'Fraid not, Sergeant." The chef pointed toward the door. "You'll have to ask the Colonel about that."

"I'll do that," I declared, stomping from the room. Of course, there was no way I could ask the Colonel. He'd made it clear that the Saigon trips were a condition for keeping quiet about his secret mission. I'd tried to get some clues from the chef, but he wasn't talking. The only other clue I had was the ARVN soldier's words…but I didn't speak Vietnamese.

As I walked through the mess hall, I spotted one of the contracted Vietnamese orderlies. Officers ate in a completely different manner than enlisted soldiers. Where the enlisted troops held out metal trays for the slopped food served from thirty-gallon pots, officers received special treatment. The Vietnamese orderly was laying out silverware on the cloth napkins. Even the tablecloth was real fabric.

"Hey buddy," I said, gaining his attention. "Got a minute?"

"Yes sir." He paused in his task and looked at me. "How may I help you?"

"What does 'conga' mean?"

"Conga, sir?" The orderly thought for a moment, then smiled. "Oh, you mean Con ga."

"Yeah, that's it. What does it mean?"

He told me. I couldn't believe it, so I told him about meeting the ARVN soldier. The orderly then interpreted the other word that the man had told me. The guy wasn't saying that "Tom" was his name; the word meant something else entirely in Vietnamese. I turned around and walked right back into the kitchen.

Colonel Lowery was there, looking like a proud new father. "Sergeant Moffett! Way to go, son! You've done one helluva job today."

I looked past the officer and watched in disbelief. The chef pulled the first one from the box that I had retrieved from the ARVN headquarters. The orderly's translation had been correct.

The Colonel had risked two lives and a million-dollar-plus Loach helicopter for his secret mission. I could only assume that the mission had the General's blessing as well; I could see where he could benefit from it, too.

The creature squirmed in the cook's hand. Water dripped off its tail and onto the floor. Now I understood why the package had seemed so off-center; it had been full of water. I also understood why there was such urgency about getting the package back to Bien Hoa. All of the pieces fell into place.

"Con ga" is Vietnamese for lobster. I watched, still incredulous, as the chef pulled six lobsters from the box and dropped them into a pot of boiling water. The delicacies would be done in time for the officers' dinner meal. Somewhere in Phan Rang, an ARVN chef had just opened a package hand-delivered by the Americans which contained "Tom"...Vietnamese for "chicken."

I kept expecting to get angry, but I didn't. It made some sort of warped Vietnam-style sense. The top brass had approved a high-dollar mission to trade a case of frozen USDA-certified chicken for six live lobsters. It was actually a fair trade. The disease-ridden Vietnamese chicken was nowhere close to the quality of American-grown, US Department of Agriculture approved chicken.

An odd thought crossed my mind at that moment. If George and I had been shot down, would we have earned purple hearts with little lobster decorations on them? Somehow, that didn't seem funny.

The Colonel seemed to sense that he might have a problem. "Remember, Sergeant," he advised. "The code word is discretion here."

He was surprised when I suddenly broke out laughing. "What's so funny, Sergeant?"

"Oh, nothing, sir," I said, turning away and heading for the door. "Just something I'd told the ARVN soldier this morning."

The officer's voice sounded concerned now. "What did you tell him, Sergeant Moffett?"

"Discretion, sir," I answered him over my shoulder as I walked from the room. "Discretion."

The Colonel didn't call me back. I'm sure that—like the poor South Vietnamese soldier in Phan Rang—he was probably wondering what discretion had to do with chicken. It was only fair, after all. He'd left me wracking my brain all day before I learned what secrecy had in common with lobsters.

I considered heading back to the hooch, but I wasn't ready to face the barrage of questions from the guys. There was no way I could tell them what the secret mission was all about. Word of it would spread across the base in days, and then we'd end up losing our unauthorized weekend privileges to Saigon.

Instead, I headed to the NCO Club. Ironically, the club was located near the base chapel. It was still early so there were few people there. I ordered my standard drink—Jack and Coke—and found a corner table to nurse it.

The hours passed quickly, and so did the number of drinks. I wanted to get angry about the lobster mission, yet I kept vacillating between anger and laughter. Somewhere out in the bush, there was probably a squad that could've used that Loach today…yet I also understood the Colonel's motivation. Everyone finds a way to cope with the silly craziness of war; if you don't, you'll end up going nuts. So what if the Old Man had discovered that food reminded him that there was more to life than Vietnam? Nobody was hurt by it.

Sometime around 2300 hours—eleven in the evening—I felt someone yanking on my arm. It was the same PFC who'd delivered the Colonel's message this morning. "Sergeant Moffett," he said, "you have to get back to the office."

"Go the fuck away," I replied.

"Really, Sarge. It's bad. They need you in the office."

I pulled my arm out of his grasp. "Let the night crew handle it."

"Everybody's there already, Sergeant. They need you. Bravo and Echo have been hit."

That got my attention. I was depressed by events of the day, but I hadn't done more than nurse my three drinks. Normally we had someone in the admin office twenty-four hours a day. The night shift was a one-man radio watch. If he'd called in the entire section then hell must've broken loose somewhere.

I ran with the Private back to the admin building. Someone had set up a squawk box—a speaker attached to the radio so that everyone could hear the transmissions instead of just the radio operator—and the news wasn't good.

The war had found its way back into our lives. For the next thirty minutes, the guys from the hooch heard from their old units.

Names of men that they had known came over the speaker or were relayed by telephone. The reports were cold and emotionless...traumatic amputation, PFC X; GSW, PFC Y. Guys that I knew, and I was writing their lives down on a piece of paper. There were close to fifty names, and all we kept hearing was "GSW." Gunshot wound.

Every one of the names was a loss. We did our job and tallied up the losses, and then we filled out the proper forms to submit to the REPO-DEPOT, the replacement center. In two days, the negative numbers would be removed as replacements arrived at the units that had been attacked. By the end of the week, the Division would be back to its normal strength.

I knew that most of the names weren't KIAs, or Killed in Action. The wounded soldiers would be sent to military hospitals, patched up and then shipped home. Yet that night, the entire war seemed very confused to me. The injured men wouldn't think it was funny to receive purple hearts with lobster devices. They wouldn't understand...and neither did I.

A week passed, then two. The guys in the hooch knew that there was something eating at me. Herb Wise was the first who was brave enough to confront me with it. "Alright, Moff," he said in a no-nonsense voice. "What's going on with you?"

I was at my desk, working through more paperwork. Every month, the 101st Airborne Division received allocations from higher headquarters for Rest and Recreation, or R&R. Units could send their troops to Vung Tao, an in-country resort, without going through us. The allocations that we monitored were for out-country R&R to places like Bangkok, Thailand. Part of our job was to ensure that every unit used their R&R slots...and to make certain that the same names didn't pop up before everybody else had their turn.

"What do you mean?" I pushed the list aside and rubbed my eyes. The last few days had been pretty sleepless for me.

Herb sat on the corner of my desk. "You didn't visit Luan Dinh last weekend, for one."

"Yeah, that." I leaned back in my chair and crossed my arms. "I had work to catch up on."

"That's bull, and we both know it."

"It's why we're here, isn't it? I'm just doing my part, man."

We were starting to draw a crowd. DiOrio took the other corner of my desk. "I've seen this before, Moff," the giant combat veteran said. "If you really want to tackle the war by yourself, then transfer up to a line unit. I'm sure they'll appreciate it."

"What the hell…?" I was immediately angry, and that wasn't like me. It took some effort, but I clamped it down and spoke in a reasonable tone. "Listen, guys, there's nothing going on, there's nothing wrong, and I'm just fine."

"That's why you've been pulling late hours here, right? It gives you a great excuse to come into the hooch after everyone else has crashed." Herb shook his head. "Listen, Moff, you've isolated yourself. We're guessing that it's because of last week's attack on Bravo and Echo companies."

I stared at the desk for a minute, thinking. Could they be right? Was I acting differently? I honestly didn't know.

"Like I said, I've seen this before," Mike said in a reassuring voice. "You knew those guys. You weren't there when they got hit, and now you're feeling guilty about it. Am I right?"

If they only knew the half of it. I couldn't tell them that I'd been transporting lobsters for the Old Man…but DiOrio was right, I did feel guilty about it. I'd wracked my brain, yet there wasn't anything I could do. The line units didn't have the advantages that we did in the rear. They never would. So what could be done to give them a little taste of the freedom that I had?

I tried to articulate that to my hooch mates. "Yeah, they were guys I knew. They slug it out every day with the VC, and I sit back here all comfy. Don't you feel guilty about it?"

"Nope," DiOrio replied. "Let me tell you what, Moff. What I'm doing here is just as important as what I did on the line. If there weren't goumbas like us, there'd be no replacements when the units get hit. There'd be no awards for the guys who become heroes. No pay, no bullets, no chow."

He picked up the paper I'd been working on and tossed it into my lap. "There'd be no R&R so they can drink, party, get laid and put their souls back together. Saying that we ain't doing our part just because we aren't getting shot at every day…that's bullshit, man, and you know it."

"Talk to Tripod if you don't believe we get shot at," Herb said, tossing in a bit of levity. He knew that I had developed an affection—I'd deny and say it was grudging tolerance—for the dog. Tripod had lost his leg to an errant grenade or mortar round. "Or you can start tracking how many rockets come over the wire around here. One of these days Charlie's going to have a short round and hit some of the barracks. That's evidence enough that we're still in the war, Moff."

Herb was an artillery man; in the artillery, a short round was one that fell short of its intended target. I understood what they were trying to do for me, but the guys still weren't getting my point. "Yeah, but look at us…we get into Saigon every weekend and what do the grunts get?"

"Like I said, Moff, join 'em if you're feeling so guilty," DiOrio stated. "Or figure out a way to make their lives easier."

"Like what?"

DiOrio pointed to the paper in my lap. "That's the R&R allocations, right?"

"Yeah." I didn't see where he was going with his suggestion. The R&R allocations were sacred. If the Division received a hundred allocations, it was our job to ensure they were evenly dispersed to all of the subordinate units. I couldn't play favorites by giving extra to Bravo and Echo companies just because they'd been hit.

"Give them ours."

I looked at Mike and then at Herb. They both nodded. The Morning Reports Group received its allotted share of the vacation slots. Then I shook my head. "Won't work, guys. Sure, I can give up my slot when it comes along. One guy off the line can go in my place. That's not going to make any significant difference."

"Damn, but he can be dense when he's in the dumps, can't he?" DiOrio asked Herb. Then he said over his shoulder, "Hey, Brunetti!"

Mike Brunetti appeared almost immediately. I started to wonder whether every guy in the infantry section was going to do a jack-in-the-box and pop up. It made me proud that the guys were looking out for me, but it had to be uncomfortable if they were hiding under the desks waiting their turn.

"Is he thinking yet?" Brunetti asked. "Or is he still doomin-n-gloomin'?"

"Getting there. So, tell this goumba about SA."

I glanced down at the R&R document in my lap. The guys were starting me to think about something. "SA? You're talking about space available, right?"

Brunetti nodded. "You bet. The flights to Bangkok always have empty seats, just in case some high-ranking brass wants to take a little R&R. Of course, the brass they're holding those seats for...."

"...have their own planes to get there," I finished, finally understanding what the guys were suggesting. I'd had recent experience with the brass using Army aviation for their own personal use. "Or they could always cabbage onto a Loach for the run."

Herb pulled the paper from my lap and glanced at it. "So that means all we need are a set of orders to fill those slots, right?"

All three of my subordinates just looked at me and grinned. They were waiting for me, as the section sergeant, to make the suggestion into policy. I leaned back in my chair and crossed my arms. "So what, are you saying that we can give the guys extra R&R slots using space available seats? What happens if they get bumped? The whole thing would come unraveled."

"Not if we give them our slots and we're the ones going SA," Brunetti replied. "The grunts will have legitimate orders. If we get bumped, we'll know what's going on and won't make a fuss about it."

"And of course," DiOrio said with a sneaky grin, "since we're the one's writing the orders...."

I thought back on the lobster run. If the brass were willing to bend the rules just for a lobster dinner, what harm was there in what we were considering? Nobody would get hurt. It would give a few extra slots to the line units, and we wouldn't actually be out anything.

The manning board hung on the wall in front of me. This war was all about numbers, filling in the right blanks with the right figures. That was the way around my feelings of guilt. The grunts would get more chances to get out of the line of fire. All we'd be doing is shifting the Morning Reports Group's allocation over to their columns.

I looked at Brunetti. "How many slots do we have this week?"

"Five," he replied, pointing to the section board in the corner. "Anderson and Ferrara from us, three from the other sections."

"Alright, let me talk to the other chiefs. Everybody will have to be read in on this or it'll blow up in our faces."

"Now we're talking," DiOrio said, slapping me on the back.

"There's only one thing left to consider," Herb said.

I felt like it would be days before my spine popped back into place from DiOrio's friendly backslap. Grimacing, I asked, "What's that?"

Herb assumed a mock-serious look. "What are you doing this weekend, Moff?"

I replied with a wide grin, "Seeing Luan in Saigon!"

RANK HAS ITS PRIVILEGES

Fall passed in Vietnam and made its way to winter. There was no change around us, though. December in 'Nam was nothing like December in New York City…it was short sleeve weather at night, stifling heat during the day. When your duty shift used up the comfortable night weather, you wanted to hit the sack and be deep in dreamland before the heat of the day made sleep impossible.

Christmas sneaked up on us; if it hadn't been for calendars then we would've never known it had come. The heat and humidity were still oppressive and the trees were still green. We celebrated it in true soldier fashion…we improvised. The Christmas tree was a pathetic looking thing. There were no evergreens available, so we used one of the local shrubs. Decorations were made from aluminum foil to make tinsel and balls. Everyone joked about the scruffy tree, but it had the desired effect. It brought us together as a family of soldiers during the Christmas season.

It was shortly after Christmas, on a hot December dawn in 1968, when we got the bad news. I had just come off guard duty from the berm, thankful that the shift was over. As I walked up to our hooch, I noticed an unfamiliar sign tacked to the front door. It didn't look ominous but the news was lousy. The heading read:

Military Directive Order:

Weekend passes to Saigon for 101st Airborne enlisted men are hereby discontinued. Officers may only visit Saigon on official business and must be in possession of written orders to be in the city.

Now that's going to cause a problem, I thought to myself. The order meant no more weekend trips to Saigon. My buddies and I were cut off from our favorite outlets for fun and mischief.

I was too tired to deal with it at that moment. The VC had added a twist to their traditional rocket attacks during the previous night. This time, they had sent in a team to probe the wire surrounding Bien Hoa airbase. A few claymore mines had ended their inquisitiveness, but we still had to man the perimeter anyway. Everybody else had pulled a four-hour shift and then hit the sack. As the section sergeant, I was expected to take the entire watch.

The guys in the Morning Reports Group had already crawled out of their bunks and headed to breakfast. I wasn't interested in food at that moment. It had been almost twenty-four hours since I'd closed my eyes, and I just wanted to crash in my bunk. It didn't take long to strip down to T-shirt and underwear. Come hell or high water, I was going to get some sleep.

It was 0700 hours in the morning, yet I could already feel the heat seeping through the tin roof. It wouldn't take long for the hooch to become a sauna. By the time I woke up, my body would feel as if it were melting.

It didn't take long for me to drift off...nor did it last long. The loud grumbling voices just outside the entrance to the hooch could've woken the dead. Annoyed, I opened one eye. The door repeatedly slammed as the loud voices moved into the hooch.

The other eleven grunts from the hooch had just read the official directive posted on the door. They were ticked. When they realized I was awake, they clustered around my bunk to express their displeasure. Regrettably my sleep would have to wait; as the senior man in the hooch, it was my job to listen.

"Hey Moff! Can you believe this!" yelled Brunetti as he thrust the sign into my face. "This stinks. If we can't go to Saigon, what're we supposed to do for a good time? Pick our noses on the front step?"

"Yeah," added DiOrio. "Looks like all we can do for fun is drink beer at the NCO club or go to the movies. That sucks!"

I was flat on my back, surrounded by the two Italian goumbas. It's intimidating enough anytime I was standing beside the two guys; they were built like linebackers. At that moment, trapped on my bunk, I felt very exposed. The two burly giants weren't the only ones who were hot about the new order. The rest of the hooch inhabitants crowded around both sides of the bunk.

They continued their complaints as I swung around to sit up on the bed. I knew I needed to come up with something to redirect their anger. "Y'know," I interrupted, "You guys really crack me up. Couple of months ago, Charlie was shooting at your heads in the bush. Now you're bitching about having nothing better to do than go to a bar or watch movies."

The whole bunch of them shrugged their shoulders and looked at each other sheepishly. I'd managed to distract them, at least. It didn't last long as Herb Wise chimed in with, "There's no date on this thing, Moff. How long can they do this?"

That started the whining and complaining all over again. I'd had enough. "Hey guys! Give me a break here, willya? I just saw the sign, too. You know as much about this as I do!"

"Well, aren't you going to do something about it?" asked Sparky Anderson, our resident mechanical genius. He was so good at getting engines to run, the guys swore he could hot-wire a B-52 bomber.

I held up my hand for silence. "Give me a chance to mull this around for awhile, okay? Maybe I'll be able to come up with something. Now get your sorry butts to the office. I need to get some sleep!"

"You know," DiOrio said as he started herding the guys away from my bunk, "*some* people get cranky when they don't get their beauty sleep."

Brunetti laughed. "If sleep can make him beautiful, he'll need to be in a coma for a long, long time."

I dismissed their parting comments with a raised finger. They laughed as they filed through the doorway. Silence finally arrived as I threw my body back on the bunk. It didn't take long before I returned to my much-needed sleep.

When I awoke, a much more pleasant sight greeted me than the one I had faced earlier. The loud slam that had startled me had come from our maid, Mai, walking into the hooch. Even with an enormous load of laundry balanced on her head, she was a vision.

"Good morning, Sergeant Pat," she said as she eased the laundry from its perch.

"Good morning, Mai."

It seemed like the laundry basket was half Mai's five foot height. The adorable fifteen-year-old flashed a smile that could melt a glacier. Throughout her months as our hooch maid, we rarely witnessed her without that smile. The ever-present glow on her face made all of us GIs perk up a little whenever we saw her.

"Do I disturb you, Sergeant Pat?" she asked, looking concerned. "I come back later. Sokay?"

"It's fine, Mai. I was just getting up." I started to swing out of bed, then realized that I was still in my underwear. Mai politely turned her back as I grabbed my fatigue pants and slipped them on. Then I plopped back down on the bunk, lingering awhile as I watched her sort out the laundry.

The tiny teenager suddenly clapped her hand to her forehead and exclaimed, "Oh, oh! Mai make stupid mistake."

"What's wrong, Mai?"

"I mix you shirt and Captain Donnelly's!" She held the starched uniform up for me to see. "Dai-uy be mad?"

The tragic look on her face was priceless. I smiled reassuringly. "No, Mai, Dai-uy Donnelly won't be mad. It's a simple mix-up, not the end of the world."

"Very sorry, Sergeant Pat!" She folded the shirt neatly and started toward the door. "I must go. Return shirt to Dai-uy Captain. Be right back, sokay?"

Something clicked in my head. There might be an opportunity here. "Wait a minute, Mai. Let me see that shirt."

She brought it to me slowly with her head held low, as if ashamed of the laundry error. I looked at the two black bars signifying the rank of captain sewn on the collar of the shirt. A plan began to form.

"Hey, Mai. While you're out, do me a favor," I said, thrusting a handful of MPCs toward her. "Go down to the accessories store and get three sets of officer's bars. One captain and two lieutenants. Okay?"

Mai cocked her head and looked at me oddly. "I think Trung Si Pat become Dai-uy very fast. Not good!"

"No comment, Mai. Just didi mau and get it done" I urged, trying to suppress the sly grin that wanted to spread across my face.

I knew that smile of Mai's could accomplish anything, and I wasn't disappointed. By the time I had finished scalding myself in the shower beside the hooch, she had returned with the new insignias clutched in her hand.

"Good job, Mai. Now sew the captain's bars on one of DiOrio's shirts. Then put the lieutenant bars on one of Brunetti's and one of mine," I instructed. It was a struggle to keep my chuckle inside.

The miracle smile disappeared from Mai's face. She glared at me much the same as my mother did when I was a kid and she'd caught me in some major mischief. "Sergeant Pat," she said, shaking her head furiously. "Beau coup dinky dao!"

"Mai!" I commanded, standing tall and trying to look fierce. "Just do as I ask."

"Sokay, sokay! I do!" she said, but not without having the last word. With a shrug of her shoulders, she raised her hands toward the ceiling in resignation. Then she turned her back to me and set about the task I had given her.

In spite of her objections and concerns, Mai made quick work of the task. She left afterwards, muttering under her breath about "big trouble." I knew she would never tell anyone about her sewing modifications, though. Mai was extremely loyal to the guys in the hooch.

When DiOrio and Brunetti walked in the door at the end of the day, they both sensed something was going on. Perhaps it was the Cheshire Cat smile on my face when I greeted them. The conspiratorial wave toward my bunk didn't hurt, either. I had formulated a foolproof plan.

"Should we be afraid?" DiOrio asked.

Brunetti nodded. "Yes, I think so. When he gets that look, there's always trouble coming."

"Aw come on, guys," I argued. "You've gotta see this."

I waved them over to my bunk again. They both shook their heads and cautiously walked to where the three modified shirts were on display. The nametags were ours; the officer bars were not.

Brunetti grasped the situation quickly. After just a glance at his new uniform, he eyed me suspiciously. "You gotta be kiddin' me."

I crossed my arms, still grinning, and didn't say a word.

"It's what happens when we leave him unsupervised," DiOrio stated. "Sleeping in this oven has fried his brains."

"You know that this is a court martial offense, right?" Brunetti asked me.

The military order that the guys had pulled off the door that morning and left on my bed now rested beside the three uniforms. I pointed to the pertinent section which I had circled earlier.

Brunetti crossed his arms and leaned against the wall, shaking his head. "We're going to impersonate officers so we can get into Saigon?"

"Unless you've got a better plan," I said, daring him to object.

"Okay, fine," DiOrio chimed in. "You've got the uniforms. But what about the rest of it? You know, the official orders that we need saying we're authorized to be in Saigon?"

"Well," I replied jauntily, "I think I've got that figured out, too. Are you in?"

"This is nuts," Brunetti stated.

DiOrio held up a hand. "Now wait a minute, Mike. Let's hear him out before we dunk his head in ice water...because I still say his brain's fried."

I patted the bunk on both sides of me and waited until they had both sat down. "Okay, here's the plan. You know that Spec4 over in Processing? What's his name...Dalton? Well, I hear one of his boys is going to DEROS back to the States. They're giving him a farewell bash—a whale of a party from what I hear—next week."

Brunetti and DiOrio, not making the connection, were looking at me as if I had lost it. I continued on quickly, before either got up to start pulling ice cubes from the fridge. "Dalton's been looking for ration cards so he can buy extra beer. He's willing to trade anything, and I mean *anything*."

DiOrio leaned back to look at Brunetti over my shoulder. "You hold him while I get the ice?"

"Hold on, now," I interrupted before either could move. "Hear me out. It's simple. He needs beer and we need authorization papers. We'll use our ration cards to get the beer and even offer to pay for it. Believe me, he'll go for it."

I counted the seconds as the two giants sat there and considered the plan. Their looks slowly turned to amazement at the simplicity of the plan. A smile slowly spread across DiOrio's face, and I knew I had them.

Turning to Brunetti, DiOrio said, "You know Dalton better than we do. Tell him what we need and what we're willing to barter."

"So you're in?" I asked.

"Yeah, we're in," Brunetti replied. "I'll go chat with Dalton now and see if he's willing to deal."

DiOrio and I didn't have long to wait. Within a half hour, Brunetti returned with a Cheshire Cat grin to rival my own…and three sets of orders in hand. The ranks matched the bars on our new shirts and the documents looked downright authentic. No one would question their validity.

"Okay," I said. "Everything looks good. Let's try them out this weekend."

Disappointment flashed across Brunetti's face. "Hell, I can't, Moff. I'm on duty this weekend. There's no way I can get out of it."

"Maybe it's just as well," I said consolingly. "You've got just three months before you go back to The World. You're too short to try a stunt like this."

"Yeah, Moff's right," agreed DiOrio. "Both of us have got 179 days and a wake-up. If we get snagged, we've got a better shot at getting off with minimum jail time."

I could tell that he wasn't happy about it, but Brunetti grudgingly concurred. He helped us brainstorm through what might happen and how we should handle it. The worst situation would be to have someone demand to see our military identification cards. We debated whether it was worth the additional jail time to forge new cards, then decided it was going too far. If the orders didn't get us through, we were sunk.

By the time Friday afternoon rolled around, DiOrio and I were ready. We donned two sets of fatigue shirts in spite of the ever-present heat and humidity. The top shirt bore our enlisted ranks and the inner shirt had the officer ranks.

We casually sauntered out the gate as we always did, with an equally casual wave to the guards in the watch towers. There was a risk that someone might recognize us as we walked the dirt road to

Highway 1A, so we kept the enlisted shirts on. Just out of sight of the two-lane highway, we stuffed our authorized shirts into overnight bags and transformed ourselves into officers.

A deuce and a half from MACV—Military Assistance Command Vietnam—responded to our extended thumbs as we hitchhiked a ride. It was only twenty miles to Saigon, but the trip took us a good hour. Highway 1A reminded me of New York City's Cross-Bronx Expressway. It moved right along unless there were trucks on it. Unfortunately, there were always trucks on it.

Just inside the Saigon city limits, the driver pulled over and yelled through the little rear window. "Captain, this is as far as I can take you. I'm going out to Tan Son Nhut Air Base from here."

DiOrio stared out the back of the truck, oblivious that the driver was talking to him and his new rank. I prompted him with, "Captain, you should thank our driver for the ride."

Mike came around quickly. "Sorry, Specialist. I was just daydreaming. Thanks for the ride. You're a good man."

"You're welcome, sir," the driver replied. "Anytime"

We jumped off the truck and wove our way through the streets of Saigon. Almost immediately, a pair of MPs—Military Police—approached us and asked us to halt. They had spotted the "Screaming Eagle" patch of the 101st Airborne Division on our sleeves. Nonchalantly, we returned their snappy salutes.

"We have new directives regarding the One-O-One in Saigon," the senior MP explained. "We'll need to see your orders."

"No problem, Sergeant," DiOrio said. We both handed them our orders. I was cool on the outside but sweating on the inside. This was our first test, and possibly our last. The MPs unfolded the orders, looked at them closely, and then handed them back to us.

"Thank you, gentlemen. Your papers are in order. Sorry about the inconvenience. Enjoy your stay in Saigon."

"No problem, officer. You're just doing your job," I mouthed with an inward sigh of relief.

Yet DiOrio couldn't leave well enough alone. As the MPs started to leave, he brought their unwanted attention right back to us. "Excuse me, Sergeant."

The senior military policeman stopped and turned. "Yes sir?"

"We were never told why the 101st Airborne enlisted men were banned from Saigon," DiOrio continued. "What happened here to create all the fuss?"

Since he assumed we were officers, the MP answered readily. "Well sir, a PFC from the One-O-One went AWOL a few weeks ago. Seems that he'd been dealing drugs down in the Cholon section of town. Two officers from CID tracked him down."

CID was the Criminal Investigation Division, a military special unit that tracked crimes like profiteering, money laundering, or similar crimes done by military soldiers. Since US soldiers typically didn't fall under local jurisdiction, the Army had established the CID to police its own.

"So this is about drug running?" DiOrio asked.

The junior MP shook his head. "Not really, sir. The CID officers confronted the soldier in an alley. They didn't expect any resistance during the arrest, but he took them by surprise. He pulled a hand grenade out of his pocket and pulled the pin."

I couldn't help it. The story was intriguing, and I wanted to know what happened. It came as a surprise to hear my own voice ask, "Was anybody hurt?"

The senior policeman laughed. "Well, yes and no, Lieutenant. The PFC kept hold of the spoon so the grenade wouldn't explode. He told the officers that if anyone came any closer, he'd blow everyone up including them. So they all backed away. But then the PFC did the strangest thing."

We both waited for the officer to continue, but he was having fun telling the story. Finally, Mike asked, "What happened?"

The helpful MP hesitated a moment longer, then shook his head as if he was still pondering the curious event. The junior officer picked up where the story left off. "The guy put the grenade back in his pocket. Only one problem with that…he forgot to put the pin back in. Within four seconds, BOOM! It was all over."

I shook my head. The mental picture created by their story was quite vivid. "Nobody else was hurt, though?"

"No sir. However, until CID finishes its investigation of the drug ring and rounds up any accomplices, the Provost Marshal doesn't want any other One-O-One enlisted soldiers in Saigon."

Satisfied, DiOrio was finally ready to move on. "Well, thanks for the info, Sergeant. I'm sure CID will wrap this up shortly. Not all enlisted men from the 101st are that crazy."

"I know, sir. Have a good night."

And that, of course, was exactly what we had in mind. The MPs continued on their rounds, vigilant in their hunt for lunatic Screaming Eagles. They were completely unaware that there were two 101st enlisted soldiers in Saigon…and they had just talked to them.

Just a few blocks ahead stood our beloved Mai Loan Hotel. It was actually a somewhat seedy old place, located on a side street a few blocks from the American embassy. Its outward appearance was commonplace. If you didn't know where it was, you could walk right by it. But that was part of its allure…anything hidden was popular with GIs.

I could still recall my first visit as we walked into the crumbling lobby. I marveled at the white marble floor, even though it was badly stained. I admired the brass rails, although they were deeply tarnished. The many chairs were old yet comfortable. There were even spittoons and small, hidden tables where you could gaze into a girl's eyes, nurse a drink, or write a letter home. The Mai Loan Hotel offered a tattered, old-world charm that drew you in and mellowed you.

As regulars at the hotel, there was always the possibility that someone on the staff would recognize us. That was the last thing we wanted. We approached the desk and I breathed a sigh of relief. The clerk behind the counter was new to me.

The Mai Loan Hotel might be old, but its staff had always been courteous and honest. That was sometimes rare to find in Saigon, and one of the reasons we came back. However, I couldn't say the same about all American GIs. There are some types who feel that everything can be haggled down to a lower rate if one yells loud enough.

Such a specimen stood at the counter. The unit patch placed him as a soldier in the 25th Division. His staff sergeant stripes meant he could afford the Mai Loan's inexpensive rates. Yet he was making a big fuss about his bill. Through sheer intimidation, he was trying to get a lower rate.

When the harassed clerk realized a captain was waiting in line, he bowed to DiOrio. "Dai-uy, pardon please. I be with you one minute."

"That's okay," DiOrio responded. "Enlisted men are always slow about adding up a few numbers."

Whew! If looks could kill, Mike would've been on a slab. The staff sergeant turned around and glared directly into DiOrio's eyes. He opened his mouth to say something as his gaze fell to the captain's rank on Mike's collar. Discretion is the better part of valor, and the man—his nametag read "McMurtry"—bit his tongue.

"That's right, sergeant!" DiOrio continued, enjoying the soldier's response. "We would like to check in today, if that's okay with you."

I feared DiOrio might be getting a bit carried away with his new and very temporary rank, but I was ready to back him up. McMurtry was a bully, nothing more. I could sense it in the way he backed down. He wasn't the type who would take on anyone bigger than himself.

We were all distracted by a noise on the stairway. A young Vietnamese bellhop was struggling down the stairs. The stuffed duffel bag on his shoulder clearly outweighed him by fifty pounds. He almost made it to the bottom before stumbling. The bag went tumbling down behind him as he fell head over heels. He landed with a thud on the lobby's polished marble floor.

Sergeant McMurtry was incensed. "Boy," he shouted, crossing the floor quickly. "What the hell is wrong with you?!"

Then the soldier smacked the kid rather hard on the back of his head. "Captain" DiOrio did not like what he saw.

"Sergeant!" Mike's voice cracked through the air like thunder. He spoke slowly, emphasizing each word. "Do you have any idea what the penalty is for striking a Vietnamese civilian?"

"You must be new in-country, sir," McMurtry hissed like a cornered rat. "With all due respect, he's just a slopehead gook. I've whacked plenty of them, and nobody's said boo about it. So until you learn the deal around here, why don't you just get off my back."

DiOrio's face turned crimson with anger. The role-playing was getting out of hand, and the last thing we needed was for my decorated combat vet friend to rip the guy's head off. I had to calm things down. Doing my best ventriloquist act, I poked DiOrio in the ribs and whispered, "You're not really a captain, remember?"

Mike was in no mood for a rank reduction. Instead, he warned me with a harsh, "Shut up, Lieutenant," and then turned again to face the sergeant.

"Let me tell you something, McMurtry," he continued in a voice that threatened deadly violence. "When you arrived in-country, you were told that you were the guest of the Vietnamese people. Nothing has changed…and if you ever strike a Vietnamese soldier in front of me again, you'll spend the rest of your time at the stockade in Long Binh. Clear?"

Through thin-lidded slits for eyes, the sergeant shot invisible bullets at both of us. Once again, though, his instinct for self-preservation kept him silent. He did not venture a reply.

"Lieutenant!" DiOrio said sharply. I looked around to see whom he was talking to, then realized it was me.

"Yessir!" I replied quickly.

"Escort Sergeant McMurtry out of the hotel. See that he gets a taxi before I get really pissed."

"Yes sir," I said, stepping forward and motioning for McMurtry to grab his duffel and follow me. That course of action sounded a lot better than watching DiOrio dust the marble floor with the weasel.

When I came back, I was seriously upset with the "captain." I said with a grimace, "I thought we were going to keep this officer thing low key."

"Relax," Mike replied. "We'll be fine. I just hate seeing kids getting treated like that by some lifer sergeant."

Now that it was over and our covers were still secure, I was willing to let it go. "All right. Let's get some sleep and hit the nightclub early."

Safely in our rooms, we shed our officer garb and became sergeants again. We were confident there would be no problems as long as we didn't leave the building. Of course, we didn't intend to…our favorite night spot was the Tiger Bar on the hotel's top floor.

The Tiger Bar was like a second home to DiOrio and me. Many times we had passed under its arched entrance and through the strings of beads that served as the door. This time was no different.

The line of bar girls pleaded as we walked past, "Hey GI! You buy me one Saigon Tea, I love you too much."

We left those enticements for the unsuspecting cherries. As seasoned veterans, we knew Saigon Tea was a major rip-off. The non-alcoholic mint tea was served in a thimble-sized shot glass and added two dollars MPC per shot to the GI's bar bill. One Saigon Tea inevitably led to another, and then another, continuing until the GI had spent more on the bar girl's "tea" than on his room.

Of course, we had to buy a little Saigon Tea to please the mamasan. We weren't about to spend a whole week's pay on it, though. As regulars, we had steady bar girl dates who followed our simple drinking rule...Jack and Coke or Ba Mui Ba beer, or get off my lap.

We had noticed a strange pattern over the months of Saigon visits. It seemed as if Saigon had an underground network of hotel spies. Soon as you checked in, they spread the word that regular visitors to the hotel had arrived. True or not, as we walked through the bar entrance that night, my favorite little hostess had already arrived. She sat at our usual table, waiting for me.

Luan Dinh was strikingly beautiful, with deep brown eyes, long straight black hair and sultry lips. With flawless makeup and her traditional Ao Dai attire—an ankle-length hot pink tunic over black silk pantaloons and stiletto heels—she created an exotic, tantalizing vision.

As soon as she saw me, Luan rushed into my welcoming embrace. "Sergeant Pat Jack, I miss you beau coup!"

I had long since given up trying to explain that my name was Patrick, not Pat Jack. It didn't really matter. As long as she wound up in my room tonight, she could call me anything she wished.

DiOrio hooked up with his girl, Suzy. We sat down at our regular table for four next to an open window. Since the girls always sat on our laps, a table for two would've sufficed. We liked our space, though. No telling when some of the other guys from the hooch might drop by with their dates.

The window overlooked the busy street. Below us were cyclos—a strange three-wheeled device that looked like a cross between a bicycle and a rickshaw—motor bikes and motorcycles. The constant ebb and flow of these serviceable vehicles never ceased to amaze me. The typical modest-sized Honda motorcycle carried a man and woman, their three kids and bags of clothes…yet never seemed to have any problem maneuvering through the heavy traffic. The economy of the vehicles was impressive to this guy from station wagon country.

We hadn't come to Saigon to watch the traffic, though. The waiter came to take our orders, and the girls predictably ordered Saigon Tea. We put our standard rule into action regarding the drink scam.

"Waiter," I instructed, handing him twenty dollars. "Give each of the girls a beer mug of that crap. Then don't come back unless you're serving booze or beer. Got it?"

He nodded and went about his job. It was good to be a regular; the mamasan who ran the girls knew where we spent the majority of our money.

By 2200 hours, the bar and the tables were all filled. The Tiger was rockin'! We'd sucked down more than a few drinks by this point and were well on our way to being stoned. As we were smooching and playing with the giggling girls, my attention was drawn to a hulk standing in the front entrance.

Through the haze of cigarette smoke, I recognized a now-familiar silhouette in the archway…Staff Sergeant McMurtry. He was in bad shape. It appeared as if his grasp on the glass beads was the only thing allowing him to maintain an upright position.

With his back to the archway, I knew that DiOrio hadn't seen his new "friend" arrive. I figured I'd break it to him gently. "Hey Mike! Don't look now, but a really good friend of yours just came into the bar."

"No kidding? Who's here?" he asked as he pivoted around for a look-see. His head quickly snapped back around as he recognized McMurtry. "Hell, I thought we'd lost that guy. Let's duck out the back door before he sees us."

McMurtry could move quickly for someone clearly bombed out of his jungle boots, though. Before I could even nudge Luan off my lap, he had staggered over to our corner. As he came close, he tottered forward and grabbed the edge of the table to keep from falling. He stayed on his feet, body flopped across our table, his nose just below one of my sergeant stripes. It turns out that McMurtry wasn't quite drunk enough. He lifted his head and his eyes lit up in recognition.

"Well, well, what do we have here?" he mumbled as he leaned his elbow on the table. From that vantage point, he peered blearily around at me first, then at DiOrio. "If it isn't Captain DiOrio and Lieutenant Moffett!"

The drunk bully giggled with menace as he realized that our ranks were lower than his. McMurtry's eyes seemed to sparkle in anticipation of his impending revenge. It took a great deal of effort, but he braced himself against the table and pushed himself up on both hands.

I knew I had to go on the offensive and do it fast. We couldn't afford to let McMurtry open his mouth in a room full of soldiers and witnesses. I grabbed him by his labels, lifted him off the table, and dragged him into the narrow hallway next to the bar. Nobody saw when I slammed him against the wall and stuck my nose right in his face.

"Nice going, sergeant," I growled ominously. "Do you have any clue what you've just done?"

"Yeah!" he replied with another sloppy giggle. "I've exposed a couple of grunts impersonating officers!"

"Wrong, you idiot!" I said with all the vehemence I could force into my voice without alerting everyone in the hotel. "You just blew the cover of two CID officers!"

"CID?" he asked. From the look on his face, one would think I'd just said we were with the Nazi Gestapo.

"Posing as 101st sergeants to find out who's part of the drug ring in this bar," I explained, drawing on what the military policeman had told us earlier. "You've heard of the drug ring, right? Guy with the hand grenade?"

"Yeah, I hearduvit," he mumbled.

DiOrio had joined us in time to hear my ploy. He chimed in. "Yeah, and now we've gotta get out of here. It's over. You've set our investigation back two months."

I glanced over my shoulder to look into the bar. "Hope we make it out of here without someone setting off a grenade. They didn't take the last guy alive, you know. That's how serious this is."

As our story penetrated McMurtry's drunken haze, his eyes grew wide. He began trembling. "Ssssorry, sirs," he said, looking back and forth between the two of us and the bar. "Guess I screwed up again. Please don't—"

At that moment, a cherry private passed near our alcove. DiOrio nabbed him. "Hey, soldier! Are you leaving the hotel?"

The young soldier nodded, unsure what was going on.

"Good!" said DiOrio. "Take this drunk with you. He doesn't belong here anymore."

"If we get out of this alive and ever see you again, Sergeant McMurtry...," I whispered in a voice that dripped venom.

"You won't," the cowed bully promised.

DiOrio pushed McMurtry toward the private, and the two disappeared down the stairs. Then we just looked at each other in disbelief. We slapped each other's back and then hugged, glad that we had been sober enough to evade trouble with some quick thinking.

As we returned to the bar for a nightcap, I said, "Y'know, this officer stuff is crazy. I'm not even sure what rank I am anymore."

With more than enough booze in our bellies, we scooped up our girls and flung them over our shoulders, caveman style, for the trip to our rooms. It was time for a little boom-boom, a little grass and a good night's sleep. We needed to return to Bien Hoa before the next day's noon roll call.

The rest of the night was extremely pleasant, as it always was when Luan and I got together. I showered the next morning and started to dress. It was two-shirt time again. This time, the sergeant stripes were underneath and the officer bars were on top. It wouldn't do to get sloppy during the return trip. We needed to slip out of the city as easily as we had come in.

Luan and I met Mike and Suzy in the lobby. We paid our room bill at the front desk and then stepped out of the charming old hotel. This was the part I always hated. We whistled for a cab to take the girls home.

As the cab pulled away, I heard Luan's sweet voice call out, "Sergeant Pat Jack, I love you beau coup!"

I smiled and waved. Until next time, dear girl. Whatever the risks, I'd take them to be in her arms again.

Mike and I hoisted our bags onto our shoulders and walked to Tu Do Street. It was the busiest thoroughfare in Saigon. That made

it the best place to catch a military ride back to Bien Hoa. We did-
n't have to wait long for a lift.

Once we were on our way, we shed the top shirts quickly. We'd
both had enough officer stuff for a long, long time. But then again,
we reminded each other while laughing madly, so had one obnoxious sergeant named McMurtry.

MIDNIGHT CONFESSIONS

"Oh, come *on*, Wise. The Jets are gonna get blown away!" I groaned loudly when I recognized the ranting voice inside the admin office. It was PFC Billy Dobler, Lieutenant Koneche's snitch, ragging about his most recent favorite subject. I let my hand fall away from the door and debated about walking into the office at all. The last thing I needed was more sanctimonious tripe from that weasel.

"You don't know what you're talking about, Dobler," Herb Wise said angrily. "Namath's on a roll, and he's going to hand the Colts their heads on a platter."

There was only one topic that could cause a fight faster than spilling someone's beer or insulting their girl. They were discussing the hottest topic at Bien Hoa base…the upcoming Super Bowl III football game between the New York Jets and the Baltimore Colts. Dobler was from Maryland and was a fanatic NFL—National Football League—supporter. He wasn't shy about deriding anyone who supported the competition.

"You think Namath's gonna be straight enough to hold onto the ball?" Dobler asked. "He's a cavalier, too busy partying to play a real man's game"

"He's the best in the AFL!" retorted Wise in defense of the American Football League.

Dobler's laugh was like a miniature poodle barking. "The AFL?! Ha! They're still in diapers. Just wait until the grownups in the NFL spank their fannies, then you'll see."

With a heavy sigh, I opened the door and stepped into the office. There wasn't anybody in the room who hadn't already heard the next part of Dobler's speech. The NFL was formed in 1922. There had been three unsuccessful attempts to form the AFL before 1959 when it finally got off the ground. That made the AFL "kids" and the NFL "grownups."

Herb beat the snitch to the punch. "Even if they're in diapers, the Jets are still gonna bomb the daylights out of your ponies."

I didn't need to see his face as I walked up behind the private. His voice carried the same smug air.

"What? The Colts are sixteen and one this year. No AFL team has ever beaten the NFL, and this year's going to be the same. You just watch and see."

Wise was starting to get ticked. "Yeah, right, keep blowing smoke, Dobler. You're just whining because the real league is forcing the NFL to play fair. What's the matter, you don't like that the two leagues have merged?"

That was another point of contention in the football debate around the base. Everyone knew about the secret meetings that took place in 1966 between the two league bosses. After unsuccessful legal attempts to steal players and handicap the AFL, the NFL had finally come to its senses. The result had been a merger of the two leagues into the two conferences playing under one league. Congress had even passed special legislation waiving anti-trust laws to allow the merger. The 1969 Super Bowl game was the last time the two would play as separate leagues.

With a smug grin of my own, I tapped the kid on the shoulder. "Private! Don't you have something to do?"

He spun around, surprised. "Wha…yes, Sergeant Moffett!"

"Then I'd suggest you get to doing it."

"Yes, Sergeant!"

While Dobler's voice was respectful, the look in his eyes warned me to watch out for him. The snitch didn't like being reminded that, in the chain of command, he was in the bottom link. One way or the other, I figured the kid would try to find something juicy on me to pass on to Lieutenant Koneche, our boss.

"Thanks, Moff," Herb Wise said after the weasel had left the room.

"Don't worry about him, Herb," I said, attempting to remove the angry beet-red coloring from my tiny friend's face. "AFVN is showing the game on Monday morning. After Namath is done with the Colts, I'm sure Dobler will be eating crow for a long time."

"Yeah," Herb replied with a wicked smile. "I want to see his face at the end of that game."

I patted him on the back and then walked to my desk. With Saigon still off-limits to us, there was little else to do over the weekend. The football game would actually be played on Sunday in the States, but we were about half a day ahead of real-World time. It 'would be around two in the morning when we got to watch the game.

The daily report was already finished and I had just come back from lunch, so there was little left to do with my day. I intended to finish the paperwork for the next "additional" R&R allocation to Bangkok, Thailand. Everyone in the section had already gone once, so it was finally my turn to go. I was looking forward to it.

The plan had worked out better than we'd thought at first. The Division still received its allocations for R&R. We simply passed ours down to the frontline battalions and then took our turn using "space available" slots on the R&R flights. It didn't cost anything extra, and it definitely didn't take anybody's authorized allotment. We were simply taking advantage of the built-in buffer within the system. It gave the combat grunts a few extra slots, which made us feel that we were doing our job...making their lives a little easier.

The process was simplicity in itself. We simply typed up the orders, submitted them through the finance division that was located right next to us at Bien Hoa, and then went. We'd only had one soldier bumped from the space available seat, but got him on the next flight out. Of course, there was one soldier who wasn't read in on the plan...the snitch, Billy Dobler.

I finished the form and gave it to DiOrio to run over to Finance. Then we called it a day and headed back to the hooch. The guys settled down to cold beer and a card game, then took a break for evening chow. We recorded, drank some more beer, sang some do-wop songs and then I headed for my bunk. The rest of the hooch continued to play more cards.

Tripod alerted us before the Air Force siren went off. The Heinz 57 mongrel mix was a better alert system, warning us before the VC launched their rockets, than the best military hardware. With dog and siren sounding so close together, I knew from experience that we didn't have enough time to make it to the bunker outside. Yelling, "Incoming!" I dove under my bed. My head slammed into something hard on the way down. The rocket attack lasted for one salvo and then the siren sounded the all-clear.

I crawled out from beneath my bunk and rubbed my face. When I looked at my fingers, they were smeared with blood. The rockets didn't hit anywhere near us, so I knew I wasn't hit. It had to have been whatever I slammed into in my dive for the bunker.

"Hey Moff, you alright?" asked Mike Brunetti as he rolled out from beneath his bunk. "You hit?"

"Nah, I ran into something on the way down." I looked beside the bed to identify the culprit, but there wasn't anything close enough to have caught me.

"You're supposed to tuck and roll, Moff," Herb chastised. To the others, he explained, "I saw him do it. He led with his head and hit the side of his bunk."

That started everyone laughing. There's nothing like the laughter to remove the tension after a few seconds worth of terror. That was our existence…awake before dawn, office work until the heat became unbearable, a siesta in the hooch during the afternoon, occasional rocket attacks and lots of beer. I was really looking forward to seeing something new. R&R in Bangkok sounded like heaven to me.

I made a run to the PX for beer the next day. We should've invested in Budweiser, considering the amount of beer we went through in a week. The guys were waiting for me when I returned. They had a present.

"This is for you," Brunetti said, extending a large newspaper-wrapped object toward me.

"What, is it my birthday or something and I forgot about it?" I asked, surprised and a little cautious about the "gift."

"Nope," Sparky Anderson, our resident mechanic, said from his bunk. "Just open it."

I looked intently at the faces of the guys around me, trying to find some hint that this was a gag or some other type of prank. Their faces didn't show me anything, so I unwrapped the package. It contained a catcher's mask.

I didn't understand the significance. "Um, thanks guys…but what's it for?"

"After watching that one and a half full gainer you did onto the floor last night, we figured you needed some protection," laughed Herb Wise.

"Yeah, that mug of yours is ugly enough already!," jibed Mike Brunetti. "We have to keep from screaming when you wake up in the morning as it is."

Mike DiOrio chimed in. "I mean, I've heard of hitting yourself with the ugly stick…but you're taking it to the extreme."

I rubbed the side of my face and grinned. The large bruised raspberry had formed after my graceless dive under the bunk the previous evening. All joking aside, I knew that the present showed the guys cared. It was just one of those male bonding rules…you never admitted to it.

My hooch mates then showed me the peg they'd placed beside the bed. Dave Corbus, our other resident vehicle expert, then gave a demonstration of how to grab the mask, drop and roll under the bunk. It was a great time, and I proudly hung the mask on the peg afterwards.

I had my first opportunity to test it the following Sunday evening as the sirens sounded. Reaching over, I grabbed the catcher's mask and pulled it over my head as I dropped to the floor. Then I rolled under my bed. I was amazed; the thing actually worked. After that, I always reached for the mask when the Tripod or the sirens sounded.

We stayed up after the attack and gathered around our small television that sat on the bar. Plenty of beer had already been consumed by the time Super Bowl III came on. Everyone was definitely pumped for the game of the season.

"Hey, where's Dobler?" asked Wise.

"He said he already knows how it's gonna end," replied Dave Motley. "He doesn't even need to watch the game."

It was a great game. The New York Jets intercepted the ball three times in the first half. Namath was incredible, passing over two hundred yards during the game. He was named the game's MVP—most valuable player—after leading the Jets to a 16-7 win over the Colts.

Johnny Unitas, the Colts' quarterback who'd been out most of the season from an elbow injury, came in during the last quarter to throw the only touchdown for the Baltimore Colts.

There's one bad thing about soldiers in a combat zone watching a physical sport like football...the instinct to act is easily triggered. Everyone was pumped full of adrenaline. Normally we didn't have any target to focus our aggression on, but this time was different. After a month of ridicule and snide comments, everyone was ready for payback.

"Where's that Dobler?!" yelled Wise after the final whistle blew. "I want to rub his nose in this!"

"He's in his hooch!" yelled a drunken voice. I was surprised to discover it had been my own.

"Let's get him!" roared DiOrio.

That started an avalanche. Everyone piled out of their seats and stormed toward the snitch's hooch. He was sleeping peacefully when we got there. That didn't last long as one of the guys screamed in his ear, "Hey, DOBLER! YOUR TEAM LOST!"

There are times when survival instinct kicks in and prevents you from saying something stupid. Regrettably, Dobler had no survival instincts. He bolted upright in his bed and was immediately barraged with haranguing and mockery. Never one to keep his mouth shut, Dobler responded with, "Get away from me, you lying sacks of horse shit! Nobody can beat my Colts!"

Soldiers have a time-honored tradition for weasels, snitches, and generally obnoxious fellows. It's called a shower party. Basically, it consists of bars of soap slipped into socks. Sometimes it actually occurs in a shower. This time, it didn't. Lucky for Dobler, he was still under his blanket. That softened some of the blows, but not by much. It was better than weighted socks thumping against bare skin, though.

I called an end to it after the first minute or so...well, okay, after about five minutes or so. Since we hadn't turned on any lights in the hooch, there was little chance that he had recognized anything more than a voice or two. We returned to our hooch, still drunk and laughing about the justice served. It may seem harsh, but that's the military for you. We take care of our own. That includes problem children.

Dobler was very meek the next day. When anyone asked if he'd heard the final score of the game, he simply replied that he understood the Jets had won. Nobody could bait him into saying anything more about it. He walked gingerly around the office, but there wasn't a mark on him. Nothing was ever said about the shower party again. The snitch had learned his lesson that he still needed to be able to live with his peers.

I took off the following day for my R&R in Bangkok. It was a relatively short flight, compared to the one I'd taken to reach Vietnam. We spent probably as much time circling the Thai airport as we did reaching the country. Turns out that an owner-driver—a cabbie who owned his own cab—had parked his car on the runway and then gone for coffee. Our plane had to circle until he came back and moved his car off the tarmac.

We were transported to the R&R center for our in-country briefing. The commander of the center was quite the character. He discussed local customs and traditions, what sites were off-limits and what would happen if we were caught there. Then he warned us about the different types of crabs that could be found in Thailand…not the type you eat, but the sexually transmitted kind.

"Finally," he said toward the end of the brief, "let's talk about katoeys. Bangkok is full of these 'lady-men,' so be on your guard. Some of them are prettier than the women! If you get into a cab with a girl, the first thing you want to do is grab between their legs."

That brought a roar of approval from the group. The commander chuckled. "You guys don't believe me yet, but you will. When you grab between the legs and feel something dangling—like the same balls and bat you got—then get the hell out of the cab!"

After that, we were reminded of our return flight time and released into the city. The first thing I did was call a cab. I'd already heard that the owner-drivers were the best source of information in Bangkok. They knew the cheapest hotels, all of the hot spots and nightclubs, and anything else a soldier might want to buy. The owner-driver had the easiest oriental name I'd heard to that point; Chet also spoke fluent English. We negotiated a rate, and then Chet became my exclusive chauffeur for the duration of my stay.

I could've stayed at the R&R Center, which was located at the Windsor Hotel in Sukhumvit Soi 20. It looked like a great place, but I didn't want anyone around monitoring my fun. It probably didn't happen; there were too many GIs coming and going to keep keep track of them all. Yet the mere thought of someone from CID looking over my shoulder was enough to make me uneasy.

My chauffeur took me to the hotel that DiOrio and Brunetti had suggested. I checked into the hotel wearing casual civilian clothes, dumped my bag on the bed, and then headed back to the street. It was a pleasant surprise to see that the driver had kept his part of the bargain…he waited for me beside his cab.

"Where to, Mister Pat?" Chet asked.

The day was still too young for hitting the bar scene yet. "I'd like to buy some clothes. You know a place like that?"

"You bet, Mister Pat!" he replied. Once again, he was as good as his word. The driver-owner had deals going with numerous shops throughout the city. He would chauffeur his clients exclusively to the shop that gave him a percentage of the sale. It was a good deal for everyone concerned.

The clothing store owner also knew how to treat his customers. As I waited with a couple of guys I'd met on the flight to try on clothes, the owner brought a tray containing the local Thai beer called Sing Ha. There was a funny thing about Sing Ha…nobody knew how much alcohol was in it, not even the brewers. One batch might have ten percent, another fifteen. I was used to chugging Bud and other domestic American beers. It didn't take long for the Thai beer to wipe me and the other guys out. It was good for the clothing store owner, though…the Sing Ha made us very happy, and we all bought quite a few sets of clothes.

After that, it was a quick trip back to the hotel for a sober-up siesta. Night had fallen by the time I finally woke up. It was time to hit the streets and see if Bangkok lived up to its party town reputation.

Chet was waiting for me outside. His recommendation was a visit to Pot Pang Road; it was actually called Patpong, but that was too close to my first name. I changed it to Pot Pang, and Chet didn't seem to care.

The street was nothing but clubs and girls. Chet parked the cab and we started walking the strip. It was incredible...a horny soldier's dream made real. Scantily clad or completely naked girls danced, waved, or simply sat suggestively behind shop windows for pedestrians to ogle. The competing blend of classical, rock, country, and oriental music blared into the night air. Neon lights flashed and glowed, rivaling the street lights in intensity. There was an air of madness and intense sexual tension that surrounded everything you touched, heard, and smelled.

We walked into one of the bars that Chet suggested. It was a rocking place. Striptease dancers leaped from table to table, danced in cages or around poles on the numerous stages. I couldn't tell any difference between the female customers, waitresses, and dancers. Every one of them seemed available and willing to do anything.

Again, there was that sexual tension in the air. The heavy rock music added to it, making it thrum like a heartbeat. I caught a scent of grass in the air; perhaps the intoxicant was deliberately released into the room, or maybe it was just secondhand smoke.

We grabbed a table and ordered a round of Sing Ha. That's when I noticed the first difference between the women in the room. There were at least a hundred girls with numbers pinned or sewn onto their clothes. The significance of the numbers didn't make any sense to me. I kept looking around the room, trying to figure out the number system. That's when I saw her.

I elbowed Chet and discretely pointed. "Look at *that* one."

"Which one, Mister Pat?" he asked, scanning the room.

"That one! In the black dress." That didn't help Chet any; there were lots of women in black dresses. I tried to find some way to identify her to him without rudely pointing. The answer was obvious. "Number forty-nine. See her, over there? She's absolutely beautiful!"

Chet smiled and nodded. Then he stood up from the table and bellowed, "Forty-nine!"

I was deathly embarrassed. It felt like the music had stopped abruptly and everyone was staring at us. Imagine doing something like that in a restaurant in New York; if there had been a mouse hole, I would've tried crawling into it.

That simply wasn't how guys got a girl's attention…I'd already worked up a tentative plan to saunter over to her, ask her name and buy her a drink. To my amazement, Chet's announcement saved me the trouble. Instead of appearing on us, a spotlight suddenly focused on the girl. She looked around the room, saw Chet waving to her, and then walked over to our table.

The gorgeous woman smiled at the chauffeur, who directed her attention to me. Her smile was stunning, and so was she. "Hello, sir," she said politely in the sultriest, most seductive voice I've ever heard. "I am Mali. You like?"

"Oh *man*, do I like!" I proclaimed. Despite my earlier embarrassment, my experience with Luan Dinh kept me from being surprised as she slipped onto my lap.

Over the next several hours, as Mali and I got to know each other better, I learned how the system worked. She was an escort…a prostitute and tour guide wrapped up into one delicious bundle. It would run me about five hundred Thai Baht, the equivalent of twenty to twenty-five dollars, per day for her services. From first sight, I knew she was worth it.

Mali didn't disappoint me. She was a master of her trade. The nights were very pleasurable, full of partying and the most sensual sex. The days spent sightseeing in Bangkok were like walking with a most precious girlfriend who knew everything about the city. Truly remarkable, really.

Like Chet and his cab, Mali was at my disposal during my entire week-long stay. We toured the standard fare of tourist sites— the Temple of the Thousand Buddhas, the Temple of Dawn, and the Grand Palace—but my tastes never ran to things. I enjoy people, and so I was more interested in doing things where people interacted. Typically that meant interaction with Mali during the late night hours and into the next afternoon, then the bars and clubs.

During one of those excursions, I got to witness an American soldier's reaction to a katoey. He was kissing "her" in the back seat of the cab, fondling all over her. Then he ran a hand down between her legs…and found out that the drop-dead gorgeous female was actually a male. The soldier jumped out of the cab, alternating between spitting and wiping his lips, then cursing and yelling. Mali and I just laughed.

The week ended too quickly. I promised Mali that I would be back in a month, and was surprised when she said that she'd have Chet keep an eye out for me at the R&R Center. She even suggested the possibility of visiting her at home. That was almost unheard of; when an escort invited you to her home, she was saying that you had become a friend instead of just a customer. I was pleased with the unexpected compliment. We kissed one last time, and then I headed for the outprocessing center.

The flight back to Bien Hoa was uneventful. It was great to see the guys in the hooch again. They listened intently—and to an extent, vicariously—to my tales of the Bangkok trip. Even though I wasn't in line for R&R in a month, they unanimously agreed that I had take one of their slots and go back.

Work didn't seem like a chore after that. It wasn't a miraculous change or anything like that; I simply didn't mind the routine anymore. Now I understood how beneficial R&R was to the troops. Just getting away for awhile gave me a new perspective on life and work.

It didn't take long for that to change. The United Service Organization, most commonly known by its acronym of USO, had organized a tour of small bands to play in Vietnam. I attended the concert after duty and had a good time. Like the other GIs in the audience, I was fondest of a Filipino band. It wasn't their music that grabbed our attention, though…it was the large-breasted blonde lead singer. She was an American beauty from head to toe.

I had just returned to the hooch and settled down on my bunk when a familiar face appeared. Even his words were the same. "Sergeant Moffett," the private bellowed in his parade-ground voice, "The Colonel sent me to come and get you! He wants you right away!"

"Oh, hell," I muttered to myself. After the lobster incident, I had hoped the colonel would've forgotten my name. I grabbed my fatigue shirt and, thinking what a strange déjà vu this was, asked the kid if he knew what the colonel wanted.

"No, Sergeant…just that it was important!"

"Fine, son. Tell the Colonel I'm on my way."

"Yes, Sergeant!" the enthusiastic kid replied as he ran toward the door.

I didn't even warn him this time. He slammed into the screen door. To my surprise, he didn't rip through the screen. Still feeling like I'd been through this already, I told him in a loud voice, "*Walk, son.*"

The trip to Colonel's trailer continued the sense of a recurring nightmare. I rapped on the door and heard the voice inside yell, "Enter!" With a deep breath, I opened the door. If the Old Man started talking about discretion again, I was going to run screaming across the base.

"Sergeant Moffett, I'm glad you could get here so quickly," the Colonel's voice said from the back room. "Come here, I need to talk to you."

I walked through the narrow trailer to the bedroom. The officer was in bed under a sheet...beside him was the blonde from the Filipino band. With great effort, I kept my eyes focused on a picture hanging above the bed instead of on the woman's large curves outlined by the thin sheet. "You wanted to see me, sir?"

"Yes, Sergeant. I have a mission for you—"

"One that requires discretion," I interrupted. "Yes, I can see that, sir."

The colonel didn't seem embarrassed in the least. "My guest is hungry, Sergeant Moffett. I would like you to go to my mess hall and have the cook whip her up a batch of chocolate chip cookies. Can you do that for me, Sergeant?"

I was absolutely dumbfounded. The army has a saying about "rank has its privileges," but this was ridiculous. However, I've always been a sucker for a woman's charms...although I never expected them to work when the gal was in someone else's arms. I discovered that I really didn't have any choice after the blonde begged, "Please?"

"Uh, yes ma'am," I mumbled.

"I think a dozen or so will be enough for us, don't you my sweetie?" the commander asked his bed partner. Then he looked at me and made it an order. "Bring two dozen cookies here, Sergeant Moffett. Don't say anything else to anyone, understood?"

I'd learned a long time ago that there's only one response to an officer when he gives a direct order. I snapped a sharp salute and said, "Yes, sir!"

Oddly enough, though, there was something missing in the translation when I gave the colonel's cook his instructions. The bearded chef wasn't too happy about having to bake twelve dozen chocolate chip cookies in the middle of the night. I was more than happy to provide a friendly ear as he vented his irritations, though.

After all, I couldn't leave until the cookies were done. The guys in the hooch were still awake when I returned. Although I couldn't explain the real story about how I got ended up with ten dozen chocolate chip cookies...the guys really loved the colonel's gift. The blonde in the trailer must have loved the cookies too because the colonel gave me one of his personal R&R slots. This one couldn't be transferred to a field grunt.

Strange how things work out sometimes. Because of the colonel's cookies, I ended up getting to go back to Bangkok sooner than I had expected. I was very surprised to see Chet outside the R&R Center, and even more surprised when he recognized me.

"Mister Pat, welcome back to Bangkok! Come, Mali will be pleased to see you."

It was strange to drive into a tropical countryside where I knew nobody would shoot at me. Some habits die hard, and I found myself scanning the tree line for an ambush that never came.

The house was a surprise. For one thing, it wasn't a hut like I expected. The building was a modern structure hidden in the woods. Mali greeted me at the door and literally gave me a breathtaking kiss. Then she escorted me through the foyer and into her home.

That's when I received the greatest shock of my life. The largest mountain of marijuana I'd ever seen sat in the middle of the living room. Mali introduced me to her family and friends. They paused in their work of stuffing dime bags to smile and greet me.

I was at a complete loss for words. Somehow I managed to get through the pleasantries without showing what I was thinking and feeling. Mali had never given me any indication that she ran her own business growing and selling marijuana.

After a pleasant reunion in her bedroom, we talked about her business. I was concerned at first that she wanted me to become a distributor for her. She just laughed at that and said that I would make a lousy drug salesman…but was a fabulous lover.

Mali didn't need her escort service job. To put it delicately, she was a devout worshipper of sexual bonding and was very selective in her partners. Nymphomaniac might be another way of describing her.

I never paid another dime to Mali for escort or tourist guide services. The week-long vacation was completely different from our first week together. We'd seen enough of the tourist sites in Bangkok, and I had no reason to visit Patpong Road. This time around, we had fun in the Thai fashion. We went bowling.

The week ended too soon, as vacations always do. Our parting was more sincere this time. I'd never expected to make a friend in Thailand, and I felt bad about leaving Mali. She took it with better grace. "You come back, Pat, I be here. No come back, I still here."

War has a bad habit of making strange friendships and then breaking them. I never returned to Bangkok. Somewhere outside the Thai capital is a woman who may occasionally think of me, but I doubt it. She lived her life by the day while working on plans for her future. That made her different from the Vietnamese, but she still had an oriental outlook on life. If I showed up unexpectedly, she would pull the past into her present life without interruption. As for the future, Mali had no plans with me in it.

I pondered those questions over the next few weeks at Bien Hoa. What I felt for Mali wasn't the same as my feelings for Luan Dinh. Both worked around the same profession. Mali played at being an escort just for fun. Luan was a prostitute so that she could put food on the table. I didn't love either of them, not in the settle-down-get-married kind of love. They were both friends in a way, and very good lovers. Yet I wanted more from a woman than that.

Time and constant work slowly refocused my thoughts and energy. It didn't matter what I felt about the girls; I was in Vietnam because of the war. Once I'd made that realization, I really didn't think about love again. That was a topic for poets, not a soldier.

The USO helped distract me as well. They brought in a tour of famous people consisting Sebastian Cabot, Billie Ray Smith, and Al Atkinson. Cabot was the bearded British actor who played "Mr. French" on the television show, "Family Affair." Billie Ray Smith, Sr., was the defensive tackle of the Colts, and Al Atkinson was from the New York Jets.

I gave Billie Ray Smith a little friendly ragging about losing to the Jets, but he was cool about it. He was a big guy who sweated constantly in the Vietnamese heat and humidity. I really respected the guy—all of them—for taking the time to come to Vietnam and support the troops.

To say that I began questioning a lot of things during this period of introspection would be an understatement. I was getting "short," the term used when a soldier was down to ninety days or less in Vietnam. My DEROS—date of estimated return from overseas—would arrive in April. I would still have five months of mandatory service left under the two-year draft requirement. The Army would assign me to another unit Stateside for that period.

I was already planning to return to my old job of lading clerk with a shipping company when I left the service. It sounded like a much better deal than what the army had offered me so far. While I felt a deep camaraderie with the guys from the hooch, that was going to end when I shipped back Stateside.

The question that kept bouncing to the front of my brain was whether I could stomach remaining in the service for five months after Vietnam. After secret lobster and cookie missions, how could anyone expect that I would be able to snap salutes and act like the stereotypical soldier once I got back to the States? I couldn't help but feel that it would be like stepping from an insane asylum into a by-the-book boarding school.

Then I found out where the Army intended to send me. I was expected to complete my last five months as a Jungle Warfare Trainer at Fort Collins, Colorado. Other than the short time I'd spent with the Recon Platoon at Phouc Vinh, I knew that I had no real jungle warfare experience. Yet the Army, in its infinite wisdom, expected an administrative sergeant like me to teach wet-behind-the-ears green soldiers how to survive combat in Vietnam's jungle.

I couldn't do it. Without real bush experience, anything I taught the Jungle Warfare students could get them killed. Their blood would be on my hands, and that was something I refused to accept. There were many things I had done, like impersonating an officer to get laid, but I had never done anything that could get someone hurt or killed.

However, the Army is not an equal opportunity employer. When it says "Go!" you go, no questions asked. There is no choice in duty assignments. To paraphrase the saying, I would have to accept whatever the army gave me "for the good of the service." Refusing to accept the assignment simply wasn't an option.

I considered the situation very carefully. At first it seemed that my only option would be to go AWOL instead of reporting for the instructor assignment. It would keep my hands clean of innocent blood, but it was really a no-starter solution.

The answer came from the experience that the Army had given me, and that I was very qualified to understand. The service had a Short Program, also called the Early-Out Program. It allowed any soldier with a hundred and fifty days or less remaining to serve after leaving Vietnam to leave the Army. All I had to do was volunteer to extend my time in Vietnam by two months.

At first, the guys in the hooch thought I had gone completely nuts. Nobody in their right mind would volunteer to stay in a combat zone. It took awhile to explain it to them, but finally they understood the method to my madness.

Sadly, it was far more difficult on the home front. I wrote my parents and explained my decision. It came as a complete shock several weeks later when I was discovered that a Congressional inquiry had my name on it. Funny thing about Congressional inquiries; they required that the military respond within forty-eight hours to answer whatever question a Congressman asked.

It turned out that my mother had contacted her Congressman after receiving my letter. She had explained that the war had hit me on the head too many times, and she wanted her son home immediately before any more mental damage was done. I was called to explain everything to the investigating officer, who then sent the report back to Washington. Everything calmed down after the

Congressman explained to my mother that I had voluntarily extended for the Short Program. She didn't like the fact that I would be in Vietnam for another two months, but she finally stopped calling the Congressman.

I was very satisfied with my solution. It meant that I wouldn't be responsible for giving soldiers bad information that got them killed. It was a bit crazy. After all, I volunteered to place my life on the line instead of the lives of students I would've had to train. Now all that I had to do was keep my head down for an extra two months. It seemed like a good plan.

However, as I was to discover over the next few months, war has a tendency to make even the best plans go awry.

SAIGON PIZZA TO GO

The weekly trips to Saigon did wonders for my morale. It was almost like I had been asleep; suddenly I woke up and started living again. Life was no longer centered around work, sleep, then more work. I looked forward to my visits with Luan Dinh. It wasn't love, but it was still incredible.

Bien Hoa didn't seem like such a bad place after that. Some of the guys who were sent to the war in Vietnam wanted to be on the front, where the action was. I was perfectly happy where I was. There were many of us administrative grunts and other personnel who were just as happy to fulfill our duties well back from the actual fighting. However, the Viet Cong didn't fight on straight battle lines; there really was no front. Vietnam is a small country. It was impossible to be there and be risk free.

Because of its high volume of military aircraft, the Viet Cong made Bien Hoa airbase a target for their rockets several times a week. It seemed as if nearly every military aircraft in existence used the base's twin runways. Our hooch was only several hundred yards from the main runway. The noise was incessant during the day. The rocket attacks were both noisy and dangerous at night.

Bien Hoa wasn't a quiet garden spot. The VC rockets weren't accurate, and sometimes they missed the runway and struck nearby buildings. Regardless of what many line soldiers believed, there was no true "rear" in the war. We did our job so that the infantry grunts up north could find and destroy the enemy. The enemy knew that logistics and support was what kept the war moving…and they did their best to interfere with that process. We took our share of casualties. Unlike the line units, though, we rarely had the chance to hunt down the attackers. We had to sit there and take it.

However, it was still life in the rear area. We had far more amenities than the combat troops. While we never bumped a soldier from their R&R trip to Bangkok, we still managed to take a few trips out-country. The guys from the hooch and I had weekly access to the pleasures of Saigon. We also had greater access to the beer from the PX and beef steaks from the EM or NCO clubs.

All told, it was the best place to be in a war...until February 1969. That's when our intelligence guys learned the Viet Cong had promised their leader, Ho Chi Minh, a special birthday gift. They promised to destroy the entire Bien Hoa military base by May 19th for his seventy-ninth birthday. The Intel guys started referring to the upcoming assault as "Tet '69." Their forecasts showed the best time for a nationwide coordinated attack would be on Tet, the celebration of the Vietnamese New Year.

The North Vietnamese had conducted a similar attack throughout South Vietnam during Tet of 1968. Government offices, ARVN and US bases were hit simultaneously. The attack had caused a great deal of damage and took quite awhile to defeat. Nobody truly believed that the North Vietnamese would try another Tet offensive...and yet that was exactly what the Military Intelligence guys were piecing together from their sources.

When the top brass heard that bit of news, they decided to spoil Charlie's birthday party. Orders went out. The next thing we knew, extra troops and helicopters started arriving to defend the vital complex. It was probably the safest period of time I knew while in Vietnam.

Billeting the new troops wasn't a problem. The infantry grunts moved into temporary tents near perimeter. Others occupied warehouses near the airfield; they needed to be close to the flight line in order to rapidly board helicopters. If the VC attacked, they would be pinned down by defenders on the perimeter. Then the helicopters would lift their troops and drop them behind the enemy. The hope was that, caught between the two forces, the Viet Cong would decide they'd rather leave Bien Hoa alone rather than stand and fight.

Well, to us Admin grunts, more people meant even more opportunities to make friends and have a good time. We watched our new neighbors arrive and move into the hooch next to ours. The twelve war-torn GIs landed their three battered Hueys at the edge of the air strip near the hooches. They came from Camp Eagle up north, where they probably saw more action in a day than we saw in a year.

The pilots and crew would be on alert status, ready at any time to scramble from their bunks and fire up the choppers.

We made friends right away. Dave Motley was concerned about having choppers—a juicy target of opportunity for VC rockets—sitting right next to the hooch. It was bad enough with the rocket attacks against the bunkers protecting fighter aircraft across the runway. Having helicopters sitting out in the open seemed like asking for trouble.

The new guys reassured him that there were patrols out already, searching for bad guys. Rockets were too bulky to move without one of the patrols seeing them. This attack, if it came, would be a ground assault. Maybe they'd have mortars, but no heavy rockets to assist.

"Don't worry about it, Motley," I told him. "These guys live like this all the time. If they aren't going to lose any sleep over it, so why should we?"

"Because they can bug out when the rockets come in?"

"And you can hide under your bunk," DiOrio admonished him. "Grow some balls, man. It's going to be fine."

"Hey," suggested Herb Wise in an obvious attempt to change the direction of the conversation, "Let's throw a real party for them. I bet those poor guys don't even know what real food looks like anymore."

"Okay. A party sounds good," I quickly agreed. "Motley, you're in charge of the beer run."

Dave turned, removing the antagonistic glare he'd directed toward DiOrio, and smiled at me. "Yah, I can do that, Patty. Beer sounds like a winner to me."

"Mike, you've got some friends over at the mess hall, right?" I waited for him to look at me as well.

"What're you thinking, Moff?"

"Steaks."

"Those're going to be hard to come by."

"If there's anyone on this base who'll be able to scrounge a few, it'll be you, Mike. Up to it?"

"Piece of cake." DiOrio grinned. "How thick you want them?"

I gave him a thumbs-up signal. "Thicker than my thumb, man.

Don't spare the expense. Breeze, you go with him. We'll need some potatoes, butter, sour cream."

Our resident stoner simply nodded.

"What about me, Moff?" asked Herb.

"Get with Mai when she comes in. See if she can't get some fresh fatigues for these guys. Then show them where the shower is. I'll take care of the tunes."

"Got it, boss."

I watched the guys head off to complete their assignments, confident that each would succeed with their mission. Then I headed into the hooch to search through my music collection. I had picked up a reel-to-reel from one of the guys heading back Stateside. When I needed to wind down, I'd load one of the many reels onto the machine, stick the headphones over my ears, and listen to the music. It had become a joke with the other guys. They thought it was hilarious to watch me dance in t-shirt and underwear to tunes only I could hear.

Three hours later, the steaks were on the grill. Beer chilled in several buckets of ice. I'd moved the reel-to-reel to a table outside the hooch. Everything was ready except the invitation to dinner.

"Good afternoon, gentlemen," I said, announcing my presence to our new neighbors. "If you don't have plans for the evening, why don't you come on over? There's steaks and hot dogs, beer and —"

That's as far as I got. The twelve guys were up and moving toward me like I was a lifeguard saving drowning swimmers. The party was a huge success. We had mastered the art of partying by this point, and we did ourselves proud. There were plenty of barbecued or grilled steaks, hot dogs, ice-cold beer and even soda…to be used as a mixer, of course. At the end of the evening, we all crashed hard but happy.

The next day, Warrant Officer Billy Barnes came to the hooch to thank us. "Great party," the helicopter pilot said, massaging his head from the hangover. "We'd love to pay you guys back, but there's no way we could match what you did."

"It was nothing," I told him, trying to rub away a hangover of my own. "Just our way of saying thanks for being here, covering our butts."

The Warrant Officer shook his head. "That dog won't hunt, Sergeant, and we both know it. What you guys did was above and beyond just saying howdy. If there's ever anything you need us to do, all you gotta do is ask."

Herb Wise and I exchanged glances. We weren't ones to let an opportunity pass, especially one this promising.

"Well, there is one thing…," Herb said slowly. Then he just sat there with a stupid grin on his face.

"Yeah?" asked the pilot.

"Well," Herb replied, drawing close to him and speaking in a low conspiratorial voice. "I've heard that there's this little pizzeria just outside Tan Son Nhut Air Base in Saigon. It's supposed to have the best pizzas in the Orient, almost as good as the ones Stateside."

"And?" Barnes asked, grinning as well. He already knew where this was leading.

When Herb got rolling, there was no stopping him. He could make a wedding seem tragic or a horror story appear comic. It simply depended on the response he wanted from the other person.

"It seems that the Air Force wants to keep it all to themselves." Herb's face changed; one would believe it was the most tragic event that had ever happened. "They've restricted the base from Army personnel. We're not allowed to travel there by truck."

Then he smiled wickedly. "They wouldn't say no to a fellow pilot, though. Maybe you could just hop down there with a Huey and pick up five pizzas for all of us?"

"Hey man, no problem!" Barnes replied, surprising us all. "We have to fly down there anyway to drop off some spare parts."

"Cool!" Herb clapped his hands together, proud of himself for convincing the pilot.

I didn't think Crash realized that it had been too easy. From the look on Barne's face, he had something up his sleeve. Flyboys had a well-deserved reputation for being loose with the rules and playing pranks. I waited for the pilot's punch line.

Barnes looked at us with his own version of a wicked grin. "We're taking off at seventeen hundred tomorrow afternoon. C'mon along for the ride. You two can take care of the pizza run while we're offloading."

"You bet, man. We'll be there!"

Barnes thanked us again, then headed for his hooch. I tried to convince Herb that there was something the pilot wasn't telling us, but he wouldn't believe it. For someone who can spin the wildest tales, Herb really was a trusting person.

I wondered what the joke would be. There were the classic pranks that pilots played with ground-pounders...like sending them off for a gallon of prop wash. It was similar to a mechanic sending a new soldier out to find a sparkplug for a diesel truck; diesels don't use sparkplugs. Or finding a box of grid squares...they were all impossible tasks designed to teach while having fun at the student's expense. The military had tons of pranks to pull on inexperienced troops.

The pilot was true to his word, though. We heard the helicopter start to rev up just after 1700 hours the next evening. Wise and I headed toward the chopper. I still didn't have a good feeling about the whole thing, but Barnes waved for us to climb onto the bird. He motioned toward the headphones. We put them on and then listened to his voice crackle in our ears.

"Gotta knock out the mandatory pre-flight briefing," he explained. "I just want to cover a couple of things before we take off."

"What's that, sir?" I asked.

"My door gunner's out sick. Moffett, you're qualified on the M-60, aren't you? Would you mind manning the gun for the trip to Tan Son Nhut?"

"Not at all, sir. I'd be glad to do it."

"Good." Barnes turned forward and began chatting with his co-pilot.

I still wasn't trusting the situation; there was a prank in the offing, I just didn't know what it was. I keyed my mike and asked, "Was there anything else, sir?"

"Oh yeah, almost forgot. There is just one more thing," the pilot added.

Uh-huh, this is it, I thought to myself. "What's that, sir?"

"We took a couple rounds in the rear rotor up in Phan Rang a couple days ago. Our maintenance boys installed new blades today. With the attack coming up in a few days, we need to test them to make sure everything is synchronized."

I was surprised. It seemed like a perfectly logical, mission-oriented task. Maybe I was wrong about pilots and their pranks. "So, what do we have to do, sir?"

"Nothing, really," Barnes replied. "I just wanted to let you know. The best way to test a new rotor is to do a cyclic climb. This short trip to Saigon tonight is the perfect time to run the test. You're familiar with this maneuver, aren't you, Sergeant Moffett?"

"Ah! Yes sir, I am." I actually had no idea what the hell the pilot was talking about, but it didn't sound good to me. My wariness returned; I had the feeling that Barnes had just told the first line in his joke. It wouldn't do any good to spook Herb, so I didn't ask any questions.

"Good," the pilot replied. "Then buckle up. We're about ready to go."

Herb and I took our assigned positions. None too fond of flying in any type of machine, Herb strapped himself in the center seat with every buckle he could find. I checked the door-mounted M-60 machinegun to ensure it was locked and loaded, then buckled myself in.

As I settled myself into the door gunner's seat, the chopper's engines revved up to full power. The wash from the propellers gusted against my face; the elephant grass around us was flattened by the strong wind. I watched the ground inch away from the landing skids.

We remained level as the Huey rose to about fifty feet in the air. It hovered for a moment, then did its typical Huey thing…the nose tilted downward as the helicopter powered up for its first burst of speed. It's amazing how fast those big birds can move.

Herb and I both knew that going on this jaunt went against the golden rule of rear area soldiers…don't put yourself in harm's way any more than you have to. This wasn't the first time I had broken that rule and it probably wouldn't be the last. Nevertheless, that still didn't make it a smart decision.

Within minutes we were over the Song Dong Nai River. Trees lined both sides of the snaking river. I guessed, correctly, that the pilot would consider this a logical place to perform his rotor test. If something went wrong, it was much less damaging to the helicopter—and the fragile people inside like me—to ditch in a river. I preferred having to swim a little over going splat in someone's rice paddy.

My door gunner position was directly behind the co-pilot. I swiveled the machinegun to cover the tree line on my side. As I looked to my left, I caught a motion from the cockpit. The pilot pointed his index finger in the air, indicating it was time to test the chopper's rotors.

From the wide grin on his face, I could tell that Warrant Officer Barnes planned to test something else as well. Namely, the metal of Herb and me. I didn't see an affirmative nod from the co-pilot as I turned to Herb to warn him.

Barnes immediately pulled back on the stick and sent the Huey straight into the air like a cannon shot. 500 feet! 1000 feet! 1500 feet! It just kept climbing. I held onto the M-60 with one hand and braced myself against the door with the other. It was actually pretty exhilarating to feel the metal bird claw higher into the sky.

I glanced back to see how Herb was doing. Not good! He was pressed into his seat from the g-forces. As I watched, his face went from pale white to a sickly green that was a near match for our jungle fatigues. He clearly wasn't having a good time.

The helicopter continued climbing. 2000 feet! 3000 feet! 4000 feet! The Huey moved steadily and rapidly upward. The metal deck under my boots started to vibrate differently, as if it now complained of mistreatment. I didn't know much about choppers, but I knew they weren't built to sustain this kind of flying. Pretty soon, something had to give.

I chided myself for the thought. Barnes and the co-pilot knew what they were doing. There was no way they would hazard themselves just to pull a prank on us. This was routine; they were just working the bugs out of the old bird. Besides, they knew the helicopter. It had carried them safely through quite a few combat missions.

That train jumped onto another line of thought. The last mission had wounded this bird…what if the mechanics hadn't healed it properly? What if the rattling and shaking was a sign that something was wrong?

I glanced forward into the cockpit. My stomach fell, but not from the continuous climb. The entire instrument panel was flashing. Red warning lights blinked on and off in every direction. At the same time, I felt the blades slowing. The big bird was about to stall. I glanced out the open door and looked at the tiny trees below us. It was a long way down.

But Barnes was an experienced pilot. He knew what to do. I felt the helicopter level out and let out a victorious yell. Turning in my seat, I have Herb a thumbs-up. We were flying straight again!

Then the pilot pushed down on the stick. We plummeted. The wind blew hard against my face as the chopper increased speed. We were going down a helluva lot faster than we went up.

Now my brain set off a whole new set of alarms as the ground screamed toward us. The vibration of the helicopter jangled our teeth and nerves. Gradually the rotors stopped their abnormal shaking and finally returned to normal operation. I was certain that Barnes would level off again and begin heading for Tan Son Nhut.

I was wrong. The chopper began dancing in the air as Barnes put us through a couple of spins on the way down. My guts began to feel like they were in a blender from all of the sudden twists and turns. I watched the ground perform a three-sixty below me, then disappear completely as the bird leveled off, then reappear again. I couldn't tell whether the chopper was behaving normally under the aerobatic gyrations Barnes was putting it through, or if he'd lost control of the bird.

As we approached five hundred feet, the Warrant Officer finally began to level off the Huey. The trees on either side of the river had grown back to their earlier size. Then they got larger as Barnes took us down to the deck.

Wise and I both held on for dear life as the chopper swooshed down over the river. It created its own version of tidal waves behind us. We zigzagged around the bends of the river and then came up on an obstruction.

I could see the startled wide eyes of two Vietnamese fishermen. The occupants of the small sampan fishing boat dove into the water, certain that we were going to crash right into them. The chopper rose slightly, clearing the boat by several feet. I looked back to see the two men bobbing in the water. They both shook their fists angrily at us.

It was sad, yet comical. I burst into laughter, appreciating the excuse to release my pent-up tension. Survival does that sometimes. After being terrified that we were going to crash, it was quite a rush to realize we'd survived. Herb looked at me like I'd gone crazy. Then the contagion hit him as well, and we both laughed wildly at ourselves for thinking we'd been so close to death.

Barnes' voice crackled in my headset. "You guys enjoy that?"

"Hell yeah!" I was feeling on top of the world at that moment.

"Want to do it again?"

"Do we have to?" Herb said into his mike. "I mean, if you still need to test things out, that's fine...."

Barnes and his co-pilot both laughed. "Nah," the Warrant Officer replied. "I think everyone—I mean, every*thing*—checked out just fine. Sit back and enjoy the rest of the trip."

Another twenty minutes of uneventful flying brought us safely to Tan Son Nhut. Wise and I gratefully stepped off the Huey. It was a good thing for us that we had to walk to the pizzeria. We left the ground crew to the task of unloading the crates of spare parts as we wobbled away. Teaching rubbery legs to stand tall is quite a task. It took ten minutes of walking before the muscle tremors stopped.

"Phew," Herb exclaimed after he finally stopped shaking. "That was quite a ride, wasn't it?"

"Yeah, quite a ride. Better than any roller coaster I've ever been on."

Herb considered the comparison for a moment. It's amazing what simply shifting one's perspective can do to make a harrowing event into entertainment. His complexion returned to normal as he nodded vigorously. "You bet. That was the roller coaster ride of a lifetime!"

We expected to be stopped and questioned at least once during our walk to the pizzeria. Army uniforms on the Air Force base should've raised a few eyebrows, but it didn't. I guess the Air Force guys figured that, if we'd made it past their front gate, we had official business on the base. Herb and I didn't correct their misperception.

Within an hour, we had retraced our steps. Both of us were laden down with boxes of pizza. I had looked into each box to verify the order of black olives, pepperoni, and extra red pizza sauce. Even if I hadn't peeked in the five boxes, the aroma alone made me eager to get back to the hooch. I wanted to savor the flavor as well as the aroma.

Herb clambered aboard the Huey first and held the boxes while I climbed up. He surprised me with his next question. "Hey, Moff," he began. "Do you mind if I take the door gunner seat on the way back? I can handle the M-60."

I had to think about it for a few seconds. It was strange to see Herb excited to change his coach seat for one in first class. For someone afraid to fly, he had come a long way on this trip. I decided it would be okay. "Sure, go ahead, Herb. I can sit in the center seat and hold the pizzas in my lap."

With no more equipment tests planned, I expected the flight back to Bien Hoa to be pretty smooth. Herb contented himself with swiveling the machine gun on its mount as he pretended to provide suppressive fire against imaginary attackers. He looked like an excited kid...which technically, he was. We all were.

The aroma and warmth from the pizzas was wonderful. I debated sneaking a piece, then decided against it. It wouldn't be fair to the others on the chopper for me to chow down. I didn't figure it would be wise to pass pizza to the pilots, either. If there were air police, they would definitely pull us over as the pilots wove back and forth. It would be hard to handle the gooey slices and fly at the same time.

The far horizon blazed crimson from the setting sun. The wind blew over my face, carrying the scent of pizza and reminding me of The World. The landscape beneath us was silent and peaceful as we flew above it. One of my best friends sat to my right, protecting us all with his weapon. It was a moment frozen in time, one that I will never forget.

The flight was uneventful until we started our descent into Bien Hoa. We were startled out of our complacency by the bright flashes of ground fire from a nearby village. It seemed to be coming from our left. Barnes banked the Huey to the right. That wasn't a good fix. We took fire from the right as well.

Herb yelled to me in a panic. "Can I return fire?"

"Negative," Barnes replied from the cockpit. "Civilians in the village!"

Suddenly rounds tore right through the middle of the chopper. I heard the ricochet and thumps of bullets slamming into the steel around me. Several rounds went right through the large stack of pizzas in my lap. I was too startled to do more than jump back into my seat. Helpless, I watched three boxes blow right out the door. I clutched frantically onto the other two.

The firing fortunately stopped as fast as it started. The chopper blades whirled in the same steady motion overhead, and there were odd mechanical thumps. It looked like we'd made it through the brief attack without any major damage.

That's when I noticed the red drops soaking the material of my shirt. Several more bright red spots were splattered across my hands and dripped from my face. A voice that sounded like my own yelled, "I'm hit! I'm hit!"

Funny, though. After the shrapnel incident that grazed my butt at Phouc Vinh, I knew what it felt like to get hit. This time there was nothing. I couldn't feel a thing.

"Where?" Herb shouted over the cabin noise as he turned at my alarmed shouting.

It was going to be bad, I just knew it. I waited for him to pale at the ghastly sight of the wound that I couldn't see. Instead, his reaction caught me completely by surprise.

He started laughing.

"What is it?" I yelled, trying to get him to tell me what was going on. "Where am I hit?"

"Shit, Moff, you scared the hell out of me!" he yelled.

"What are you talking about?!" I knew that you were supposed to reassure a wounded man after an injury so he didn't go into shock. You never told him how bad it was; instead, you were supposed to do anything to let him know that he was going to be okay. At that moment, I didn't feel Herb's method was working correctly.

"That's not blood," Wise said through his laughter. "That's pizza sauce!"

Having bullets appear through the floor beneath my feet had been a shock. I wasn't over that close call yet, so I didn't quite believe my comrade. Gingerly, I licked a few drops of red liquid off of my hand. It didn't taste like blood. Sure enough, it was thick tomato sauce from the pizzas in my lap.

"Everybody okay back there?" Warrant Officer Barnes yelled back at us. "Anybody hit?"

"Nah," Herb replied, grinning. "Only casualties are the pizzas. Looks like three missing in action and two wounded."

"Well, hold onto them then. We're landing shortly."

The moment the chopper touched down, our hooch mates came streaming toward it. From the look on their faces, they were ready for the promised pleasures of pizza. I handed Brunetti the two torn-up boxes.

"What's this, Moff?" Mike asked, looking at the boxes. "That's not gonna be enough for all of us."

After being shot at, I was in no mood to listen to complaints about the delivery service. "Shut up and take them. We had a little problem on the way back."

"It was nothing, really," I told Brunetti when he noticed the splatter of red on my face and uniform. "I'll tell you about it when we get to the hooch. I need a beer."

Barnes and his co-pilot yelled for us to save them a piece, then headed for the helicopter unit's operations shack. Since they had received fire on the trip back, they had to report it to Military Intelligence. I was confident they would leave out the details of their unauthorized pizza delivery boys.

By this point, the guys from the hooch were getting the impression that something nasty had happened. Herb and I steered them toward the hooch. The first thing I did was grab a beer from the fridge, pop the cap and slug about half of it down before coming up for air.

Brunetti placed the pizza boxes on our makeshift bar and lifted the lid. He stuck a finger through one of the four holes. With a wry grin he said, "Looks like the VC are learning Italian skeet."

DiOrio tossed me a towel, then joined in the jest. "Italian skeet? What's that?"

"Italians toss their pizzas in the air. Skeet shooters try to hit as many clay pigeons in the air as they can. I guess Charlie has combined the two."

I pointed a warning finger in his direction to get him to stop, but it didn't do any good.

Mike looked at Herb and me in mock serious and asked, "So, which one of you two yelled 'Pull!'?"

There's a funny thing about beer and pizza. When it's around, there's an atmosphere of camaraderie and friendly joking. Getting shot at can take a lot out of a guy, yet it didn't take long for the other guys to get me laughing. Especially after we dug into the pizza and DiOrio turned to me.

"Hey, Moff," he said in the booming voice of a barroom conspiratorial whisper. "Is pizza supposed to have nuts in it?"

I shook my head, not quite getting what he was driving at.

"Then you'd better check your family jewels, man, 'cause there's something strange tasting about this pizza."

The jokes continued in that vein for quite awhile. I had to admit that there was a strange taste to the pizza, though. It tasted great except for the trace of burnt lead in it. Warrant Officer Barnes arrived sometime after that. He informed us that a patrol was going out in the morning to check out the village where the ground fire had originated. Then he regaled the group with his imitation of the sounds from the cargo area—in other words from Wise and me—as he took the chopper through its cyclic climb. There were howls of laughter as we celebrated living through both harrowing adventures. I got the pilot back, though. I vowed to never go cycling with chopper pilots again.

The sergeant in charge of the patrol dropped by the pilots' hooch the next day. I happened to be heading back to our hooch after calling it quits for the day. Barnes saw me and called me over to join the conversation.

"Yeah, like I was just telling the Chief," the sergeant said, "everything went fine. We searched the village and didn't find any weapons or ammo. It was probably just a few stoned VC passing through. You guys were in the wrong place at the right time so they figured they'd mess with your Huey."

"That's good to hear," Barnes replied. "I'd hate to have to worry taking potshots from the ground every time we had to lift off."

"So they're gone?" I asked. "No Tet party for Ho Chi Minh's birthday? It's a bust?"

"Yep. I don't think Charlie could manage to get enough troops this far south to pull it off. They're taking quite a pounding up north right now."

That was reassuring to hear. The last thing I wanted was to be anywhere near live rounds. I'd had my close call of the war and didn't care to go through it again. Yet I could tell there was something bothering the young infantry sergeant. "Is that all?"

"Well, there's this one thing. Don't laugh, man. It was really weird."

"What was that?" Barnes asked.

"Well, as we swept through the village, we noticed something really bizarre. Two of the village huts had these…objects sitting on top of them."

"Really?" I was curious. We hadn't seen anything strange on the village roofs when we'd passed over. "What did they look like?"

The sergeant scratched his head, as if embarrassed. "I can't swear to it, but they looked like pizzas. Pepperoni and everything!"

Barnes and I looked at each other. The sergeant followed our gazes and waved his hands. "No shit, man, I'm telling you the truth! They looked exactly like pepperoni pizza."

"What do you think, Moff?" Barnes asked with a serious look on his face. "Sound like these guys have been too long from the world?"

There was no way we could let the sergeant know that his guess was correct. The pizza run had to remain a secret. I joined in with, "Hallucinations maybe?"

"Come on, fellas," the sergeant pleaded. "You gotta believe me!"

"Well, I guess it could've been part of some Vietnamese ritual," Barnes suggested.

"Could be," I agreed, watching the hope appear on the patrol sergeant's face. "Although if I were you, I think I'd leave that part out of your report."

"Yeah," he said, nodding at my suggestion. "You're probably right."

Barnes and I watched the infantry soldier walk away. We could tell that he was lost in thought over how to write up his patrol report for the Intel guys.

I smiled at the pilot and motioned toward the hooch. "Want a beer?"

"Sure," Barnes replied. "Got any pizza to go with it?"

"Sorry, boss. We scarfed it down last night, remember?"

The Warrant Officer grinned wickedly. "Well, it just so happens that we have to go back to Tan Son Nhut tomorrow…."

"Don't even think about it," I replied. "Our pizza delivery days are over!"

It turned out that the patrol sergeant was correct in his assessment. There were a few skirmishes on February 22-23, but Bien Hoa was left alone. The nearby base of Long Binh received a heavy probe from an unknown number of VC during the night, but the enemy never penetrated the wire. Attack helicopters, fighters and Puff the Magic Dragon—the AC-130 gunship version—dealt out more damage than the VC wanted to contend with. After five hours being pinned down by the Army and Air Force, what remained of the enemy force turned tail and ran. Ho Chi Minh did celebrate his 79th birthday in May of that year, but never saw another one. He died on September 3, 1969.

A week or so after the failed "Tet '69" offensive, Barnes and his fellow chopper crewmates headed back north. Their airlift services were critically needed by the grunts fighting the shooting end of the war. We never saw them again…and we never made another pizza run, either.

EASY MONEY...? MAYBE NOT

There are often inequities in the military. It's just part of being in the service. There are times, though, when things become so blatantly unfair that something has to be done about it. That was the case after the 101st Airborne Division was banned from Saigon.

It wasn't that we thought the ban was unfair. That was just an inconvenience. We knew that the restriction would be lifted eventually. There were also ways around it, like becoming officers for the weekend.

The true injustice was expressed by our unit commander, Captain Miller. We were heading to the base theater one evening and he had joined our small group for the walk. Other than going to the NCO Club, drinking and playing cards at the hooch, our only source of entertainment was watching movies.

"You know, Sergeant Moffett," began Captain Miller as we walked. "I've heard that the Air Force isn't taking care of the vehicles in their motor pool. I don't think those things have moved since I first saw them."

"You're right, sir," I replied cautiously, not certain where he was leading the conversation. "They're just sitting there collecting dust."

That's when the commander broke one of those cardinal rules for officers. He expressed his displeasure at the system to his soldiers. "It isn't fair do you think, Sergeant Moffett? Here we are having to walk everywhere, and the Air Force lets its vehicles rust. Such a waste."

I provided a sympathetic ear. "Yessir, I agree totally. It just isn't fair. When I arrived, the Air Force refused to give me a ride to the Army side of the base. I'm not the only one, either. We've all had to dodge airplanes while lugging our gear across the runway to the hooch."

"That's a safety issue, don't you think?"

"Yessir, I do believe it is."

Captain Miller's face was expressionless as he looked forward and stated, "Someone really should do something about that. Find a couple vehicles that we can use to carry troops and gear around. Can't have soldiers run over by our own aircraft, after all."

"I agree totally, sir." In my time in the Army, I'd already learned that orders come in three types. While Captain Miller hadn't given me a direct order, it was most definitely an indirect order. The good news was that it wasn't an impossible order, either. A plan began developing in my head as we walked.

I waited until all of the guys had returned to the hooch that evening before telling them of my conversation with the Captain. They didn't see the significance of the conversation at first. I turned to Sparky Anderson, our resident mechanic. It was time to test his reputation that he could hotwire a B-52 bomber. "Sparky, we're going to need your help."

"What do you need, Moff?" the cigar-chewing mechanic asked.

"You've seen the Air Force motor pool, right?"

That got everybody's attention. Brunetti waved his hands. "Oh no, Moff, I ain't got nothing to do with this."

"Relax, Mike," I replied calmly. "We're just following orders."

"Orders? What're you talking about?"

"It's simple. Captain Miller said someone should do something about finding a couple of vehicles. Well, guess what?" I grinned mischievously.

"What?" Brunetti predictably asked.

"I found some. They're sitting in the Air Force motor pool, gathering dust."

"Hell, let's do it," Mike DiOrio said loudly. "It's not like they're using them or anything."

Herb Wise provided the clinching argument. "Yeah, and it will save us having to hitchhike to Saigon."

We brainstormed what was needed. It didn't take long. Sparky Anderson had access to all of the tools we needed, and Dave Corbus was a licensed truck driver. We decided that we should find two vehicles, a deuce for troop transportation and a quarter-ton jeep for the commander.

Under cover of darkness, our small group of raiders sneaked across the base. A pair of bolt cutters took care of the lock holding the Air Force motor pool gate closed. Then we slipped through the gate and into the parking lot. We found the two best vehicles and then waited.

Lookouts let us know when it was all clear. This was the riskiest point of the whole venture. Deuces have diesel engines, and you have to let them warm up before driving one of the large trucks. The noise of the engine starting sounded like a siren to our ears. Nobody came running out yelling "Thief, thief!" though, so we moved to the next phase.

I jumped behind the wheel of the jeep and led our convoy of two vehicles through the gate. The lookouts secured the chain on the gate with a new padlock—we were even courteous and left the key for the Air Force—and then they jumped into the back of the deuce.

We made it safely to our motor pool. The final phase began. Every maintenance section stocked green, brown and black paint used for camouflaging vehicles. We repainted the bumpers on both vehicles to cover over the Air Force bumper numbers. The deuce and jeep were still relatively new, so the fresh paint didn't stand out too badly. Then we added our own unit bumper numbers. After the paint dried, we rubbed mud and oil on the bumpers to make them appear aged.

Sparky Anderson found a tire cover for the jeep. While the paint dried on the bumpers, we each took a hand at painting the Screaming Eagle crest and the words "101st Airborne Division" on the tire cover.

We knew it was all superficial window dressing. There was no way to modify the serial numbers etched on the engines, but we weren't going to go that far. The sheer number of deuces and jeeps on the post would work in our favor. Nobody was going to pull over every vehicle to check the engine numbers.

Captain Miller was extremely surprised to see his new jeep parked in front of the admin office the next morning. He didn't press for details about where it came from; a good officer knows that there are times when one simply should not ask. It tickled him pink, though. The other adjutant officers didn't ask any questions, either. Like a Christmas present found under the tree, they simply accepted that some green-suited Santa Claus left it there for them.

It took awhile for the Air Force security police to even discover that the vehicles were missing. I was on my bunk one afternoon when one of the guys came into the hooch. "Hey, Sarge, there's an Air Force MP out here, wants to talk to you."

My heart skipped several beats. How could they have tracked the midnight requisition to me so quickly? I rolled out of my bunk and nonchalantly stretched. "What does he want?"

"Hell, I dunno, Sarge. He says he's related to you."

That was intriguing. I knew that one of my second cousins was at one of the airbases in Vietnam, but I'd never heard he was a military policeman. I walked outside to see if it was true.

The Air Force cop was leaning on the bumper of the deuce that we'd left parked in front of the hooch. "Hey, Cuz! Can I talk to you for a minute?"

Sure enough, it was my cousin. I gave him the traditional hug and we caught up on life for a few minutes. Then I asked, "So, what brings you over here? I thought you Air Force guys kept to your side of the base and didn't fraternize with us grunts. Hope nobody saw you or it could ruin your reputation with your pals."

"Well, it's sort of official business."

I leaned on the bumper beside him. "How's that?"

"Someone stole a couple of vehicles from the Air Force motor pool. We're pretty sure it was one of the infantry units around here."

"You know grunts," I replied. "If it ain't nailed down, it's fair game. So how do I fit in?"

"I know that you're familiar with everything that goes on over here," my cousin said. "I was hoping you could give me a hand. It would be a big scoop for me if I can make an arrest."

It was a relief to know that he didn't suspect me. I placed a serious look on my face and nodded. "Of course, Cuz. You know I'll help out however I can."

He smiled broadly. "Thanks, man. You don't have to do anything. Just keep your eyes and ears open, willya?"

"You bet. I'll let you know if I find out anything."

That concluded our conversation. It was probably cruel of me, but I had my cousin hang around for a minute. I wanted a picture of us together to show my parents back home. One of the guys snapped the photo…of us leaning on the stolen truck. Then my cousin returned to his side of the base. I never saw him again while we were in Vietnam.

About a month after the enlisted ban to Saigon went into effect, we received the news that it had been lifted. Our days of having to impersonate officers were over, so the timing couldn't have been better. We had wheels to get us to the Big City, and it was time to be ourselves again. The guys in the hooch all agreed that we need-ed to make a trip to Saigon.

There was only one thing that put a cramp in our style. We couldn't just park the huge vehicle on the streets in Saigon. Someone had to guard the vehicle or we'd never see it again. We put together a four-hour roster and then drew straws for the detail. Luckily for DiOrio, Brunetti and me, we didn't end up pulling deuce duty for the entire weekend.

Dave Corbus, our heavy vehicle driver, dropped us off at Le Loi Square in the center of Saigon, right in front of the Continental Palace Hotel. By Vietnam standards, the Continental Palace was expensive. Mostly senior officers and embassy staffers frequented the plush hotel. There was no real rule about it, though. If you had the bucks, the Palace would take your money. It also wasn't the most expensive watering spot in town, either. Just across the square was the newer, plusher Caravelle Hotel. The Caravelle could make the Continental's drink tabs seem almost reasonable.

We piled out of the back of the deuce and waved to our hooch mates. They would meet us at this spot on Sunday morning. In the interim, though, they were off to find a hotel with a parking lot. That was a challenge in Saigon. There weren't too many places who would let soldiers park military vehicles beside their other customers' cars.

"C'mon," I said to Brunetti and DiOrio. "Let's go into the Palace and have a beer."

"Are you nuts?!" DiOrio asked, giving me a disbelieving look. "You know us. We'll get carried away and blow our budget for the whole weekend."

"No way," I argued. "We'll just have a beer and share a pizza. I hear they use some kind of strange cheese and bury the top in black olives."

DiOrio shook his head. "That's all we need. It's probably water buffalo cheese or something."

"No, it's not—"

"Could be goat cheese," Brunetti teased.

"Come on, guys. Get real here, okay?" There were times with those two goumbas when it felt like I was talking to a brick wall. "It's cheese, there's tons of it, and it's really good. If we close our eyes and dream a bit, we'll think we're eating an old-fashioned New York pizza."

"Okay, fine," DiOrio grudgingly agreed, jabbing a finger right at my nose. "But after the pizza, we're gone!"

"Yeah, yeah," I said reassuringly. "Just a beer and a pizza, then we're out of there."

We walked into the hotel and headed for the bar. It was still early, so the big crowd hadn't begun to arrive yet. There were plenty of seats at the bar. We planted ourselves on the soft barstools and ordered beer and pizza.

The beer disappeared quickly and we still hadn't seen the pizza yet. I ordered another round and received a "told you so" look from DiOrio. Those were rapidly consumed, and still no pizza.

That started DiOrio on a tirade about money. We didn't have a lot to burn. If it hadn't been for my mom sending some my way occasionally, I wouldn't have had any more than the other two guys. It seemed as if we always had a chronic shortage of funds. To hear Mike DiOrio tell it at that moment, most of it was my fault.

The Vietnamese bartender picked that moment to place three more Buds in front of us. "No way!" DiOrio exclaimed. "We didn't order those. All we want is our pizza!"

Before he got any further, the bartender explained. "Beer on American guy over there."

I followed the bartender's index finger to see a man dressed in civvies seated two stools away. Holding up my glass, I said, "Good luck, and thanks for the beer!"

"My pleasure," the stranger said as he climbed off his stool and moved toward us. "My name is Kurt Kloman. What're yours?"

"I'm Sergeant Moffett," I replied, then waved a hand toward my two cranky partners. "These two are DiOrio and Brunetti."

Meanwhile, I was trying to figure out Mister Kloman. He was dressed in civvies—of course, so were we—but for some reason he didn't look like he was in the military. Maybe it was the way he was dressed, more IBM than weekend military leave. He was a wiry sort of guy. His small, thin glasses—which weren't really "in" back then— were definitely not Army issue. Partly it was the way he moved. He was just a bit too smooth and comfortable in civvies as compared to those of us who changed into uniforms when we went back to work. I estimated his age at somewhere around forty years old.

My first question was, "Are you in the service?"

"No," he replied easily. "I'm with a construction company under contract with the US government. We build runways, buildings, big stuff like that."

Brunetti was impressed. "I hear you boys make some great money working over here."

Kloman spoke confidentially and let his gaze cross over us. It was like he somehow managed to look each of us in the eyes at the same time. "Frankly, we do. We practically double our salaries from anything we were making in the States…and those six figures weren't bad to begin with."

DiOrio whistled softly. "Must be nice."

The civilian scooted his barstool a couple inches closer. "I hope you don't mind my eavesdropping, but it was kind of hard to miss it. Sounds like you guys have some money problems at the moment. That's why I bought you the beers."

"Yeah, we're always bitchin' about money," Brunetti said, leaning against the bar. "But if you don't have it, you don't have it. Nothin' nobody can do about that."

"Well," Kloman said, lowering his voice and wiggling his stool even closer. "I know how you grunts can make some serious money if you don't mind taking it in piasters."

Piaster was the common name for the Vietnamese currency. It was actually called a dong, but everyone used the old French colonial term for the money. We didn't have any problems spending piasters, but something about the way he said it tripped warning alarms in my brain. "If this is anything illegal," I said, "you can stop right there."

"No, no, nothing like that!" he protested, shaking his head and raising both hands up, palms forward. "But I can't have everybody trying to get in on this deal. I probably shouldn't be talking to you about it, either…but I really believe in supporting our soldiers whenever I can. Let me tell you about it. Are you willing to listen?"

I glanced at my two companions. Like me, they reluctantly nodded. "Alright, go ahead."

Kloman pulled a pen from his pocket and started jotting numbers on a coaster. "Let's say that you have one dollar in greenbacks in your pocket. That would be worth about forty piasters under the authorized exchange rate. It's also worth about a hundred and sixty piasters on the black market here in Saigon. Everybody knows that, right?"

We all nodded. He hadn't told us anything that we didn't know already. I waited for the slip that would let me catch him in a lie. There was something that I didn't quite trust about the man.

"Well, the reason for the high rate of exchange is because piasters—like Korean won and Thai baht currency, just to name a couple—aren't recognized on the international monetary exchanges. Their value fluctuates too much to be considered 'standard' currency. They can only be spent within the country where they originated, or in neighboring countries that accept it. Once you cross out of the orient, they're worthless. Unless you have recognized status as a charity of some sort, that is…and I'm guessing you guys don't qualify for that."

I considered making a crack about the three of us being a charity case, but I kept my thoughts to myself. "Okay, I think you made your point. So where do you fit into all of this?"

Kloman leaned back in his chair and smiled. "In the scope of doing business, there are other ways to convert currency. There have to be in order for big companies like the one I work for to make a profit. We use the authorized commercial rate. It goes basically like this. When we receive money from the locals, it goes into petty cash. That gets lumped together every week and sent to our bank in Hong Kong."

The civilian reached for the bar coaster and started jotting more numbers on it. "Let's say we send up a thousand piasters; that's worth twenty-five dollars on the authorized exchange. At the *commercial* rate, though, it's only worth about eight dollars. That's because we construct tangible things like buildings that don't change their value. Follow me so far?"

My two Italian friends beside me nodded with me. I hadn't realized there was such a difference between the commercial and retail rates. It was something like a three hundred percent difference!

Kurt Kloman scribbled like he talked, fast and furious. "So okay, Hong Kong banks accept regional currency. All my company's finance guys do is wait until the piaster goes up…and then they trade it for one of the other local currencies. When the new currency goes up, they trade it to greenbacks or another solid currency. Now, large companies can hold onto thousands of dollars worth of piasters or other oriental currency at a time without breaking a sweat. We just wait for the Hong Kong market to start buying piasters and then sell them for a profit."

"That's about it, boys," Kurt Kloman said as he pocketed his pen. "Right now my company is selling piasters at a huge profit. Usually we don't let individuals get involved, but I can see you guys are honest types who deserve a break. Still, I've got to tell you that there's no way I can deal on the ten or twenty dollar levels. If you can give me a minimum—let's say, a hundred dollars each—then I can get you a thousand piasters for every five bucks. How does that sound to you?"

DiOrio and Brunetti both whistled sharply. "For five bucks?"

Kloman stopped talking and shrugged his shoulders, indicating it was no big deal to him. The three of us quickly exchanged looks. That could be a very big deal for us. DiOrio was the first to speak. "That's huge money, Mr. Kloman. Only problem is, greenbacks aren't so easy to come by. The army only gives us military pay certificates, no hard cash."

"You don't need actual greenbacks," Kloman said casually. "I've got plenty of cash for that. All you need to do is pay me using money orders. You guys can buy them easily at the PX using your MPCs or getting an advance."

"Okay," I said, still wary but really wanting to go for this deal. "Let's say we go along with this. What happens to the money orders?"

"Well, that's really quite simple," Kloman said. "I'll cash them when I get back Stateside. A buck's just a buck over there, right?"

"Yeah, but what do you get out of this?" I asked.

"I get the good feeling of knowing I'm doing something for the war effort when I help out guys like you. That's worth a lot more than the bit of extra work for me. It's all legit, believe me." He leaned closer. "Nobody gets hurt. You make some money just like I have. But if you don't feel a hundred percent okay about this, don't do it."

The three of us looked at each other again. DiOrio shook his shoulders just a bit, signaling "Why not?"

"Okay," I said to Kloman. "When do we start?"

"Right now, if you want," Kurt said, smiling pleasantly. "You guys can do down to the PX in Tan Son Nhut for the money orders. Just remember, don't endorse them. I'll go get the piasters and we'll meet back here in…say, two hours?"

When we shook our heads in assent, he asked, "How much do you want to exchange?"

"Two hundred apiece," Brunetti replied.

"Okay, great! I'll see you in two hours, then," Kurt concluded, leaving his barstool and heading toward the door.

We finished our beers quickly, told the guy behind the bar to cancel our pizza, and jumped in a cab that was idling outside the hotel. Somehow I always had to laugh when the three of us buddies got into the blue and white Saigon taxis—all prewar Citroens— because I knew what would happen.

Each of us weighed well over two hundred pounds. We could see the driver wince when he sized up his new load. Our total weight would have the car banging against the pavement and our heads bumping against the cab's ceiling for the whole trip.

We made it down to Tan Son Nhut Airbase in about half an hour. The cabdriver said he'd wait as we bailed out. The teller's window was about to close as we skidded up to it. After a bit of paperwork to obtain an advance—the regulations limited us to one third of our base pay—we got our $600 worth of money orders. We were back in the taxi within a few minutes, heading back to the Continental.

When we got there, we sidled up to the bar. Kurt Kloman had not yet arrived, so we decided to finally have the pizza we'd been longing for since first leaving the base. We placed a new order and polished off a few beers while waiting. The pizza finally appeared. We took our first bites and knew that—no matter how much we fantasized—a Saigon pizza was never going to challenge one from New York. This one was dreadful, but we were hungry. Before we had finished choking down the slices, we noticed Kurt making his way through the maze of tables and potted palms sprinkled about the restaurant.

"So, how'd you guys do?" he asked cheerfully, pulling up another bar stool.

"We did fine." I said. The others had nominated me as the spokesperson since I was the one holding all the money orders. As I reached for my pocket to pull them out, Kurt grabbed my hand and said quietly, "Not here! Follow me out through the kitchen. There's an alley out back where we can make the exchange."

The two Mikes and I made eye contact. Without saying even one word, we agreed…this had all the makings of a classic rip-off. But somehow we didn't think our skinny little friend was up to the challenge of trying to put one over on us, unless he had a small army waiting outside. So we threw back our shoulders and followed him out through the kitchen. The cooks looked at us strangely, murmuring in their own language.

Once out in the alley, we looked around. No support team for Kurt in view, just a couple of busboys crouched down along the wall while eating their nuoc mam. I took the money orders out of my pocket and said, "Okay, Kurt. Here ya go!"

Kloman took the money orders and handed over a fair-sized brown paper bag. "And here you go! If you want to count it, I'll wait. But it's all there."

Brunetti had already opened the bag. He flicked through the stack of piasters and said, "Looks good to me."

"Good," Kurt said, smiling, "Listen, I won't be around for about two weeks. I've been assigned to a job up in Nha Trang, but I'll be back by the end of the month in case you guys want to do this again."

"Okay, fine," DiOrio said. "If we're in town, we'll look for you back here."

A misty rain started falling as our little friend Kurt turned away. He walked through the rain and the steam from the kitchen vents, eventually disappearing into the night. Definitely strange. We just shook our heads and decided that—since we were in the alley anyway—we might as well split up that bag full of Vietnamese cash. By the time we were done, the pockets of our jungle fatigues were bulging on all sides.

At that point we decided the best move was to get back to the Mai Loan Hotel, our hooch-away-from-home, where we routinely stayed in Saigon. After checking in, we headed for our rooms and stashed most of the piasters in our bags We kept out only what we wanted for the evening. That meant a bit more than usual, because we'd agreed we might just as well celebrate in honor of our new-found cash.

We skipped the Tiger Bar on the hotel roof and opted for the Iguana Club, a little more pricey and a few blocks away. Not that you would confuse the Iguana with some classy Stateside bar. It was like just about every other street bar in Saigon. It had its share of bar girls, each one hanging onto her GI catch of the day. The air was always pungent with the aroma of marijuana.

As we walked in this time, the scrub Vietnamese band was crucifying our "anthem," a tune called "The Letter" made famous in the States by the Boxtops. But for us, this was about as good as it got. After muscling our way up to the bar, each of us ordered a "Jack and Coke." No Ba Mui Ba Beer for us tonight; we were going to party with our cash windfall.

After about four rounds of Jack, we were all fairly well sloshed. But when an Australian master sergeant came up next to us, he and Brunetti seemed to hit it off right away. "Give our Australian friend anything he wants!" Brunetti said grandly. "And put it on my tab!"

Amazing! I thought. Yesterday we didn't have two nickels to rub together, but today we had a running bar tab.

"Hey, thanks for the drink," the Aussie said, hoisting his current half-empty glass in appreciation. "My name is Gladstone. Trevor Gladstone."

We made the usual introductions. Brunetti motioned for him to pull up a chair.

"Where are you lads stationed?" he asked.

"101st Airborne in Bien Hoa," I said.

"Not a bad duty assignment," Trevor replied. "But you look like you're celebrating something tonight."

In my semi-drunken stupor, I said, "We're celebrating money orders!"

The three of us hugged and patted each other on the back, proud of our big score.

But Trevor wrinkled his forehead. "I hope you mean the kind of money orders that you buy and send home to your families…NOT the ones involved in the scam going on here in Saigon."

"Scam?" DiOrio said. "Nah! We met this guy Kurt and he gave us 200P to the dollar for our money orders. Ya see, he buys piasters here, then sends them through his company—"

"Who has some kind of banking connection in Hong Kong," Trevor said, breaking in. "Then the piasters are converted or sold on the currency exchange for US dollars and no one gets hurt. Did he say something like that?"

"That's almost word for word." I said, suddenly feeling almost sober. "But how did you know that?"

"I love you Americans," Trevor said, grinning, "but sometimes you can be so naïve."

"Whattaya talkin' about?" DiOrio said, leaning on the bar and looking at Trevor. "It all seemed to make sense to us!"

"I'm sure it did," Trevor said. "But the way he told it isn't exactly the way it works once he gets those money orders."

"Keep talkin', Sgt. Gladstone," Brunetti said. "We're all ears."

By now we had begun to realize that this was not going to have a good ending.

"Well, your buddy Kurt was partially telling you the truth," Trevor said as he signaled the bartender to pour another Jack Daniels. "Instead of him taking those money orders home with him, he sends them directly to a bank in Hong Kong. Through some very creative banking transactions, the cash winds up in the hands of the military in the Peoples' Republic of China."

Our party faces were quickly becoming frowns. Each word out of Trevor's mouth was a sobering smack across the face.

"What else?" Brunetti asked quietly.

"Well," Trevor continued, "the Chinese, now having the strongest currency in the world—that you boys so aptly handed over to them—go out and build more rockets and other fun ordinance, stuff they could never finance with their own currency."

"Keep going, Trevor," I said. All three of us knew where this was heading. "We're still listening."

"After that it's pretty simple, lads," Trevor said as he knocked off yet another shot of Jack Daniels. "The Chinese turn the rockets over to the NVA and VC, who conveniently fire them at Bien Hoa Air Base, or any other base, hoping to hit a fighter jet or a Huey. But if a rocket happens to fall short and land on your little heads, the mission is still accomplished because some damage has been done."

The three of us just sat there, too stunned to even speak. We were slowly realizing that we were young guys who clearly got hustled by a real pro.

By now, Trevor was about bombed out of his socks. At one point he almost fell off his barstool. He finally managed to stand up, hold up his empty glass and offer a toast with a wry grin. "Here's to my three American friends who helped finance the Vietnam War…for the other side!"

His mock toast crushed us three, but he wasn't quite done. Trevor was one of those guys who could get a bit nasty in his cups. "Now, lads, here's some more potentially bad news. I understand your CID is close to finding out who these guys are that are playing the money order game. When they arrest them, you might just be involved as accessories to the crime."

"Wonderful!" we thought. We didn't have any idea that our little deal was anything bad, and now we were facing possible time in the stockade. By now Trevor almost seemed to enjoy rattling our cages. "What's the matter, lads?" he said. "Did I take the wind out of your sails?"

"You sank the whole boat, sergeant!" DiOrio answered quietly.

"Sorry, men," Trevor said, with no real remorse. "You've got to be a little more attentive about who you deal with here in Saigon. Everyone is out for just one person—himself—and nobody else."

The three of us had heard enough. We thanked Trevor, threw a bunch of piasters on the bar to cover the drinks and walked out. As we were leaving, the Iguana's ragtag Viet band was playing another GI favorite, "We Gotta Get Out of This Place." How appropriate, I thought dourly.

It didn't help that, when we stepped outside the bar, the monsoon rains were coming down in buckets. We pulled on our boonie hats, but otherwise made no attempt to cover ourselves from the downpour. We didn't even walk very fast. I think we felt that the rain might wash away our sins of the day. But realistically, we knew better.

We didn't talk much on the way back to the Mai Loan Hotel, just went to our rooms. The next morning we agreed that it had been hard to get to sleep. Each of us felt we were carrying a massive load of guilt.

We checked out early, skipped breakfast and headed for Le Loi Square. Corbus was there with the deuce, but we weren't in the mood to wait for the other guys. We hitched another ride and headed directly to Bien Hoa. Maybe the faster we got out of Saigon, the better off we were going to be. We weren't sure if it was paranoia or not, but we had the strange feeling we were being watched.

By the time we got back to the base, it was close to the time we had to report for duty. We went straight to the office without stopping at the hooch. It was a Sunday morning, which was usually a slow day. But a load of newbies had arrived during the night, so it was going to be a busy day at the office.

We wanted to tell the other guys in the hooch about our weekend debacle, but we thought it would be best to tell everybody as a group. That meant holding off until the evening. Actually, we didn't talk to the guys much at all during the day. We got the feeling that they knew something wasn't right about our weekend.

Finally, around 1830, just after chow at the mess hall, the twelve of us made our way back to the hooch. When everyone was there, I said, "All right, everybody grab a beer out of the fridge and take a seat."

As sergeant of the hooch, I felt it was my responsibility to tell the story. "I have to tell you what happened to us over the weekend before you find out some other way."

"Damn," our buddy Chuck Johnson said. "You guys were acting strange all day. So what's the problem?"

I talked for about thirty minutes non-stop, trying not to miss any details. At the end, I said, "So that's the whole story."

Then DiOrio, Brunetti and I waited for a reaction. Nobody said anything for about twenty seconds. Even our three-legged dog Tripod seemed to express everyone's feelings. He tilted his head in apparent disbelief.

Dave Corbus was the first guy to speak. "Hey, Sarge, faced with the same situation, I think all of us would have done the same thing. Hell, big bucks coming at ya like that, I'd have bought in hook, line and sinker, no question."

"Yeah, Dave's right," Breeze Anderson said. "We're always short of money. Anytime we see a chance for a quick buck, we have the tendency to move too fast without considering the consequences."

Each of the other guys in the hooch chimed in with encouraging words, and we all shook hands and hugged each other. This made the two Mikes and me feel much better. But Herb Wise put the finishing touch on the whole incident.

"Tell ya what," Herb said, "the next time the VC drop some rockets on us, we'll consider them compliments of you three. After that, your sins are forgiven as far as we're concerned."

"Thanks, guys" Brunetti said. "We appreciate the support- as stupid as we were."

"I have just one question," Bobby Ferrara said. "What are you going to do with all those piasters?"

"The orders for all three of us came through for 'in country' R&R at Vung Tao next weekend," DiOrio said. "Hopefully we'll be able to put the money toward something good."

"I'll bet you will!" Willy Kylander teased. "That many piasters buys a ton of Saigon tea. The girls will be all over you guys."

"Wrong, Kylander," I said. "This money is tainted. I guarantee all of you that it'll be put to good use."

"Well, I can't wait to hear what wonderful things you do," Kylander jibed, grinning.

After that snide remark, we all went to the fridge and each of us grabbed a can of beer. Not one of us got his can open, though. At that moment, Tripod began barking followed shortly by the air base siren suddenly went off. It meant only one thing…rocket attack!

We all yelled the same thing, "INCOMING!" The hooch was surrounded by sandbags and the tin roof offered little protection from rain, never mind rockets. Tripod's warning gave us just the time we needed. The bunker was the place to be.

Everyone dropped their beers, grabbed flak jackets and helmets, and made a mad dash for the bunker that was fifty yards away. As sergeant in charge, it was my responsibility to see that everyone got there safely. I was the last one out, still standing at the doorway of the hooch with Tripod at my side, when *KABOOM!* The first rocket hit in an open field between the runway and us.

When the siren went off, I'd only been wearing a T-shirt and boxers, and flip-flops. This was definitely no time to be worried about my outfit, though. I pulled on my helmet and flak jacket and headed toward the bunker. Tripod—I'd swear he knew as much about rocket attacks as we did—dashed across the field and made it safely to the bunker.

I was moving as fast as I could to catch up with the dog. At the exact moment, when the guys pulled Tripod into the bunker, I thought I might have lost it forever. The flip-flops twisted under my feet. I went skidding face first into the dirt, removing large sections of skin on the right side.

KABOOM! The second rocket hit…thankfully, not me. But this time it was much closer to the hooch. I knew the way the VC fired rockets; the next one could land in my pocket. I tried to pick myself up but couldn't get my footing and fell again.

Tripod, seeing that I was in trouble, ran out of the bunker and gripped my flak jacket with his teeth, trying to pull me toward the bunker. What a dog! But he was actually making it harder for me to get up. Finally I did get to my feet, then grabbed Tripod and made it the rest of the way.

The bunker was basically a hole in the ground with sandbags and plywood piled over the top. When I got to the opening, I leaped in headfirst without even considering my mangled face. Heavy rains had fallen over the previous several days, and there was about two feet of standing water and mud on the bunker floor. I landed right in the middle of it.

The other guys were standing in the water and muck. They all broke into applause, but I wasn't about to take any bows. For one thing, just as I raised my head to wipe the mud from my eyes— *KABOOM!*—a third rocket hit, right in the spot Tripod and I had vacated moments before.

We waited uneasily for about ten minutes after that. The rockets had been coming closer each time, almost as if the VC were walking them toward us. One or two more and they'd have the right range to drop a rocket right on top of our bunker. It was tense until the siren went off again, this time indicating "All clear." The rocket attack was over. We had all survived.

Dave Corbus came up to the two Mikes and me as we walked back to the hooch. I could see he was in a good mood. Well, to be honest, we all were. We'd just been a few feet from turning into rocket fodder, and now we were safe.

With a slap on our backs, Dave spoke for the rest of the guys. "Like Crash said, the next rocket attack and then you're forgiven. Now you guys can clear your heads and start fresh."

Everybody else went back to their drinking and card playing. But somehow, even though our hooch mates had forgiven us, there was still something wrong. We felt a black cloud was going to hang over us as long as we had those piasters. The answer? Get rid of them! We were going to do just that next weekend in Vung Tao.

TRIP TO VUNG TAO

The week after our deal with Kloman passed with terrifying slowness. Brunetti, DiOrio and I were each sitting with forty thousand piasters in our possession. It was a small fortune by Vietnamese standards. Had we chosen to cash them in at the PX for the authorized rate of forty piasters per dollar, our two hundred dollar "investment" would've earned us a thousand dollars.

However, there were two things standing in our way. The first was our integrity. We hadn't realized that we were dealing with a black market weapons dealer in Kloman. There was no way we could use the dirty money for our benefit. We either had to hand it in and confess, or we had to make the money clean somehow. The second obstacle was the Criminal Investigative Division, or CID.

We went to work each morning with the fear that CID agents were waiting for us. Anytime Lieutenant Koneche called my name, I jumped, fully expecting to be called into his office to begin the interrogation. It was a constant pressure of guilt and fear.

There was also a moment of heart-stopping fear each time we walked back to the hooch. The cash was safely hidden until we could figure out what to do with it, but we would pause before opening the door to the hooch. The only way we could get seriously busted was if CID caught us with the cash. What would we find inside the hooch? Had the agents ripped apart our bunks and searched through our belongings?

It was paranoia, but rightly so. That kind of cash would have us in Long Binh Jail for a long time. Then we'd receive dishonorable discharges. My chances of getting the job back in New York would be tossed right out the window. All because of one incident when we believed a civilian's pie-in-the-sky plan, our lives would be ruined.

Thursday afternoon finally arrived; it was the end of the work week for the three of us. We all breathed deep sighs of relief. All we had to do now was get back to the hooch and crash for the night.

In the morning, we would head to the Air Force side of the base and our flight to Vung Tao for R&R.

Vung Tao was a coastal resort area that the military had set aside for in-country R&R. The pearl-white beaches, sparkling waves and all-night parties would be a good restorative for our souls. There was a better reason for us going, though. Vung Tao would let us get rid of the dirty cash in an area where nobody knew our names.

We headed back to the hooch. Brunetti was the first to notice the briefcase in DiOrio's hand. "Hey Mike, what's that for?" he asked.

"I'll show you when we get to the hooch," was DiOrio's mystifying answer.

I assumed that it was for carrying the cash, and I was partly correct. The briefcase could be locked, which would safeguard the money inside. I didn't anticipate DiOrio's other precaution, though.

When he opened the case in the hooch, there was only one thing inside. It was a standard army issue Colt forty-five caliber pistol. DiOrio had a ton of combat experience and made it a policy to never go anywhere unarmed. I thought this was taking things a little too far, though.

"Why are you taking that thing along?" I asked, pointing to the automatic.

"Because my M-16 wouldn't fit," was DiOrio's deadpan response.

"That's not what I meant. Why do you need a gun? We're going to one of the most secure places in Vietnam!"

DiOrio closed the case. "Ain't no such thing, Moff. You know that."

In our hearts, we all knew that no place in Vietnam was "totally" secure. We always seemed to live our lives knowing that the odds of us disappearing off the planet in a second were pretty high. Some places were better than others, though. Vung Tao was one of them. At least, that's what I'd been told.

"It's going to be bad enough if we get caught with all that cash on us," I argued. "Having that pistol will just make things worse."

Brunetti shook his head. "I've gotta go with Mike on this one, Moff. Carrying around a lot of cash is dangerous enough without packing some protection. It's worth the risk."

I just shook my head in disbelief. There was little I could do about it, though. I'd been outvoted. "Just keep that thing hidden, okay? I don't want to see you pulling it unless it's a life or death situation. Are we clear?"

DiOrio tossed a half-assed salute. "Yessir, sergeant sir."

"Goumba," was my reply. I headed for my bunk and a restless night attempting to sleep.

We retrieved the case early the next morning and were at Bien Hoa Air Base by 0700. The old tin-roofed terminal seemed strangely empty considering that this was the only scheduled flight to Vung Tao today. We walked up to the Air Force check-in counter and handed our travel orders over to an airman.

"We're going to Vung Tao," DiOrio said.

The airman shook his head as he looked over our orders. He then raised his gaze to me and said in a bored voice, "I'm sorry, Sergeant Moffett. Not today you're not."

That was enough to make my heart stagger. Was there some reason we were being kept from leaving the base? I used my best drill sergeant voice to ask, "What do you mean? Our papers are in order!"

"Your papers are fine," the airman replied. "The problem is that all the Caribou aircraft flew up north yesterday for a big troop redeployment. There won't be another plane to Vung Tao for at least four days."

"You've gotta be kiddin' me," Brunetti said in disgust. "We waited all these months for an in-country R&R and now there are no planes?"

DiOrio swelled to his very intimidating height. "Yeah, what's the deal here? They won't change our orders. It's a use it or lose it opportunity, and we'll lose our chance!"

"Sorry boys, that's the deal. There's nothing I can do," said the airman, raising his hands in surrender. "You might try MACV and see if they have a shuttle heading in that direction."

"Yeah, thanks for nothing," DiOrio said as we turned away from the counter.

It didn't quite feel right to me. The orders for our one-shot in-country R&R had been cut several weeks before our meeting with Kurt Kloman last weekend. It just seemed awfully convenient that the flight to Vung Tao had been cancelled, thereby restricting us to the base. Hitching a ride through MACV—Military Assistance Command Vietnam—was possible, but it would require some coordination. I was willing to bet that the answer would be the same…nothing heading to Vung Tao for us.

I knew we were cooked. The money was the only evidence CID would have to nail us as accessories in Kloman's scheme. If we couldn't dump the cash off post, it would be found eventually. It was just a matter of time.

Dejectedly, we walked out of the terminal, threw our bags on the ground and sat on them. My mind was racing as I tried to figure out what to do next. That's when I noticed that the hangar where the Caribou planes were normally parked was standing wide open. I couldn't tell, but it seemed like there was something large sitting in the shadows.

"I guess we'd better start hitching a ride back to the hooch," Brunetti said. "Doesn't look like we're going anywhere today."

"We'd better figure out something and quick, guys," I replied, pointing toward the hangar. "Call me paranoid, but I think they're onto us."

They followed my finger, then looked at me questioningly. "I can't see nothin' from here, Moff," said DiOrio. "Might be a plane in there, might not. I really can't tell."

Brunetti nodded in agreement. His tone didn't carry much conviction as he said, "Besides, what does it matter if there's a Caribou in there? It could be down for maintenance or overhaul or something."

I didn't say a word, just looked at them patiently. They understood the ramifications of having a Caribou in the hangar and the Air Force airman's calling me by name. We needed to get off the base.

At that moment, the three of us looked up and saw a Vietnamese bus loading civilian passengers. The sign on the bus read Vung Tao. Once again, fortune had shone on this soldier. We looked at each other, looked at the bus, then looked back at each other. DiOrio summed up our thoughts when he said, "What the hell! Let's do it!"

The bus had a strange coloring, consisting of a sick-looking pea soup green with rust marks from front to back. The tires were in poor condition and didn't look like they'd make it to the front gate, never mind its two and a half hour destination of Vung Tao.

We walked around the back of the bus and got in line with the other passengers. Each rider handed their money for tickets to the bus driver, who waved them onto the bus. He saw us and shook his head. Like the three of us, he knew that we were breaking several hefty regulations if we stepped one foot on his bus.

When we reached the driver to purchase our tickets, he volunteered some friendly advice. "GI take bus to Vung Tao beau coup dinky dao!"

Fear is a healthy motivator, and we were too afraid of not getting on the bus. It didn't matter that military regulations forbade soldiers from riding on a public conveyance outside of a secured area. We had to get to Vung Tao, and no bus driver was going to stand in our way.

"You just drive the bus," DiOrio commanded the driver. "We'll take care of everything else."

Still shaking his head, the driver took our money. He turned his head so that he could honestly say he never saw us board the bus. We noticed that there were three empty seats in the very last row. Our luck was holding; we needed to blend in, and the seats were perfect for camouflage.

We made our way through the bus to the back. It was a typical civilian Vietnamese transport. The overhead racks were filled with cages of live chickens that squawked and smelled to high heaven. There were boxes filled with the stomach-churning Nuoc Mam sauce. Several wooden cages contained cats that could either have been family pets or the evening meal. The passengers themselves were dirty and grimy, unwashed and smelling of many days laboring in the rice fields.

When we reached the back of the bus, we squeezed into the last row. There was hardly any leg room. Brunetti took the window, I sat next to him and DiOrio was to my right. With the size of those guys, I felt like the center of an Italian hero sandwich.

DiOrio threw our small travel bags in the overhead rack. I kept the attaché case containing the troublesome piasters and the forty-five caliber automatic. My earlier concerns about carrying the pistol seemed completely unfounded now. That had been when we were flying to a secure area by airplane. There was no way of knowing what kind of trouble we could run into on the bus.

Then something occurred to me that I thought I should share with my two goumbas. "Excuse me, boys. I hate to bring this up, but don't you think we're gonna stand out a little bit going past the Air Force security gate? After all, we're not exactly four foot four like everyone else on this bus."

"Moff's right," Brunetti said to DiOrio. "We have to think of something real quick."

"I have an idea," DiOrio said. He began talking to three mamasans sitting next to him, each wearing their lampshade conical hats. The bus started pulling out, and I couldn't hear what DiOrio was saying to them over the rickety-rackety rattling of the motor. He pulled out a few piasters and gave them to the women. They in turn gave him their hats, which he handed to Brunetti and me.

"Got it covered," he said, grinning proudly. "It's the best I can come up with on short notice. Just crouch down as low as you can. The hats should take care of the rest."

Brunetti and I—realizing we really had no other choice—put our boonie hats on the floor. Then we put on the lampshades and tugged the chinstrap into place.

"I really feel ridiculous!" I said.

"Not to worry, man," joked Brunetti. "You look it, too."

The bus had filled up completely by this time, and it was standing room only for the last few boarders. We hadn't realized it until I looked up...but all of the Vietnamese on the bus were looking at us like we had totally lost our minds. Little did they know how right they were.

The three of us hulking Americans tried to squeeze down into the lowest crouch position possible. It was extremely difficult, as the seats were spaced close together for passengers a lot smaller than the three of us. I tucked my knees up into my chest and pulled the conical hat down low. DiOrio and Brunetti followed suit, and soon the only things visible to anyone looking through the windows were our eyes.

The other passengers chattered away as the bus belched smoke and lurched forward. There was no way to tell what they were saying because not one of the three of us could speak the language. Crunch time came when we paused at the main security checkpoint leading out of the base. The bus was waved through the main gate without incident. Within ten minutes, we were on Highway 15 heading south to Vung Tao.

The first thirty minutes of the trip were uneventful. Then a chicken got loose, most likely startled by one of the nearby cats. Chicken feathers flew all around the bus as the bird tried to simultaneously run and fly away from the passengers who grabbed at it. A wing whacked a box in the overhead, and a jar of Nuoc Mam crashed over a guy's head. He wasn't hurt, but—being covered with armpit sauce—you would've thought he had died and gone to heaven. Since the only ventilation was the breeze through open windows as the bus was moving, the rancid odor streamed steadily to the back of the bus. I thought I was going to lose my breakfast, but after awhile the odor became part of the other scents and I didn't notice it anymore.

I wondered who had put together the bus's route. It seemed to stop at every tiny village and intersection. I wouldn't have been surprised if the driver had stopped because someone working in the rice paddies had waved him down. What should've been under a three hour trip was promising to take all day.

The bus stopped in a village called Long Thanh, and that's when things started to get hairy. Several passengers got off, but one Vietnamese guy got on. He maneuvered his way to the center of the bus and then started scanning faces. When he saw us, his features changed from a stunned look to something else. It wasn't like the curious or indifferent faces of the others who had boarded the bus. This was something else. It was a look of pure hatred, one that we knew well. He had to be Viet Cong.

For the next hour, he openly glared at us and we stared back at him. He was dressed in a white gauze-like shirt with green pants. There was no place for him to hide a weapon in that get-up, but I wasn't taking any chances. I pulled the attaché case off the floor and placed it onto my lap, then unlatched both locks. Opening the briefcase only enough to fit my hand inside, I calmly closed my grip around the butt of the automatic pistol. It gave me a feeling of confidence.

Keeping my face expressionless, I whispered to my buddies, "If he moves toward us, he dies!"

DiOrio said, "Hey, Moff, be cool. Let's just see what he does."

The head games and Wild West stare-down continued without either of us backing off. We reached the village of Phu My and, with what had to have been a curse or insult, our little Viet Cong friend got off the bus. We weren't sure if that was the last time we would ever see him, or if he was going to get some friends and meet us further down the line by attacking the bus.

It was tense, but the next half-hour passed without any sign of our VC buddy or his pals. We finally sighed in relief, knowing that we had escaped a bad situation. The bus made its way through the village of Phouc Le and then headed southwest on the final leg to Vung Tao. I calculated that we had another twenty minutes or so before we hit the gates and could start our R&R.

Then we ran into trouble. As Brunetti was sticking his head out the window, trying to clear his lungs of the nuoc mam and other nauseating odors, an Army jeep flew by. It was a Military Police patrol heading north, providing security on the main supply route with its fifty-caliber machine gun. The three of us ducked down, but it was too late. The three MPs in the jeep had spotted us.

The jeep started to make a U-turn on the highway to head back in our direction. The bus driver caught the motion in his rearview mirror. He knew what was going to happen, so he began slowing down.

I pulled the forty-five caliber pistol out of the briefcase and ran to the front of the bus. It didn't take anything more than showing him the weapon, and then the bus driver decided that slowing down wasn't the best idea after all. The bus went back up to its top speed of about fifty, and then we caught a big break.

As was known to happen with jeeps on a routine basis, the MP vehicle stalled in the middle of the road. I looked back to check on the jeep, then forward to see how far we had left to go. We passed a sign that read "Vung Tao 5 km." Things were looking up.

MPs can be tenacious, however. A flashing light caught my attention. Sure enough, the policemen had managed to get their jeep started again and were driving like maniacs to catch up with us. DiOrio and Brunetti grabbed our gear and joined me at the front of the bus. When the MPs finally caught up with us, we had just passed a very large sign that read, "Welcome to Vung Tao."

"Okay now, GI?" asked the bus driver.

"Yeah, sure," I replied. DiOrio held the briefcase open for me and I tossed the pistol inside. Something about it seemed strange, but I couldn't put my finger on it. I had other troubles to worry about. With an apologetic smile, I turned to look at the driver. "Sorry about that."

"Sokay, GI," the little man said, head bobbing. "Important you in Vung Tao, I know. No ploblem."

I patted the guy on the back in gratitude. He pulled the bus over onto the shoulder and opened the door. Our boots hit the ground before the bus had stopped rolling. When we were all clear of the door, the driver released the clutch and continued moving right on down the road.

The MPs let the bus continue on its way. The most they could've done to the driver was chew him out or hold him until the local Vietnamese police showed up. That could take hours. Instead, they had bigger fish to fry...namely, us.

"You stupid grunts!" yelled the ranking policeman, Lieutenant Shively, as he ran up to us. "What'n'the'hell do you think you're doing?"

We came to attention and saluted. It wasn't that we were truly being respectful. It was just a way to buy some time and calm the irate lieutenant down. As the ranking soldier, I answered the officer's question. "Sir, we're going on R&R, sir!"

"Lemme see your orders, Sergeant!" barked the lieutenant. When we failed to move immediately, he returned our salutes and held out his hand.

I pulled the orders from my pocket and extended them to the officer, then resumed the position of attention. The driver had left the police jeep and—with one hand on his holstered pistol as he walked past—he took a position behind us. The third MP stayed in his position, manning the fifty-caliber machine gun.

"Sergeant Moffett, huh? And you two, DiOrio and Brunetti. Do you have any idea how many regulations you've just broken?" The lieutenant returned the orders and placed his hands on his hips. "I'm of a mind to let you spend your R&R in the local jail."

"Sorry sir," I explained in my most reasonable voice. "This is our only chance for R&R, and they canceled our flight this morning. We had to get here somehow, sir."

The officer was watching my face closely. I put on my best "stupid grunt from the field" look and smiled. He wasn't impressed. "That's a strange thing for an infantryman to be carrying, Sergeant Moffett. What's in the briefcase?"

I have no idea how I managed to keep my thoughts from being transparent. It wasn't a good sign that he had repeated my name twice, almost as if he knew it beforehand. If my guess was correct, we were about to find ourselves in the local clink waiting for the CID guys to catch up with us.

"A forty-five pistol, sir," replied DiOrio before I could open my mouth. "That's all."

"Open it, Specialist DiOrio," ordered the officer.

This wasn't looking good at all. I watched DiOrio place the briefcase in the palm of one hand as he opened it with the other. There should've been an eyebrow raised or something to see 120,000 piasters sitting there. The lieutenant showed no reaction except for a grunt, then a dismissing wave as he said, "Put it away, specialist."

"Yessir." Mike complied quickly, snapping the lid shut and lowering the briefcase to his side.

I was lost, not understanding what had just happened. The officer's next question caught me off guard as he asked, "Where are you staying in Vung Tao, Sergeant?"

"The Grand Hotel," I replied quickly.

Lieutenant Shively looked me straight in the eyes. "I don't think that's a good idea, Sergeant Moffett. Here's a better one. I suggest you stay at the R&R Center so you don't get into any more trouble."

Damn, I thought to myself. Now he's done it. An officer's suggestion carried the same weight as an order, and we had no choice now but to comply. Although he didn't know it, though, Lieutenant

Shively had just done us a favor. After receiving an order, there's only one thing a soldier is expected to do.

I saluted and said, "Yes sir, we'll do that right now."

Shively returned the salute. A puzzled look appeared on his face as I grabbed my bag and repeated his order to my comrades. I honestly don't think he was finished with us, but I didn't give him much choice.

"Alright you two," I barked in a command voice to DiOrio and Brunetti. "You heard the man! To the R&R Center, double time!"

Double time is a cross between walking and running; all three of us started double-timing in order to put as much distance between us and the lieutenant as possible. There was still a chance that he could stop us—all he had to do was order us to halt—yet the confused look on his face told me that we were almost home-free.

The three of us were soon out of the MP officer's line of sight. By some miracle, we made the proper turns and ended up in front of the R&R Center. It was only a few blocks away from where the bus had dropped us off. Just in case Lieutenant Shively decided to check up on us later, we checked in and decided to take three beds on the second floor.

The Center's accommodations were spartan to say the least. I knew from first glance that we wouldn't be staying long. Other than a tile floor with ceiling fans, the quarters were nothing more than a giant open-bay barracks similar to the ones we'd lived in during Basic Training. Our floor looked just like our hooch, right down to the same style of bunks.

"Damn, that was close," I said as each of us threw the bags on our respective beds. "I thought we were done for sure."

"Me too," echoed Brunetti.

"There's something I don't get, though," I said as I pulled the briefcase toward me. "Why didn't the el-tee bust us when he saw all the cash?"

Before either could reply, the answer became obvious as I opened the case. The only thing in the container was the Colt 45. I looked up at my two companions, a definite question on my tongue. "Where's the money? You didn't leave it on the bus, did you?"

DiOrio shook his head and laughed at my confusion. "I stuffed it in my bag when the MPs were chasing the bus."

"We figured the first thing they'd want to check was the brief-case," Brunetti helped explain. "If they didn't question the forty-five, then they wouldn't have us dump out the rest of our gear."

"Yeah, that way the lieutenant couldn't rag on us about getting on the bus unarmed," DiOrio said, finishing their explanation.

"Well, I'll be the first to admit I was wrong about bringing this thing," I said, pulling the pistol from the briefcase. "No telling what would've happened if that VC had done something and we'd been unarmed."

DiOrio and Brunetti didn't say anything. They just looked at each other. That should've been my first clue. I started to clear the weapon by popping out the clip…and noticed there were no bullets in the magazine. My two companions were still silent as I pulled the slide to the rear. No round popped out of the chamber. The gun had been unloaded the entire time.

"Of all the stupid…!" I was shocked and angry. "What was I sup-posed to do with the VC on the bus, huh?! Use harsh language? You idiots, you could've gotten us killed!"

"Hold on a minute, Moff," Brunetti chided, "you're the one who didn't want Mike to bring it along at all. Now you're pissed because he didn't have it loaded?"

"Damn straight! Did you expect me to pull the trigger and—on hearing the click, click, click of an empty chamber—throw the gun at him in true Hollywood fashion?!"

"That Viet Cong wasn't gonna do nuthin', Moff. And besides," DiOrio said, reaching into his pocket and pulling out a loaded clip, "he wasn't the one we would've needed to worry about. I've seen you shoot."

"He's right, Moff. I'd feel safer standing behind the target!" Brunetti grinned and slapped me on the back. "We had it covered, man. Don't sweat it."

The fear and adrenaline finally crashed as I realized that I'd had no control over the situation whatsoever. There's only one thing to say at moments like that, so I said it. "I need a drink. A really strong drink."

"Would it improve your aim?" teased Brunetti.

"Let me see that," I said to DiOrio, pointing to the loaded magazine. "I'm suddenly in the mood to kill something."

"Nothing doing, man," the giant Italian replied, laughing. "I'll take you up on that drink offer, though."

We kept a very low profile that evening just in case Lieutenant Shively decided to visit the R&R Center to check up on us. The movie was boring but free, and it killed several hours. Finally, around 0200 hours, we threw our bags out the second-story window and jumped from the fire escape to the ground. It was simply time to go. We made our way through a back alley to the beach road, then about a mile up the road to the Grand Hotel.

After checking in, we decided to hit the sack as soon as we got to our room. It had already been a day of too much fun and games for me. The last thing we needed was to venture out and get into more trouble.

We also didn't need to blow the stash of our ill-gotten cash. I had the definite feeling that spending it on our own pleasure would come back to haunt us. Perhaps it was wishful thinking, but I honestly felt that we had to use it on something worthwhile…a good deed or cause that could balance the karmic scales.

It was strange to wake up to the sound of the ocean splashing against the beach. The smell of salt water was invigorating. We woke early, had breakfast, and headed straight to the beach which was just across the street from the Grand Hotel.

We spent the day playing touch football and volleyball with a bunch of other GIs who were also on R&R. There was even the opportunity to get in a little surfing, if the pansy waves could justify the name. We slugged Ba Mui Ba beer all day. It was great.

However, the real treat was having pineapples. A Vietnamese girl came down the beach with a basket of pineapples and a machete. It was impressive to watch her skillfully remove the pineapple husk; she swirled the fruit under the edge of her machete, peeling it like a potato. Then she would skewer the bottom with a wooden stick. Ready to eat.

There's a funny thing that happens after a day at the beach, surrounded by all that water…you become incredibly thirsty. As we headed back toward the hotel around 1700 hours that evening, we passed several roadside beer stands. An ice-cold beer sounded like the perfect thing to quench our parched throats.

Only one problem with that plan; the street bars were strictly off limits to American GIs. That rule had been stressed on multiple occasions when we checked into the R&R Center. The street bars were for ARVN—Army of the Republic of Vietnam—soldiers only. So, in true fashion when DiOrio, Brunetti and I were told not to do something, we did it anyway.

We walked up to one of the bars and ordered a beer. Before the echo of our words could even fade, one of the South Vietnamese soldiers standing at the bar began yelling at us. "GI no drink here! Go!"

"Hey, buddy," DiOrio replied in the same loud tone, "if we can share your war, we can damn well share your bar!"

That didn't go over too well. Another Vietnamese soldier standing near Mike said something that sounded very loud and rude. DiOrio reacted as any good soldier would if he thought his mother had just been insulted...he picked the guy up and threw him over the bar.

Three guys jumped DiOrio, two came at me, and four headed for Brunetti. We didn't want to hurt anybody, so we were careful with how far we threw our allies. After all, they weren't that large to begin with; average height seemed to be maybe five foot. It was like tossing bags of potatoes.

The next thing we knew, what had started with a simple request for a beer turned into a street brawl. American GI reinforcements arrived from the beach. South Vietnamese soldiers came running up from the other bars. From a distance, it probably looked like some kind of judo match. Two Vietnamese would try to wrestle an American, who would flip both over into the sand.

Flashing lights caught my eye. I slapped DiOrio and Brunetti on the shoulder and pointed to the approaching MP jeeps coming up the road. By that point, the melee had lost any semblance of organized combat and had turned into a free-for-all. We grabbed a couple of beers from the stand—it was a matter of principle by that point—and managed to separate ourselves from the fracas.

We made it safely to the Grand Hotel and walked through the rear entrance. Our injuries from the altercation were minor. I had a black eye from getting hit with a banana, Brunetti had a cut over his nose, and DiOrio had a bump on the head. Other than that, we were none the worse for wear. We decided to lay low for the rest of the evening and headed back to our room.

Our room had a great view of the beach. There were no regrets as we watched the military police restore order with practiced ease. Although each military service has their own traditions, there is one shared by every branch...the bar brawl. It simply wouldn't be a satisfying R&R without one. We chugged the beers captured from the street bar, acting like sports commentators as we watched the MPs break up the street brawl. It took them about thirty minutes. Then we polished off a bottle of Jack Daniels, played cards for awhile, and finally went to sleep.

Perhaps it was the fact that we got to bed earlier than usual, or that we didn't have the traditional hangover from a long night of partying. Whatever the reason, Sunday morning seemed especially beautiful. We woke early and decided to enjoy the sunrise by going for a walk...this time, far away from the beach.

We had only walked a short distance when we ran into another early riser. DiOrio saw the eagle on the officer's collar and saluted first. Surprisingly, the officer simply waved down our salutes.

"As you were, gentlemen," the Colonel said jovially. "It's too early for army stuff, so let's just pretend we're civilians this morning."

"Sounds good to me, sir," I replied, shaking his extended hand. "Sergeant Pat Moffett, sir."

"Pleasure to meet you, Pat. I'm Mark Wallington. Colonel Wallington, when I'm on duty...which I'm not at the moment, so rest easy."

The man wasn't like any officer I'd met to that point in my military career. He seemed almost grandfatherly in his bearing and tone. Then he said, "It's good to see three young men heading to services while you're on R&R."

"Services, sir?" I asked. Then I recognized the branch insignia of a cross on his collar and understood what he meant. "Oh, you mean *church* services. Of course, Chaplain Wallington. Is that where you're heading?"

"Not at the moment," he replied. "Chapel services are at ten. This is my time to enjoy God's handiwork, and to rehearse my sermon."

The sun had risen over the eastern horizon enough for the elderly priest to get a close look at our faces. I'd never met a man who could read another person so quickly or accurately. He simply pointed to my black eye and said, "I'd invite you to my morning service, but something tells me you need some religion in your lives a little faster than that."

"Sir?" I asked, not understanding.

"There's a church about a quarter mile up that road, the Church of Saint Francis." The chaplain pointed toward a steeple in the distance. "Go see the pastor there, Father Wildredo. Everyone around here knows him as Padre Willy. He's a devout man, and he'll be able to help you."

It had been awhile since I'd stepped into a church. Was it that obvious, or was this simply canned advice that the chaplain gave to everyone he met? I honestly couldn't tell. The glowing dawn now seemed to carry an air of mystery about it. Perhaps it was just my own guilt and paranoia over the dirty money still in our possession that was causing me to wonder. Nobody ever called me "Sergeant Moffett," yet this was the third stranger who had stressed my name. Was I being paranoid again, or did the Vung Tao base chaplain know something?

"He's a Filipino priest and a civilian, Sergeant Moffett. Everything you say to him is kept strictly confidential, even if it's something that a chaplain might have to report." The Colonel laid a friendly arm over my shoulder. "So whatever burden is in your heart this morning, go to him and release it. Then go see the orphanage that Padre Willy runs. Perhaps some good can come of it, if you know what I mean."

If you know what I mean.... The words sent a chill down my spine. If someone had laid a bet that the chaplain wasn't reading my soul at that moment, I would not have taken it at any odds. I managed to find my tongue and said, "Thank you, sir. It sounds like a good idea to me."

"I thought it would," the base chaplain said with a broad smile, "and of course your companions should join you. I'm sure they have something to contribute as well."

Colonel Wallington patted my back twice, then began walking away. After about ten feet, something seemed to make him pause. He turned back, looking mysterious in the dawn light as he spoke to the three of us. "Just remember, boys. God works things in His own time, and in His own way. Have faith that nothing happens except according to His grand plan."

I had no idea what to say to that. So, following the Army maxim of "when in doubt, whip it out," I snapped to attention and gave a sharp salute. DiOrio and Brunetti followed suit beside me. The Colonel returned the salute, smiled, and then continued on his morning walk.

"What in God's name was that all about?" Brunetti whispered into the morning air.

"I have no idea," I said in the same low tone. We stood there for a moment, and then I came to my senses. In a louder voice I said, "Well, all right then. Let's go get some religion, shall we?"

The other two didn't argue. We found the Church of Saint Francis without any problems. The building wasn't impressive, just a small white stucco affair with a tiny steeple. We walked through the foyer and into the chapel. The inside contained about fifty splintered and worn pews. There really wasn't much to the place at first glance, but my opinion changed as I walked toward the altar. It was carved of wood, and truly a remarkable thing of beauty.

We knelt down in the empty church and said a few prayers. I discovered that, if nothing else, the sense of peace that comes from prayer made the trip worthwhile. Then I heard the rustling of cloth. A priest in a white cassock approached us from the sacristy. It was none other than Padre Willy. After chatting for a few minutes, the Padre asked if we would like to visit the orphanage.

Perhaps it was the man's charisma and devout passion for others…I found that I was truly interested in seeing his young charges. The Padre led us across the church lawn to a nearby building. It was actually in better condition than the chapel; I could tell where the priest focused his resources.

There were ten cribs in the first room we entered. Each crib contained a Vietnamese child no more than three years old. I noticed the small signs hanging from the foot of each crib. The signs bore the names of different states…Montana, Arizona, etc.

"That's a good idea," I said to the Padre. "I would've never thought of using states when you don't know the children's real names."

"No, no," replied Padre Willy, chuckling. "We know the proper names for each child. The states are where the child's adopted family lives. It helps to keep them separated that way, considering that we have to watch our funds."

"Watch your funds?" asked DiOrio. "I don't understand. What does money have to do with it?"

"Transportation costs, my son," the priest replied. "It costs more in transportation to send a child from Vietnam to Maine, for example, than it does to send one to California."

Brunetti smiled at the young boy who played peek-a-boo through the slats in his crib. "The adopting families pay those costs. Shouldn't be a problem."

Padre Willy shook his head. "Were that the case, but it isn't. There aren't many American families who want a Vietnamese child. If they had to pay travel costs, that number goes down to almost zero."

DiOrio, in his typically blunt manner, summed up all of our feelings exactly. "That sucks."

"The Lord provides, brother," the Filipino priest responded.

My attention was drawn to something moving near the back door that lead to the courtyard outside. I walked closer, curious. It turned out to be a young girl about the same age as the other children. A nun was combing her hair. The young girl had the biggest brown eyes I'd ever seen.

"And where is this little cutie heading?" I asked the priest as I knelt in front of the beautiful baby girl.

He stepped up behind me and placed a hand on my shoulder. "Nowhere, I'm afraid."

"What?" I twisted around to look up at the priest. "What do you mean?"

"Her name is Thanh. A family in Oregon is waiting for her. We'll get her there eventually."

I stood and, taking the Padre by the arm, led him far enough away from the little girl that she wouldn't be able to hear what we were saying. "Why can't she go now?"

"We have enough money for nine children, Pat. One of them has to stay." Padre Willy waved his hand toward the other children. "Some of these infants have been waiting six months or longer. I had to make a choice. I could send Thanh to Oregon, or I could send the young boy your friend is playing with over there to Massachusetts. It's easier to gather enough donations to send Thanh to Oregon, so she stays for awhile. Maybe next month, or the month after, we will have enough."

I didn't envy the holy man and the choices he was forced to make every day. It was an incredible burden to carry, deciding which child would stay in the war-torn country while another traveled to peace and freedom in the States.

It still didn't seem fair. I looked down at the innocent young child and thought of everything I had been through in her country. There was no safety in Vietnam. Would Vung Tao remain free of rocket attacks? It didn't seem likely. The VC considered any place containing American troops to be a legitimate target. Did the little baby have another month of peace before the war came here?

Perhaps it was the obscure way that Colonel Wallington spoke to me in the predawn hours on that Sunday morning. Maybe it was Padre Willy's good works helping the orphaned Vietnamese children find a place of safety. Most likely, though, it was the innocence in Thanh's brown eyes. Whatever the reason, I found that I truly wanted to help get the little girl to her new home in Oregon.

"I wish that I had dollars to give you, Padre, but all I have are these." I began pulling piasters out of my pocket. "Will they help?"

The priest nodded, surprised. "Every little bit helps. The Church can—"

"—change them because you're a charity!" I didn't mean to interrupt, but I had remembered probably the only honest thing Kurt Kloman had said.

I began emptying my pockets of piasters and placed them into the shocked priest's hands. Then I looked at DiOrio and Brunetti and put out my hand. They grinned, understanding what I was doing. By the time we finished pulling the cash from all of the hiding places, Padre Willy had a sizable fortune in his hands.

"God bless you, my sons," the priest said, smiling gratefully. "There's more than enough here to put Thanh on the flight. We leave tomorrow on a flight for Bien Hoa where the children will connect with a flight to the States."

"Incidentally, Father," DiOrio said, wistfully looking at the pile of bills. "How much *did* you need for the little girl's plane ticket?"

"Oh, about $500," Padre Willy replied as he handed the cash to a nearby nun. "Thank you again, good brother! God has surely brought you to us this morning in our time of need."

DiOrio's sad look was amusing as he watched the nun carry the pile of cash out of the room

I couldn't stand watching my giant friend appearing so distressed. As the base chaplain had said that morning, nothing happens except according to God's plan. Maybe whoever was looking out for us from above would be able to grant just a minor miracle. I smiled at the Filipino priest and said, "You say that you're flying to Bien Hoa in the morning, Father?"

After the priest nodded, I asked for the favor. "It just so happens that we're stationed in Bien Hoa. There aren't any flights for the next few days, and I was wondering...?"

"Of course!" the holy man replied, understanding. "There's a C-123 coming to pick up the children. If you wouldn't mind helping me keep the children organized on the flight, I'm certain that I can obtain boarding passes for you."

I was beginning to feel like there was an invisible pattern in life after all. The coincidences were too incredible to believe. A nagging question rose in my mind—were the opportunities given for the three of us misfits, or was it solely for the young child?—but I pushed it down quickly. I was simply a soldier, and war didn't leave much time for philosophical deliberations.

We spent a few hours more talking with the priest and playing with the children, then headed back to the hotel. It took awhile to pull DiOrio out of the dumps, but we managed. After all, it is extremely hard for a practical person to hand over that amount of money without feeling some regret.

The Padre was as good as his word. We met him at the Vung Tao airport early the next morning, and he had our boarding passes ready for us. It was almost comical seeing three giant GIs towering over the excited kids. We boarded the C-123 and made the short hop to Bien Hoa.

It was strange to feel so sad afterwards as I watched the children lining up to board their flight for the States. I'd only known them less than a day, and yet it felt like I was losing something precious. It didn't help when Thanh wrapped her arms around my neck and gave me a goodbye kiss.

She was crying. I didn't understand how anyone could grow so fond of each other in such a short time. "Don't worry, little Thanh," I told her reassuringly. "There's nothing to be afraid of. You're going home."

We waited until the plane had lifted safely into the air before turning toward the hooch. Our adventure in Vung Tao had come to an end. Little did we know that trouble was waiting for us in Bien Hoa.

A DAY OF PEAKS AND VALLEYS

Our hearts were lighter as Brunetti, DiOrio, and I hitched a ride back to the hooch. We had just said our farewells to the children from the orphanage. Padre Willy's parting words before the airplane had risen into the air had been heartfelt and made us feel good about our deed. "Bless you, my sons and get home safely."

The tainted money had been cleansed and, with its use for a good cause, so had our souls. It was a wonderful feeling to be free of guilt. We couldn't wait to get back to the hooch and tell the rest of the gang. They wouldn't believe it.

Sadly, though, our mates were all at work. We didn't have to report for duty until the next morning, so we showered and tried to kill the time until Herb Wise and the others came off shift. After half an hour of doing thumb swivels—twiddling our thumbs—we couldn't take it anymore. The news was just too good.

"Hey, Moff," Brunetti said as he stood beside the open fridge. It was the third time that he had eyeballed the cold Bud and then turned away from it.

I pulled the earphones off my head. I'd been trying to listen to music on the reel-to-reel, but I couldn't get into it. For some reason, I was too impatient and excited. Time seemed to be crawling. "Yeah, what?"

"What're we doing?" Brunetti asked, closing the door to the refrigerator.

"Waiting," announced DiOrio from his bunk. He sat up and looked at both of us.

"What for? I mean, come on. I want to tell the guys about what happened."

I placed the headset on top of the reel-to-reel and turned off the tape. "You realize that it'll mean we'll have to work, don't you?"

Both of my Italian friends nodded simultaneously.

"Then what're we sitting around here for?" I grabbed my cap and pointed toward the door. "Let's go to work!"

The first warning we had that anything was wrong came as we neared the office. The commander's jeep—still stolen and looking new with its Screaming Eagle tire cover—wasn't the only occupant in the grass parking lot. Another jeep sat beside it. Stenciled on the bumper were the letters "CID." We stopped almost simultaneously, hoping that nobody had seen us.

DiOrio hitched his thumb back toward the hooch. "Maybe we don't want to go in there right now."

Although it didn't match the sinking sensation in my stomach, I said reassuringly, "It doesn't matter, man. They can't prove anything. We don't have the cash anymore, so there's no evidence. We'll be fine."

"I've gotta agree with Mike," Brunetti said. "Why don't we just head back to the hooch?"

"Why?" I asked. "If they're here for us then that's their next stop. Unless you guys are talking about going over the fence?"

"You're probably right, Moff. We can't run, so let's just get this over with." DiOrio wasn't afraid of anything, yet it took him a great deal of courage to agree with me. There were only two things that would bring CID to our office doorstep. They had parked beside one of them, and Kurt Kloman was the other.

My heart was pounding like we were in the middle of a rocket attack. I stepped forward first and was relieved to hear the footsteps of my two comrades behind me. After inhaling a deep breath, I opened the office door and stepped into the room.

The Lieutenant's snitch, Billy Dobler, was the first to see us. He ran straight to Lieutenant Koneche's office, apparently to tell the boss that we had arrived. Herb Wise looked up from his paperwork; the stricken look on his face enough warning. He held his hands up as if riffling imaginary bills.

That made me feel a little better. Like I'd told my two friends, there was little that CID could pin on us. After all, in barracks lawyer terms, if there was no evidence then there was no crime. The three of us continued walking toward the officer's door when we heard him yell, "Moffett! Brunetti! DiOrio! Get your asses in here."

I stepped through the doorway first, ensuring that the primary blast of the officer's wrath would be focused on me. DiOrio followed and came to attention on my right. Brunetti closed the door behind him and then joined us on my left.

Lieutenant Koneche was furious. "How could you three be so stupid as to get involved in this kind of stunt?"

"Which stunt is that, sir?" I asked from the position of attention.

"Money laundering." A lieutenant, one of two officers seated in chairs in front of Lieutenant Koneche's desk, turned to face me. "Black marketeering. You know, that stunt."

I looked at the Lieutenant's face and answered honestly, "Sir, we have had no involvement in the black market."

"That's true, Sergeant," spoke the other officer, a Captain. "The only black thing you've been involved with were the olives on your Continental Palace pizza."

His statement told me that we were screwed, blued and tattooed as the saying goes. If he knew about the pizza we had ordered at the hotel before running into Kurt Kloman, then someone had been watching us. There might even be photographs, and that was all the CID needed for a conviction. We were looking at a long tour in Long Binh Jail.

"Yes sir," I replied cautiously. "We ordered pizza with black olives at the Palace when we were in Saigon a week ago."

The Captain's face was expressionless as he watched my eyes. Then he nodded once and said, "You're not stupid, Sergeant Moffett. I'll give you that. You know how much trouble you're in right now...don't you."

He said it as a statement and not a question. I wasn't sure what to say to that. A verbal confession would result in us being arrested...yet it almost seemed as if the officer was offering us a way out. If I could only determine what it was before getting trapped by my own words.

I nodded. "Yessir, I know what we'd be facing if we had been involved in money laundering."

"So let me tell you what *I* know, Sergeant." The Captain stood and walked to the window. He spoke toward the lawn outside instead of directly to me. "I know that three soldiers were approached by a man at the same time you were at the Continental Palace bar. We've been following this man for about a month on suspicion of money laundering. We thought we'd got him that time, but he managed to lose his tail."

I let out a slow sigh of relief. If Kloman had lost the CID agents trailing him then there was no evidence. We might be able to get out of this after all. There are times when silence is the best policy. I kept my mouth closed and let the officer talk.

"You see, Sergeant Moffett—and I'm speaking to you as well, Specialists—this Kloman character is very slick. He's willing to let patsies take the fall for him, but we've never caught him in anything dirty. That's a shame, wouldn't you say, Sergeant?"

"Yes sir," I replied, fervently hoping that DiOrio and Brunetti would stay quiet and let me do the talking. If I failed to get us out of this, at least they'd know which story didn't work and could create their own. "Not being able to catch a criminal would be a shame, sir."

The Captain continued speaking to the world outside. "So what I have, Moffett, are three soldiers who—after meeting this man we believe is involved in black marketeering, arms smuggling and money laundering—immediately went to the closest military PX and purchased three $200 money orders."

The officer turned and stared into my eyes again. "Tell me, Sergeant Moffett, what happened to that money?"

There are times when only the truth will save you, so I told him the truth. "Sir, we had a scheduled in-country R&R in Vung Tao. We'd heard of a priest there named Padre Willy. He runs an orphanage and needed money to send Thanh, an orphan girl, to the States. If I were one of the three soldiers in your situation, that is what I would do with the money."

"I assume that if I were to contact this priest through the MPs at Vung Tao that he could confirm such a story?" the Captain asked, his eyes never leaving mine.

"Absolutely, sir."

"Then I have a problem, Sergeant." The officer returned to his seat and looked up at me. "You see, I don't give a rat's ass about the three soldiers. From what the agents overheard during the conversation with Kurt Kloman, it was obvious that these three weren't going to make this a long-term deal. Sound about right?"

I shook my head and did my best to appear confused. "I'm sorry, sir, but what was the problem you're referring to?"

"Just this. I want to put Kloman away. If I had three soldiers who'd been approached by him to do something illegal, then I could use their written statements to arrest him. I know he's a smooth talker, so I'm willing to waive any charges against the three. They'd be innocent victims of a crime, not accessories…and if necessary, they would be material witnesses. Are you following me, Sergeant Moffett?"

"Yes sir. It sounds like a sweet deal." I wasn't ready to come completely clean at that point. We were only talking a hypothetical situation, after all. I'd believe the CID officer when he showed me his promise in writing.

The Captain waited for what seemed like an eternity, but was probably no more than several minutes. His hawk-like gaze never left my face. Then he smiled. "There are at least a hundred GIs involved in this money laundering operation. They've got enough money to buy houses in Saigon and keep their own harem of hookers. From what I've seen and heard, these three soldiers aren't from that strain. I'll bet they're honest guys who got pulled into something dirty, and now they want a way out of it."

I watched with a great deal of interest as the other CID officer opened a briefcase and placed three stacks of paper on the desk. If this was a legitimate offer then the military wanted Kloman really bad. I had to make certain, though. I nodded toward the papers and asked, "What are those, sir?"

The Captain didn't even look back at the papers on the desk. "Those are depositions. If I had three soldiers who'd been approached by Kloman, could identify him in a photograph and were willing to sign those depositions about what happened…well, they'd be free and clear. Lieutenant Koneche, would you please tell Sergeant Moffett what we discussed earlier?"

"It's exactly as he says, Moffett," replied our boss from behind his desk. He had been completely silent and refused to look at us. Now he looked stern…but there was also a pleading look in his eyes. "No

Article Fifteens, no bust in rank, no payroll penalty, no nothing. If you, DiOrio and Brunetti were approached by this Kloman guy, all you have to do is identify him and sign the statements. It's that simple."

I was almost ready to believe our incredible luck. However, I've learned to always keep a wild card…and so I asked Lieutenant Koneche for one. "What would you suggest, sir?"

The Lieutenant looked as if I'd offended him with the question. It was obvious that he didn't understand what I was asking for or why. He replied through clenched teeth, "I'd sign the damn statement, Sergeant Moffett."

That was all I needed to hear. An officer's suggestion carried the same weight as an order; he had essentially ordered us to sign the statements. I nodded to the CID Captain. "I'll need a pen, sir. We'll sign the statements."

The CID officers showed a photo to each of us. Not surprisingly, it was Kurt Kloman. DiOrio, Brunetti and I then signed the depositions, which were frightening in their accuracy. Either the agent tailing Kloman had an photographic memory or he'd been sitting on Kloman's lap. The statement contained parts of the conversation that even I had forgotten.

"Thank you, gentlemen," the CID Captain said after placing the signed statements into his briefcase. He waved his partner toward the door and followed, then paused in the doorway. "I hope that we'll never see each other again under these circumstances… because if we do, not even a Padre or an orphan girl will save you."

"You won't, sir," I promised. DiOrio and Brunetti echoed the words as the Captain walked out of the office.

Lieutenant Koneche had a few choice words for us, but we always had a good relationship. He basically told us not to get involved in that sort of thing again. Then he told us to get back to work and sent us to our desks. We acted like nothing happened. It was difficult, as everyone from the hooch was concerned and stopped by my desk. I put on my best mask and reassured them. Inside, though, I was still shaking from the encounter.

The day seemed to move almost routinely for the next two hours. It seemed like we had truly escaped our predicament without any serious repercussions. Then a Command Sergeant Major—a CSM—named Vaughn stormed into the office.

"Where the hell is Sergeant Moffett?!" he yelled.

Everybody froze. Our nerves had just begun to unwind after the tension of the morning. The last thing we needed was some senior ranking NCO to come screaming in on a ballistic trajectory.

I stood up from my desk and, dreading whatever the CSM wanted, replied, "Right here, Sergeant Major."

The CSM stormed over to my desk. With the ability that senior sergeants develop over the years, he leaned almost nose to nose into my face and roared. "Son! You're an Eleven Bravo Forty! Is that correct?!"

"Yes, Sergeant Major," I replied meekly.

"What in the hell are you doing here?!" It was a trick question; luckily, the CSM didn't even give time for a response before bellowing, "This is bullshit, son! There's no damn way any Eleven Bravo in the 3rd/187th Infantry is going to sit behind a typewriter when they're needed in the field!"

I tried to explain to the Sergeant Major how I got the clerical job, and that I had already served twelve months in-country. Even the fact that I had just extended my tour for sixty days to take advantage of the Army's Early Out Program didn't matter to him.

"That's the lamest excuse I've ever heard!" The CSM slammed two fists on the top of the desk. "You're done hiding from this war, Sergeant. I don't care whether you've got two weeks left in-country, your place is out in the bush!"

I broke the cardinal rule of dealing with sergeant majors...I interrupted him in the middle of his tirade. "Sergeant Major, I—"

His face purpled. "Shut your mouth, soldier, and listen up! You're going to meet me at 0700 hours tomorrow at Bien Hoa airbase. Then we're going to travel together, just the two of us, up to Camp Eagle near Phu Bai. Is that understood, Sergeant?!"

"Yes, Sergeant Major."

"It damn well better be, son, because if you don't show up, I'm reporting you AWOL as a deserter! You'll find screwing around with a Sergeant Major isn't as easy as fooling CID folks. We'll see if you can weasel your way out of those charges!"

Now I understood what was going on. Word had already made its way through the chain of command and—even though I'd never seen CSM Vaughn before in my life—he had decided that I needed to be punished. I was both terrified and furious at the same time.

Sergeant Major Vaughn stormed out of the office as fast as he'd come in. I stood there, fists clenched, until I finally managed to calm down. The other guys in the office gave me that "you're screwed" look.

It was early in the afternoon, but that was the last straw. I gave what I assumed would be the last order I'd ever give to my section. "Alright, boys, I think we've been through enough today. Close up shop and go home."

I walked out of the office before anyone could say anything to me. The day had been too much. I couldn't believe how close I had come to going to Long Binh Jail…but compared to the combat I'd see in Phu Bai, maybe jail wouldn't have been such a bad thing after all.

There was nobody in the hooch when I finally arrived. I figured that the guys probably sensed that I needed to be alone. It was a welcome relief, actually. I didn't think that I could handle their sympathy just yet.

I laid down in the sweltering midday heat and had just barely managed to close my eyes when the door slammed. A familiar voice once again yelled in his best parade ground voice, "Sergeant Moffett! Is Sergeant Moffett in here?"

It was the same PFC, so I knew what was happening. I rolled over on my bunk and said, "What does the Colonel Lowery want this time?"

The PFC seemed surprised that I remembered him. He shrugged and said, "The Colonel wants to see you on the parade ground."

The way I was feeling, it couldn't be anything good. I considered for a moment the methods of punishing soldiers—like public flogging or drumming out—but those had been abolished for at least a century. There had to be some other reason. "What for?"

"I don't know, Sergeant."

"Tell him I'll be right there."

I wondered what the Colonel wanted of me this time. Undoubtedly it had something to do with food...but why meet on the parade ground? Why hadn't he ordered me to report to his trailer again? I considered the possibility that it was nothing more than a meeting to discuss how discrete I would be about his indiscretions. After all, I could always blackmail him into overriding the Sergeant Major.

That wasn't my style, though. Whatever the Colonel had done, whether legal or illegal, didn't matter to me. He had ordered me on two missions, and I had accomplished them to the best of my ability. Now CSM Vaughn had ordered me on another mission...and I had no choice but to comply.

I shrugged into my uniform and headed for the parade field. It came as a complete shock to find myself called in front of the formation...where General Barnett pinned a bronze star on my chest and told me what a great job I was doing. It seemed bitterly ironic to me. Little did he know that the CID was rattling their handcuffs that morning, or that I'd been ordered to the combat zone.

There were about twenty other guys called in front of the formation with me. It turns out that General Barnett had made a surprise visit to the base and wanted to give out some medals. Since we had all been in-country for more than eight months, we were qualified for the bronze star.

The day had reached the point of being surreal...like I was walking through somebody else's dream. Nearly arrested, chewed out and disgraced in front of my soldiers, and then awarded the bronze star. I kept expecting to wake up at any moment, but I didn't.

After the formation broke up, I decided that I wasn't tired. To be perfectly honest, I just wasn't ready to face the guys in the hooch yet. Instead of returning to my bunk where I was supposed to be packing, I decided to tackle the hard tasks first. In my position as a section sergeant, I had worked with tons of people at Bien Hoa. I wanted to tell them all goodbye.

It wasn't an easy task. Most of my professional acquaintances hadn't heard that I was leaving. They were stunned by the quickness of the Sergeant Major's action, and by the injustice of it. All offered to intercede on my behalf, but I politely turned them down. There was no need for anyone to step into the line of fire between CSM Vaughn and myself.

Things became a little more complicated when I decided to visit Master Sergeant Huer, the Chief of Records Branch. We had always worked well together. He had been my immediate supervisor until SSG Williams had arrived; now he was my boss's boss on the enlisted side of the chain of command.

I knocked on MSG Huer's trailer door. By this point, I was a complete wreck; it is emotionally draining to say goodbye to so many people. I heard the senior sergeant yell something that sounded like "Enter!" so I opened the door.

Two Adjutant officers, Lieutenant Fitzgerald and Lieutenant Davila, were with MSG Huer. The scene could've been an after-hours working meeting or just chillin' out together; the three sat back in big easy chairs, smoking cigars and drinking Remy Martin brandy.

"Moff! What brings you here, looking like somebody just broke your favorite toy? Sit down, man, and have a drink!" MSG Huer grabbed an empty glass and started to pour brandy into it.

"I can't, Sergeant Huer," I replied, still standing. It was hard for me to force the words past my tight throat. "I just came by to say thanks for everything you've done for me. Hopefully you'll be able to find a suitable replacement on such short notice."

MSG Huer froze, then looked up at me. "Suitable replacement for whom, Sergeant Moffett?"

"Me, Sergeant. I'm heading to Phu Bai in the morning."

He replaced the brandy bottle on the table and leaned back in his chair. "What are you talking about, Moff? I haven't seen any request to ship you up north."

"Command Sergeant Major Vaughn ordered me to meet him tomorrow morning at the airbase," I explained. "He feels that all Eleven Bravos belong with the combat units and not in the rear."

"Vaughn, huh?"

"Yes, Sergeant."

MSG Huer didn't say anything else for about thirty seconds or so, then he looked at the two officers beside him. "Have you heard anything about this, gentlemen?"

The two lieutenants looked at each other, then at Huer, and shook their heads. Both officers watched the strange transformation occurring on the senior sergeant's face. Then they smirked as if they knew what was going to happen next.

MSG Huer took a big swig of brandy and a long toke on his cigar. It was completely silent in the room as he blew several smoke rings into the air. Then he stated emphatically, "Son, you aren't going anywhere."

"But Sarge, Sergeant Major Vaughn made it very clear that I would be reported AWOL if I didn't—"

"I don't care what Vaughn said," Huer declared. "You aren't going anywhere until I say so. Is that clear?"

I opened my mouth to object, but caught Lieutenant Davila shaking his head in warning. That's when I remembered something. There's a difference between rank and power in the military. Just because a person has a lower rank doesn't mean they don't have more power. As Chief of Records Branch, MSG Huer had an incredible amount of power if he chose to use it. Feeling like I was trapped between the proverbial devil and the deep blue sea, I simply nodded and said, "Yes, Sergeant. It's clear."

MSG Huer took another toke on his cigar and said, "Moffett, tomorrow you report to the office just like you've done every day since you've been here. I'll take care of old Sergeant Major Vaughn."

His voice was calm, which made it far more frightening than the Sergeant Major's in-your-face screaming tirade. I decided not to press the matter any further. If Huer said he'd take care of it, he would...I just hoped he didn't get too drunk and forget about everything he'd promised. I said goodnight to my boss's boss and the two lieutenants, and then departed.

Tripod the Wonder Dog was waiting for me when I stepped out of the trailer. I knelt down to pet him and said, "Well, little dog, with a little luck you and I may be hanging around each other for another two months."

I started walking back to the hooch with Tripod at my side when suddenly the dog started to bark and run around in circles. He'd done this in the past; it usually meant he sensed a rocket being fired at the base. Tripod was better than Lassie and Rin-Tin-Tin combined. He could pick up a rocket attack before the Air Force knew it was coming.

Sure enough, Tripod made about two spins before I heard the siren go off from the airbase, indicating "incoming" rockets. The dog and I made it to the bunker near our hooch just as three rockets hit the airbase in quick succession. Thankfully, the rockets didn't come close to the hooch or our bunker.

As I lay in the bunker, huffing and puffing and completely out of breath, I mumbled to myself, "What a day!"

After the "all clear" siren sounded, I headed to the hooch for a well-deserved can of Bud. The guys seemed to sense that something was in the air with my situation. They kept their questions to themselves.

We were sitting back, watching AFVN on our fifteen-inch black and white TV, when a surprise visitor came into the hooch. It was none other than Command Sergeant Major Vaughn. I knew he could only be looking for me, so I met him at the front door of the hooch. CSM Vaughn stepped back into the darkness outside. I followed, figuring that he wanted privacy to cover whatever he had to say to me.

"Sergeant Moffett," he began, "I've had a change of heart regarding sending you up north to a field unit."

"I don't understand, Sergeant Major. I was just packing my gear and getting ready to go tomorrow." It was a little white lie. With the afternoon and most of the evening spent saying farewell to my friends at Bien Hoa, I hadn't packed a thing.

CSM Vaughn's face was unreadable in the dim light. "Well, I spoke to the admin officers at Camp Eagle. They told me you were doing a great job keeping the infantry strength up to par...sort of keeping the books balanced so the 101st gets its fair share of replacement troops."

"Thank you, Sergeant Major. I've always tried to do my—"

"Let me finish," the senior sergeant interrupted. He couldn't look at my face as he continued. "I also want to apologize for being insensitive to the fact that you extended your tour for sixty days because you were a clerk. I don't think you would've done that if you'd been out in the bush chasing Charlie around."

It was starting to sink in…for whatever reason, Vaughn was rescinding his order. I knew that I had to be careful, though. It isn't wise to tick off a Sergeant Major, especially after he's been forced to eat crow. I kept the jubilation from my voice as I replied, "That's for sure, Sergeant Major."

"In any case, I just wanted to tell you to keep up the good work." The Sergeant Major raised his head to look at me. "You'll finish your tour right here in Bien Hoa."

At last, the words I'd been waiting to hear. I almost succeeded in keeping my voice neutral as I replied, "Thanks for reconsidering my position, Sergeant Major…and best of luck to you."

CSM Vaughn either didn't know what to say or he bit back his response. Either way, his only acknowledgement was a quick nod. Then he turned and walked into the darkness, leaving me alone in the night.

There is rank, and then there is power. Curiosity had the better of me; I had to know what MSG Huer had said to get the Command Sergeant Major to reconsider sending me to Phu Bai. I went to Huer's trailer, feeling pretty good after Vaughn's visit. My boss's boss was a little bombed but completely coherent.

"Well, well, if it isn't Sergeant Moffett," MSG Huer said from his easy chair. "You look like a man that has some good news to tell me. Would that be right?"

I grinned like the Cheshire Cat. "I do, Sergeant Huer. Sergeant Major Vaughn showed up at the hooch tonight. He said I was more important down here than I could be up north. He also apologized for not being more understanding about my tour extension."

"Is that right? Well, I'll be damned," Huer said in a sarcastically comical voice.

I sat down on the edge of an easy chair and looked him straight in the eye. "That's right, Sergeant Huer. He told me that I'd be staying right here. I know you had something to do with the Sergeant Major's sudden change of heart. What I'd like to know is…how did you do it?"

Huer swirled the brandy in his glass, sipped some, and then grinned. "It's real simple, Moff. The Sergeant Major was way out of line ordering you to transfer to another unit. He didn't follow the chain of command, and the bastard never should've walked into the office and told you to go anywhere. Yes, he can pull you out into the field…but not until he's talked with your company commander, who then would've talked to me. Since neither of us had seen a request for your transfer, it wasn't going to happen."

"I understand that, Sarge. But there had to be something else to it," I said.

"There is," Huer replied as he poured brandy into another glass. He held it out for me as he said, "Vaughn screwed with the wrong person."

My Cheshire Cat grin grew even wider. "Hell, I could've told him that. What did you do to him?"

MSG Huer leaned back in his chair and lit a cigar. Then, with one hand holding the brandy glass and the other twirling the cigar in the air, he explained what happened. "The Sergeant Major's 201 file is about five inches thick. It has every award, promotion, and everything he's done in this man's army for the past twenty-five years."

Having worked in the personnel section, I knew about 201 files. Every soldier has one. The documents inside the folder were exactly as MSG Huer explained; they created a history of the soldier's career.

The senior sergeant continued. "After you came in this afternoon, I had a little chat with Vaughn. I reminded him that he's due to retire after this tour in 'Nam, and that I was really proud of my staff—like a certain Sergeant Moffett—who help me keep those files in order. I told him that, since he's due to retire soon, I had pulled that file for safekeeping. Then I suggested what a shame it would be if that file somehow disappeared. It's been known to happen, you know. There's supposed to be a duplicate file at Personnel Records Branch in St. Louis, Missouri. They're so messed up, though, that it would probably take them years to reconstruct all the information."

I was impressed. Soldiers hand-carried their 201 file to their next duty station, and the personnel section was always cautioning them about taking care of their 201 file. At first glance, that was all MSG Huer had done with the Sergeant Major. The threat was obvious enough to anyone who knew what Vaughn had done to me, yet subtle enough not to be considered a threat by anyone else.

"What did he say to that?" I asked, laughing.

"He said he got the message." Huer took a toke from his cigar, holding the smoke in his lungs as he sipped his brandy. Then he exhaled into the glass, watching the smoke swirl. "Then he asked what he would have to do to make sure that the file didn't get lost. I told him, 'Moffett stays!' and to apologize to you for his mistake. He said, 'Deal!' and left."

There definitely was a difference between rank and power. Huer had used it for my benefit, and I was extremely grateful. I chugged the brandy, then placed the glass on the table and stood. "Thanks, Sarge. You really saved my ass from getting shot up in Phu Bai. If there's ever anything—"

"Don't mention it, Moff," Huer interrupted, brushing off my gratitude with one hand. "It's part of the job, remember that. Take care of your troops and they'll take care of you."

"Well, still…thanks for taking care of me."

"My pleasure, Moffett!" Huer grinned to let me know that his next words were only teasing. "Now get your ass to bed."

"Yes, Sergeant!" I replied, tossing a half-assed salute his direction.

I went back to the hooch and threw myself onto the bunk. Everyone else was already asleep. It had definitely been a day of peaks and valleys. Little Thanh was going to the States because of the money we'd donated. The CID had come close to arresting Brunetti, DiOrio and me for money laundering. I'd been ordered to the combat zone, then given a medal, said farewell to everyone I knew and then apologized to by a Command Sergeant Major.

As I laid back, hands laced behind my head, I whispered to myself, "Maybe today wasn't such a bad day after all."

LEAVING ON A JET PLANE...
NOT SO FAST!

The last two months of my Vietnam tour seemed to fly past. It was a time of anticipation because I was getting short. Each day that passed was another date scratched off the calendar. I was truly looking forward to the approaching day when I would catch the Freedom Bird and fly home.

Yet it was also a time of sadness and farewells. Mike Brunetti hit his DEROS—the date of estimated return from overseas—one month before I did and happily headed home. It wasn't the same after that. DiOrio, Wise and I still took our trips to Saigon, but our partying seemed muted somehow. A part of our group was missing and nothing could replace him.

I had gotten used to it, though. Hellos and farewells were just part of life in Vietnam. A group of soldiers had just enough time to become friends before one of them would head home. A stranger would arrive and become integrated into the group just as another would leave. The only constant was the unit itself; the faces were forever changing.

Then it finally arrived...my last night in Bien Hoa. What had started fourteen months ago in Phouc Vinh was now coming to an end. The following morning would see me on my way to Long Binh processing center. There I would get my boarding pass and assigned to a flight going back to the States or, if I preferred, any free-world country.

I recalled meeting a GI in Bangkok on one of my R&R trips there. The soldier didn't have much of a family back in the States, so he opted for a ticket to Bangkok instead. He had already nailed down a job as a Budweiser salesman there and was looking forward to starting his civilian life. I had a good family back home but, even if I didn't, there was no way I was going anywhere but the USA.

That last night in Bien Hoa found me with mixed feelings about leaving. It was like…well, it's extremely difficult to describe what it was like. Perhaps the closest would be considering a young bride on the night before her wedding. She feels great joy for the approaching day, yet at the same time a great sadness. It is the last night of a significant part of her life. She is surrounded by family and familiar things, but she knows all that will change the following morning. After that, everything she knew will be gone. The home that she grew up in will become a place to visit, nothing more. Her entire life will change.

All soldiers feel something similar. A great part of me, of course, wanted to go home. I couldn't wait to see my parents and friends. My old job waited for me, and I was ready to get on with my life. Yet I also had strong feelings of camaraderie for a bunch of friends and cherry clerks that I was leaving behind. We had lived together, shared the fear of dying and the joy of surviving the turmoil of Vietnam together. Brothers all, those men who surrounded me that last night.

Everything was tugging at my heart strings. Thankfully, the army has traditions for everything, even farewells. The guys in the hooch had modified the farewell party to match our own unique quirks and personalities. There would be no tears because it was time for the traditional DEROS hooch party.

The first part of the tradition was called the "beer blast," and it was taken very literally. The soldier about to DEROS would stand in the middle of the hooch, dressed in fatigues. The other fifteen or so hooch brothers each had a can of Bud with the tops completely cut out. On the count of three, everyone would chuck their beer on the guy leaving country. With fifteen cans of beer hitting him at the same time, the departing soldier was left feeling like he was going to drown in suds.

The next tradition was much more tame. We called it the "farewell hooch punch." The mess hall loaned us a giant five-gallon pot on the condition that we return it clean and shiny. We dumped in four quarts of vodka, two quarts of orange juice, one quart of gin and twenty-five cans of fruit cocktail. After stirring with a giant spoon and throwing in a bag of ice, the concoction was ready to drink. The empty Bud cans served as drinking mugs.

We always seemed to have enough booze and juice, but we never had enough fruit cocktail. When our parents wrote to us, asking what we would like them to send to us, our response was the same...fruit cocktail because we just couldn't get it in Vietnam. I remember that my mom sent ten cans in one of my packages, along with a note saying fruit cocktail was very healthy for me and that she was glad I was eating so much fruit. If she only knew....

When the hooch punch pot was completely dry, we sat around, shared a few joints and told "war" stories. When we got bored with that, we broke into our "doo wop" mode and sang oldies for awhile. We sounded like alley cats howling in the night to the other hooches, but for us we thought we were better than Little Anthony and The Imperials. Tripod the Wonder Dog got drunk too, licking the pot. We all passed out sometime during the night.

Of course, Charlie had to send a farewell present of his own. I remember hearing the siren going off at the airbase for a rocket attack. I barely managed to get one leg out of bed and didn't get any further. Fortunately, none of the rockets landed anywhere near the hooch.

I was dressed, packed and ready to go by 0800 the next morning. It was so strange to see my home—a tiny space consisting of a bunk, a foot locker and a small table—completely empty and sterile. There was nothing there to show that I had ever lived there. I glanced around the room that had been my home for so many months and smiled wistfully.

"Keep everyone safe," I whispered to the empty barracks. I sketched a brief salute, then lifted my duffel bag to my shoulder and walked out of the hooch.

All the guys were waiting for me outside the hooch. My throat was dry and scratchy as I hugged my brothers in arms; it was hard to say goodbye without choking up. As I finished the farewells, a jeep pulled up that belonged to the Company Commander, Captain Miller.

"The CO wanted you to leave in style," the driver explained, "so he sent his jeep."

I had to laugh, as did several of the other hooch-mates who knew the story. It was the least the commander could've done, considering that I was the one who organized stealing the jeep for him from the Air Force months before.

After I threw my duffel into the back of the jeep, I realized that Tripod was nowhere to be found. "Hey guys, you seen Tripod?" They shook their heads. Several offered to look under the nearby hooches for the dog, but I waved them off. "Don't worry about it, fellas. He's probably off in the bush, chasing some tail of his own. Just give him a hug for me, willya?"

There was nothing left to say. My heart was torn...my life at Bien Hoa had come to an end, and it was time to do the hardest thing I'd ever faced. I turned away from my friends, climbed into the jeep, and motioned for the driver to move out. With one last wave goodbye, I left them to whatever fate and fortune had in store for them.

After only going about fifty yards, I heard the faint sound of barking over the jeep's noisy engine. When I turned back and looked, sure enough there was Tripod. He was running at full three-legged speed to catch up with us.

"Pull over," I told the driver. Without even bothering to wait for the jeep to come to a complete stop, I jumped out to greet the dog. Tripod started licking me all over my face. He had never done that before. It was like he knew that I wasn't just heading for a weekend in Saigon...he seemed to sense that this time I was leaving for good.

There was no way that I could take Tripod back to the States. Vietnam had too many parasites and diseases; US Customs and the USDA prohibited shipping any animal from Vietnam into the US. I had to leave him behind.

I hugged the silly, faithful, rocket-early-warning dog. "Go back to the hooch now, Tripod. You've got to take care of those cherries just like you took care of me. You hear me? Make sure they've got a chance to go home someday."

Tripod barked once and did a little three-legged dance around my legs. Then he headed off in a slow trot in the direction of the hooch, head held high and tail wagging. It seemed like he knew his assignment.

I climbed back into the jeep and exhaled a long breath. It was the only thing keeping the tears out of my eyes. I'd said farewell to everyone and so there was only one thing left to do. I motioned for the driver to move out, and we headed to Long Binh.

There was a lot of traffic on the highway that day. What should've normally taken twenty-five minutes turned into a forty-five minute ride. The driver dropped me off at the DEROS section, where I checked in and handed in my orders.

The next couple of hours were spent waiting around, filling out forms and getting a bunk assignment for the night. By the time I was finished with the outprocessing rigmarole, it was time for noon chow.

The lunch meal was nothing remarkable. I was slightly disappointed; it seemed to me that the Army should've laid out a major farewell banquet for the soldiers who had served their time in Vietnam.

There was nothing for me to do after chow. I'd already been told that I wouldn't be leaving on a flight that day. Still, I wanted to know what the routines were. I headed to the DEROS muster tent where the actual boarding passes were handed out. It had to be a hundred and ten degrees in the tent. Nobody seemed to care, though. For the soldiers sitting in that tent, it was the last time they would be sweating in Vietnam.

The process was very simple. A senior sergeant called names from a roster and held out a boarding pass. The soldier whose name had been called stepped forward, took the pass, and headed out of the tent. It didn't take long for the muster tent to empty out.

I headed back to the transient hooch after that. It was totally boring. With nothing better to do, I slept on my bunk for a few hours. The only thing I had to look forward to was the evening meal. It turned out to be as blasé and boring as lunch.

Later that night, I went to the enlisted men's club. It was a giant beer hall with a fifty-foot bar and about seventy-five tables scattered throughout. There were roughly three hundred GIs there that night, all having a rip-roaring time. No sad faces in this group, though…because the next stop was the USA. Everyone was free to blow off some steam as we wasted away our few remaining hours in Vietnam. "White Room" by Cream was blaring out of the jukebox. It was followed by a Beatles song that seemed to epitomize my fourteen months in Vietnam… "Magical Mystery Tour."

Most of the guys were dancing by themselves, some on the table tops. Everyone else was either playing cards, arm wrestling or just hanging out at the bar. Not too many of us knew each other personally, but it didn't matter. On this night, we were all brothers just having a good time.

Swapping stories at the bar helped kill a few hours, but I didn't linger too long. If everything went without a hitch, I would be on the Freedom Bird flying out in the morning. It wouldn't be wise to be too hung over when they called out my name to get the boarding pass. I went back to the hooch around midnight and crashed into a deep sleep.

I awoke early and hit the showers before any of the other GIs had crawled out of their bunks. It didn't take long to repack my duffel bag…the only thing I'd removed was my shaving kit. Then it was off to wolf down breakfast.

The DEROS muster tent was empty when I arrived at 0900 with a fully packed duffel bag. I took a seat in one of the folding chairs on the front row. It didn't take long for the tent to fill up after that. Within twenty minutes, two hundred and fifty GIs were seated. We were ready to get our boarding passes.

A big Master Sergeant stomped down the aisle to the podium at the front of the tent. His nametag read Kazanski, and the "Big Red One" patch on his sleeve identified that he was from the 1st Infantry Division. Some people were born big and ugly, but this guy had worked on improving his natural gifts. As wide as he was tall, he looked like he was going to explode right out of his jungle fatigues.

"Alright, listen up!" he roared. "When I call your name, come up for your boarding pass. Then move out smartly through that door. If your name isn't called, don't come up here whining to me. Get to your hooch, then get your butts back here at 1300 hours for the afternoon manifest call."

After about fifty names, MSG Kazanski called mine. I bounced right up and headed for the podium. The boarding pass was tantalizingly close. I reached for it, then looked up in surprise as it was suddenly yanked away.

Kazanski glared at me. "Son, I guess you weren't listening to the orientation yesterday. Let me refresh your memory. I said your haircut had to be 'high and tight or you're off the flight.'"

My hair was nicely trimmed, well within regulations, and nowhere close to touching my ears. I looked at the sergeant and said reasonably, "With due respect, Sergeant, I wore my hair like this the whole time I was in-country. It's within regulations, and I've never been told to get a better haircut."

"I ain't responsible for the failings of your superiors, Sergeant," Kazanski said as he looked down at the roster on his clipboard. He bellowed the next name and gave my boarding pass to the soldier who ran forward.

I didn't understand what was going on. "Sergeant, why can't I leave it like it is? I don't have any plans to stay in the Army once I walk out of the Oakland Army Terminal anyway."

The Master Sergeant looked up at me as if surprised that I was still there. His eyes narrowed like he was getting pissed. "Son, I really don't care what you do once you step out of this tent. I'm not letting any soldier leave this station looking like some hippie weirdo when you step off the plane Stateside."

This was a complete exaggeration, and bitterly ironic coming from an overweight lifer like Kazanski. However, I was a little duck in the sergeant's pond. There really was no other choice; I had to quack in whatever manner he wanted. If I got into a brawl with the sergeant, I might never get out of the country.

Kazanski's face started turning purple as I continued standing there. In a cold voice, he said, "Now, I suggest you visit the base barbershop just down the road. Tell the barber you want a 'high and tight.' Then get back here for the next muster at 1300 hours looking like a real soldier. Until then, son, get out of my face."

There was no use arguing. I picked up my duffel bag and threw it over my shoulder. As I walked past them, other soldiers offered encouragement and sympathy. They said things like, "That sucks!" and "You got the short end of the stick, man." I dejectedly walked out of the tent as the fat man resumed calling out names for the early flight.

The injustice of it all burned through me as I headed back to the hooch. I was sick and tired of petty people with their childish power games. After throwing my duffel bag on the bunk, I didn't even bother to unpack. There was no way Kazanski could keep me off the next flight. I would be on it…or would I?

I trudged down to the barbershop and jumped into a chair. A "high and tight" haircut was a buzz almost to the skin on the sides of the head, and a very short cut on top. The last time I'd had that type of haircut was during Basic Training. I wasn't buying into Kazanski's game, so I told the barber to trim a little more hair. When he was finished, I thought it looked pretty good...at least good enough to get my boarding pass.

After another disappointing noon meal, I returned to the hooch for my duffel bag. Then I made my way back to the muster tent for the 1300 hour call. As soon as I walked through the doorway of the tent, there stood MSG Kazanski.

With a fiery look in his eyes, he immediately came toward me and got right in my face. "Boy! You've gotta be deaf or just plain stupid! When I say 'high and tight,' that's exactly what I mean. Looks like you just got a little faggot trim, trying to get over on me. Well, don't bother taking that duffel off your shoulder. You're bumped from the late flight as well!"

By this point, I really didn't care what the sergeant thought of me. "Let's face it, Sergeant Kazanski, you're just playing games here! Half the guys going home don't have hair any different than mine. So let's hear your real bitch!"

"Maybe I just don't like your face, Sergeant!" Kazanski bellowed in response.

Before I could dump the duffel off my shoulder and tear into him, the fat boy abruptly turned and walked away. I was left with nothing but a cold rage and the feeling that I'd never get out of Long Binh. With nothing else to do, I went back to the hooch.

I sat on my bunk and tried to calm down. It didn't help when I realized the hundred and fifty day Early Out Program that I'd extended for was now down to a hundred and forty-eight days. Basically, I was in-country for two more days than I should've been. I decided that I would be back in the barber shop early the next morning. It didn't matter if I had to get my whole head shaved...by hook or by crook, I was going home on the next flight out. If Kazanski messed with me over some bullshit power play after that, I was going to beat the living hell out of him. Having made that decision, there was nothing more for me to do except go back to the EM Club and hang out for the night.

As I walked up the dirt road toward the club, I found it almost desolate. Either the grunts were already in the club, or they'd caught one of the Stateside-bound flights during the day. I was staring at the ground, thinking about the past twenty-four hours of army nonsense, when suddenly I heard a familiar voice from my past.

"Damn! Now there's a grunt I never thought I'd see again!"

When I realized the words were being directed toward me, I looked up and saw Platoon Sergeant Leroy Dardy. It was like seeing a ghost. Dardy was from my Phouc Vinh days. I hadn't seen him since the original 101st guys went back to Fort Campbell, Kentucky, and I had transferred to Bien Hoa. He was one of the best NCOs I'd ever known.

"Moffett!" Dardy said, sticking out his hand. "What the hell are you doing here? I thought you would've been home months ago."

I couldn't help but grin as I took his hand. We had a hearty handshake as I replied, "Same with you, Sergeant Dardy! I hung around for the Early Out Program. What's your excuse? Did you sign up for another tour in this godforsaken place?"

Dardy nodded. "Yeah, I signed up for another tour. Now, before you go looking for a shrink, don't worry. I'm not going out to the field."

It was great to hear the old bantering again. I couldn't help but tease, "Yeah, what…you got a nice cush job in the rear somewhere?"

"You bet," Dardy laughed. "In two weeks, I'll be taking over as manager of the NCO Club right here in Long Binh. But for now, I'm just filling in at odd jobs until the present manager DEROS's out of country."

"Well, Sergeant Dardy, you'd better hold a job open for me at the NCO club. At the rate I'm going, I may never get out of 'Nam."

"Why's that, Moff?"

"This Master Sergeant, Kazanski's his name, has already bumped me off two Freedom Birds. Says my hair's too long. It's all b.s., though. He just doesn't like my pretty face."

"Kazanski?" Dardy asked, then broke into laughter. "You won't have to worry about him anymore, Moff. He went on R&R and I'm taking over the DEROS tent tomorrow."

"Are you shitting me, Dardy?" I asked, astonished at my good luck. "That's the best news I've heard in days!"

"Don't worry, Moffett, you'll be the first boarding pass on the first flight out. That's a promise." Dardy wrapped one arm around my shoulder and started steering me away from the NCO Club. "So, unless you got something better to do tonight, why don't you drop by my private hooch and have some Jack Daniels? I've got a friend dropping by."

"That didn't take you long," I replied, falling into step with my old comrade. "Is she cute?"

Dardy chuckled. "Wish that was the case, but no. He's a Marine Major by the name of Craig Johnson. We knew each other from my previous tour, and I happened to run into him at the Caravelle Hotel in Saigon last night. He had to come up here today—doing some Intelligence work or something—so I invited him over."

I've never been one to turn down the offer of free drinks, and Dardy knew it. I replied, "Fine by me...but you're buying."

He just laughed. "It's already chilling."

When we walked into Dardy's hooch, I was totally astonished. Even the Colonel at Bien Hoa didn't have it that good. There was a full-size refrigerator/freezer and a small dinette set in the kitchen. A bar with two stools separated the kitchen from the living room. The bar had an overhang with oriental lanterns draped on all sides. The small living room contained a small couch and two reclining chairs. Beyond that was the bedroom with a beaded entrance and a twin-size bed. All the walls were covered with camouflage poncho liners to give the hooch a military atmosphere.

"Whatd'ya think, Moff? Pretty cool place, huh?"

"It looks great, Sarge," I replied, truly impressed. "Hell, I know apartments back in Brooklyn that don't look this good!"

We sat down at the bar and caught up on events in the other's life while having a few Jack and Coke's. The Major showed up shortly after that. He was tall, about six foot five, and dressed in civvies. Perhaps it was the way he carried himself or the 'high and tight' haircut, but there was no mistaking it...he didn't need a uniform to announce he was a Marine Corps officer.

For the better part of the evening, Dardy and Johnson swapped war stories on their experiences in the bush. Both were working on their second tour. I couldn't compete; my strange fourteen-month tour didn't give me any combat tales to pass on. Most of my stories that Dardy would find hilarious weren't appropriate to tell in the presence of an officer.

Perhaps it was because I wasn't truly a participant in the conversation, but I noticed that the two combat vets were becoming morose. Their stories were about men they'd known…and the tale typically ended when Dardy or Johnson were reminded that those men had later died in combat.

Dardy abruptly slammed his drink onto the bar. "Dammit, Craig, why are we doing this?"

"Doing what?" the Major asked, surprised at the outburst.

"Laughing about all this hard-core blood-n-guts crap." Leroy Dardy looked down at his glass. "Why aren't there any heartwarming or even funny stories about Vietnam?"

I considered telling the two men about some of the funny things that happened to me during my tour, but the serious look on their faces told me it wasn't the best time. They were struggling with something that I didn't quite understand. Sometimes it's best to remain silent and let the other guys just talk it out.

"I know what you mean, Leroy," Major Johnson replied. "Too much death and pain in our stories, isn't there?"

Dardy emptied his glass in one swallow, then poured another. "Is there any other kind? I mean, when this war is over and just another section in the history books…are those stories the only ones that will survive?"

"God, I hope not." Johnson grabbed the bottle and refilled his glass.

"Maybe someone will write a book that'll be different," Dardy suggested. "One that lets us remember the good times in Vietnam…one that'll let us laugh instead of wanting to cry. Wouldn't that be something?"

Major Johnson looked at both of us kind of strangely, then nodded. "Yeah, that would be something. Hell, I've even got a story for them. It's sort of sad, but heartwarming nonetheless. Took place about four months ago, when I was assigned to S-2 Intelligence with 5th Marines up in An Hoa."

I waited for the major to continue with this story, but he did-
n't…at least, not immediately. He stared at his drink, then raised it
to eye level. With forefinger held straight, he poked the glass toward
me and Dardy.

"This ain't a war story, got it? I wasn't there when this first started. Most of it I heard later." He took a gulp from his drink.

"It's a fairy tale, then?" I teased.

"Yeah, a fairy tale," Major Johnson replied, laughing at the old
joke about the difference between a fairy tale and a war story. "So,
once upon a time there was this small hamlet. It was just outside the
main base camp. Now in this hamlet, about fifty Vietnamese lived in
total squalor. That wasn't including the nearby orphanage…there
was another twenty-seven children who lived there, under the care
of a Laotian nun who was also a nurse. The orphanage hooch was
the worst of all the hooches in the hamlet. When the monsoon rains
came, mud and raw sewage ran right over the orphans where they
slept on the ground."

I could visualize the scene. There were plenty of villages
throughout Vietnam like the one Major Johnson described. It had
always seemed to be a cruel pecking order to me; families lived at
the top of the hill, then further down were the elderly and
infirm…and at the bottom were the orphans. There were no sani-
tary facilities; the toilet was wherever the person squatted. Since the
village was on a hill, the torrential monsoon rains would uncover
everything. All of the garbage, feces, and other junk would flow
downhill and through the orphanage. Rampant disease typically
killed the majority of the children.

The major continued his story. "Well, there was an American
who really cared about that orphanage. He was a Lance Corporal
named Jimmy Sullivan, assigned to Bravo Company. Each time
Corporal Sullivan came in from the field, he would collect unused
C-rations from the platoon and whatever medical supplies he
could scrounge. All of this stuff he would carry down to the
orphanage. If Bravo Company was in base camp for a few days,
Sullivan would spend his free time taking other stuff down. He'd
cabbage onto empty pallets—the kind that carry supplies to the
units—and haul them down. Then he'd use the wood to build beds

out of the pallets so the children wouldn't come in contact with the ground. Mattresses were made out of old poncho liners sewn together; he'd stuff them with cleaning rags or anything soft to make soft bedding for the kids."

Dardy poured us another Jack Daniels as the Major went on.

"Now, it didn't take long for the other guys to notice what Sullivan was doing. After awhile, they got tired of watching him work while they drank and played cards. So one day, one of the guys asked what he could do to help…then another, and another, until finally the orphanage became the pet project of the entire base."

I raised my glass in salute, assuming the story was about over. "With that kind of manpower, it didn't take long to save the orphans, did it?"

"Longer than you think," the major replied. "You see, Sullivan wasn't satisfied that the kids were out of the muck. The children lacked the bare essentials like clothes. When the other guys heard that, they wrote home and asked their families to send hand-me-down children's clothes. Before we knew it, boxes of clothes started arriving almost daily from the States. Corporal Sullivan then tackled the next challenge…getting some decent food for the kids. He got the idea to have his buddies ask their families for those giant packages of goodies from the mail-order house, 'Wisconsin Cheeseman.' Within a couple of weeks, big boxes of cheese, salami, and jars of peppers started flowing into the daily mail call."

Dardy and I were mesmerized by the major's story. We hoped the tale would end "and everyone lived happily ever after" at this point, but that didn't seem to be the case. Major Johnson took a big slug of Jack Daniels, indicating that the rest of the story would be difficult to tell, even for a hardened combat vet like himself.

"Life was moving along pretty good for the orphanage. They had food, clothes and were doing well medically. We were all proud of Lance Corporal Sullivan and what he had accomplished. It was clear that his love for the children greatly exceeded his hatred for the enemy."

Major Johnson then stopped. He looked down at his empty glass as if wondering where all the Jack Daniels had gone. Dardy didn't say a word; he just tilted the bottle of whiskey and refilled the offi-cer's glass. I held out my glass as well, then the three of us drank. It was obvious that the major was clearly building up to a climax, and that it was one which required a stiff drink.

"Lady Luck can be a real bitch sometimes," Major Johnson declared. "She definitely was with Sullivan and the orphanage. First, a NVA rocket attack aimed at the base camp fell short and hit the hamlet. One of the rockets hit the orphanage and completely destroyed the hooch. If it hadn't been for them hiding in the bunker that Sullivan had built under their beds, everyone would've died. As it was, only two children were hurt. Nothing serious, mind you, so I guess you could say Lady Luck gave them a break."

I thought that was the end of the story, but I wasn't even close. Dardy, the major and I were pretty shit-faced by this point, and the alcohol was making our emotions run high. I truly wanted a happy ending.

"Corporal Sullivan was very upset about the orphanage being destroyed. We all told him that we would help him rebuild it to the fine building he had created." Major Johnson emptied his glass, refilled it, then downed half of the new mix. "Then Lady Luck turned nasty. While Bravo Company was patrolling about four klicks outside base camp, they ran into a full contingent of Viet Cong. Corporal Sullivan was killed during the firefight."

Tears began to fill my eyes. I took a big swig of my Jack and Coke to disguise the raw emotions. There was no need to play the tough guy, though. There were tears streaming down the major's face.

He wiped them away brusquely, then pointed his finger at us again. "That's not the end of the story, though. I was sitting in S-2 doing some work about a month after we'd lost Lance Corporal Sullivan. That's when our chaplain, Tom Ahearn, came into the office with a letter in his hand. He was crying, too, and he didn't need no drink to disguise it."

I didn't say anything. There was no need. After everything Dardy and Johnson had been through, they had earned the right to cry whenever they wanted. I just wished there was something I could do to make them laugh instead.

"It had to have been something truly miraculous or horrible to make a chaplain weep," Dardy said quietly. "So what was he crying about?"

"The letter," Major Johnson replied. "It was from Corporal Sullivan's parents. They said that Jimmy had written them often about the orphanage. Those kids meant the world to him, and they were very proud of his efforts to save every child there. I thought that was pretty cool, and said so to the chaplain. That's when he showed me the other thing he'd found in the envelope. It was a US Treasury check for ten thousand dollars."

My breath caught in my throat. I'd worked personnel and administration for the past fourteen months, and I knew the significance of a Treasury check for that amount. There was only one thing it could be. Swallowing down the tears, I said, "It was the death benefit check…wasn't it."

The Marine Corps Major nodded. "Yes, it was. A ten thousand dollar check sent to the Sullivan's upon Jimmy's death. They could do whatever they wanted with it. The Sullivan's explained exactly what they wanted done. It would do nothing to make up for the loss of their son, so they wanted it to be used for rebuilding the orphanage that Jimmy loved so much."

Dardy and I couldn't have been more moved.

"So, what do you think? Is that the kind of story you think people back in the States would care to hear?" Johnson asked.

"It was perfect, Major. Thanks for sharing it with us." I said.

There wasn't much said after that. Major Johnson glanced at his watch and announced that he needed to hit the rack. It was already well into the early morning hours, and all of us needed to get some sleep.

We finished our drinks and said good night. I thanked the Major again for his story and wished him the best during his current tour. After the officer left, I reminded Dardy about his promise that I would be the first plane ticket handed out in the morning. Then I headed back to the hooch and crashed in my bunk.

As I drifted off to sleep, all I could think of was the Jimmy Sullivan story.

TICKET TO RIDE

I hurried toward the muster station the following morning, my overloaded duffel bag slung over my shoulder. It contained all of the remaining items that tied me to the Army—uniforms, the wool green socks, green underwear and tee-shirts—everything from the olive drab squeeze bottle of bug juice to my Class-A uniform.

It wasn't surprising that the duffel didn't seem to weigh that much. This was June 19, 1969. It was my own personal D-Day, my DEROS, the date of estimated return from overseas. My step quickened at the thought, and the burden on my back seemed lighter still. After spending fourteen months in Vietnam, it had finally arrived. Today was the day I was going home.

A slight breeze moved the warm moist morning air. It had rained the night before, but then again it always seemed to rain every night and every other day during monsoon season. The sun was halfway into its daily climb up into the sky, a dull pale-yellow orb that was slowly turning to white. I could already feel the heat and humidity as sweat began to pool under my arms and across my back. It was going to be another hot one, a tortuous mix of near ninety degrees and ninety percent humidity. It didn't matter, though. Today I was going home.

The roadway squelched beneath my heavy strides and the reddish clay from the unpaved street stuck to my black combat boots. There were no sidewalks here. For that matter, there were no real roads here either. The red clay and khaki-yellow dirt mixed with gallons of rain to create the multipurpose sidewalk, street and obstacle course.

I reached my first stop of the day. I knew that this time I would make my way past the gatekeeper and onto the plane that would take me home. The hand-painted sign beside the front door read "Muster Station." I paused briefly, stomping my feet on the wooden pallet that served as a doorstep in a futile gesture of removing the mud from my boots, then entered the building.

Naked wiring and the occasional bare bulb dangled from the wooden center support beam, looking like a five-year-old's first attempt to decorate a Christmas tree. The floor consisted of plywood laid over wooden pallets. The slats creaked as I moved past the battleship-gray metal desks in the front office and stepped into the briefing room.

A few others had arrived before me, but I found a seat in the front row reserved for the lucky soldiers who were going home. I dropped the duffel bag and sat anxiously in the steel folding chair, like a parishioner waiting for the revival to begin.

Voices chattered behind me and the volume in the room rose as more soldiers entered and took a chair. I recognized some of the voices, turned and greeted the men I had met at the EM Club. Men I would most likely never see again after today.

"Got a hangover yet, Moffett?" yelled someone from the back of the room. "Or are you curing it with the hair of the dog that bit ya?"

I grinned and waved. "Bigger than Brooklyn!"

A conversation from two soldiers in jungle fatigues caught my attention. One held his hand toward the other, thumb and forefinger pressed tightly against a long black hair. Probably a gift or reminder from the soldier's fling last night with a local mamasan.

"Come on, man, pull it!"

The second soldier grabbed one end of the hair, tugged. "I can't move it."

"Just goes to show how short I am!"

I laughed, as did several others around the pair. The common army hand signal of thumb and forefinger was used to signify how much time a soldier had left in-country. As another day passed, the soldier could move his forefinger closer to the thumb to show how "short" he was. We were all short-timers here in this room, some with several days left and some like me who had reached our DEROS and were going home today.

The voices in the room continued to grow louder and more restless. Heads turned to follow a tall figure in the pickle-suit green uniform as he strode to the front. One hand held a clipboard, the other a tall stack of boarding passes. Anticipation grew as he stepped behind the podium and adjusted the microphone.

"Alright, men!" Sergeant Dardy bellowed into the mike. Speakers squealed at the volume, and the room instantly grew quiet. "When I call your name, step up to get your boarding pass and move out smartly through the door to my right."

Now that he had everyone's attention, his voice had taken its normal tone. The speakers still squealed. "Jump on any of the buses outside and they'll take you to Bien Hoa Air Base. Your flight back to the states on Flying Tiger Airlines will depart at thirteen-hundred hours."

I grinned. Back to the states. What beautiful words they were, absolute music to my ears.

A man of his word, the first name that Sergeant Dardy called was, "Moffett!"

I stood, grabbed the duffel by one strap and slung it over my shoulder. My heart was racing as I stepped the short distance to the podium. I grasped the boarding pass with one hand and clasped the other around the sergeant's, shaking it warmly.

"Thanks for everything, Sarge. I really appreciate it."

The stern army demeanor lifted for a brief second as Sarge grinned. "My pleasure, Moffett. Have a safe trip home."

The duffel slipped a little, and I had to release the handshake before the bag fell from my shoulder. I shrugged the weight until it settled securely on my back.

"I will, Sarge. And don't forget that this is going to be your last tour in 'Nam. If you re-up, you're really pushing your luck."

"Don't worry about me. Another year and some Jody back home is gonna be entertaining my woman. Ain't gonna let that happen." The sergeant's business-as-usual look reasserted itself, then was broken with a wink. "Hell, with my luck that Jody'll turn out to be you!"

"Never can tell what'll happen in a year," I said, stepping toward the door.

The thought of Jody, the army's fictitious bogeyman who would steal wife or girlfriend while the soldier was away at war, ran through my mind. I turned to face my friend one last time and—with a mischievous grin—asked, "Is she cute?"

"Wait a minute, soldier," Sergeant Dardy said as he picked up the clipboard and pretended to read. "What's your name again? I can't seem to find it on the passenger list."

I pushed the door open and tossed a wave over my shoulder. "Too late, man. I'm outta here!"

I stepped into the muggy sunshine and let the door slam behind me. Four fifty-passenger buses waited beside the street, their doors open and inviting. The drivers were smoking cigarettes in the shade of the first bus.

"Hey," I called as I stepped toward the group. "Which one has air conditioning?"

One of the drivers laughed. The nametag and rank identified the young man as Spec4 Foyt. He was still chuckling as he said, "They all do. Can't you see the windows are down?"

I flipped the boarding pass up, holding it as if it was an invitation to an exclusive party and the young specialist in charge was the bouncer at the door. The soldier nodded and motioned toward the first bus.

"Take any seat you want, Sergeant," Specialist Foyt said. "I'd recommend the one by the door. You get a breeze and don't have to smell everyone around you."

A gray portable radio sat on the black engine cover beside the driver. I could hear the Armed Forces Vietnam Network playing "Stoned Soul PIcnic" by The Fifth Dimension as I threw my duffel bag onto one of the overhead racks and took the seat opposite the driver.

An hour of the Army's hurry up and wait drill went by and the bus was already hot and muggy. It grew more so as soldier after soldier climbed in and claimed a seat. I glanced occasionally at my watch. The minutes continued to creep by, each one another closer to one o'clock and my plane ride home.

There were only enough seats for fifty passengers, and that didn't include one duffel bag per soldier. It was soon standing room only, with soldiers sitting on their duffels in the aisles. The moist hot air now carried with it the pungent odor of sweat and stale cigarettes. I was glad that Sergeant Dardy had called my name first, and that I had heeded the young Specialist's advice to take the front seat.

The mood was still jubilant. The only grumbling occurred when a soldier would apologetically announce he had to take a leak. The soldier's progress toward the front could then be measured by the muffled curses of soldiers moving themselves or their baggage out of the way. Finally the man would reach the door, disappear for a few minutes, and return. Then the process would start in reverse as he made his way back to his seat. An irritated voice finally called out, "Just whip it out the window!" and was greeted with cheers and applause. I didn't know whether anyone heeded the advice, but I did notice a decrease in the number of pissers who worked their way forward.

The drivers were milling around outside the buses when I saw Sgt. Dardy step out of the muster tent.

"Alright, move em out!" Dardy yelled to the drivers. Each of them quickly jumped on their respective buses.

The passengers cheered when the engine came to life, and Specialist Foyt gave a thumbs up.

"I hear that you guys want to go home. Is that right?" Foyt glanced up at the rear-view mirror and was rewarded with a roar. He shifted into gear and said, "Then I guess it's time we were on our way!"

I couldn't help the grin that spread across my face. It stayed there as I watched our little convoy make its way through the compound and past the machinegun turrets at the front gate. I had been on this route so many times in the past that it was second nature to me. Yet this time there was a difference, a sense of loss that I couldn't quite place. It wasn't just leaving the place I had called home for fourteen months, or leaving the fragile friendships that had developed and been nurtured in this strange, hostile environment. There was something else moving through me.

The smile slowly faded as we drove through the countryside. I watched the small huts and villages pass by like telephone poles, saw the Vietnamese workers and families disappear behind the convoy. They never once lifted their faces to see us, never once lifted a hand in farewell. It was as if to them, this was just another day. Same as the one before it, and the same as the one they would face tomorrow. Another busload of GIs going past had nothing to do with them, wasn't part of their world.

For a brief second I could almost sense how they might see me, if they chose to see me at all. Perhaps they saw me as a tourist or spectator. Here for a moment, perhaps to spend a little cash and throw a fine party. Then gone, leaving them behind to pick up the broken glasses and set the furniture aright.

Perhaps they saw me as a ghost, flitting briefly through their lives and bringing unwanted chaos and destruction. Or maybe they saw me as a traveler who had stopped for a moment to help them build something new and different with their lives. I preferred to believe the latter, but well I understood the saying about oriental faces being inscrutable. I was left wondering…if you could not read the face, how could one ever know what was going through their minds?

I would have been reassured had I known that I wasn't the first to have thought this way, nor would I be the last. These thoughts had crossed the minds of soldiers passing through foreign towns on their way home since America had first sent troops to fight in other nations' wars. From France in the war to end all wars, from pacific islands and Europe in World War II, from Seoul after the Korean War—in all these places and more, soldiers had viewed the devastation left behind and asked, did we help or harm? Did we do enough? Did we accomplish anything at all?

The answers from those distant battlefields would be the same ones spoken here in the midst of the jungle. Both yes, and no. Some of the people affected by the war would remember the soldiers with fondness, and others with bitter hatred. The Americans had done too much, or too little. They had built or destroyed a critical road or bridge or hospital—had saved or killed a family member. For each positive view that one person held, another could hold the opposite. And for each individual, their argument would be true.

Victory was never truly determined by battles won. It was determined by what was left behind when the guns had finally fallen silent and peace had started taking root. With Vietnam, perhaps the victory for American soldiers would be found in the strangest of places. Perhaps it would be in someplace like Jimmy Sullivan's orphanage. I didn't know. Time alone would tell.

A concrete structure came into view and slowly drifted past my window. The building was a French bunker built on the outskirts of Bien Hoa airbase. Tall grass surrounded it and the firing ports stood empty. It had long since been abandoned and was too far outside the perimeter to be included as part of the base's defenses. Mute and vacant, it was a reminder of other soldiers who had stood watch on this ground and a testament to what they had left behind. A structure without purpose or function in peace. The French had not found victory here.

Several more miles passed. The convoy was cleared through two checkpoints, and then the lead jeep was at the main gate to Bien Hoa airbase. I watched the Air Force security policeman at the gate wave us through, his partner holding a tight leash on the German Shepherd guard dog. It always impressed me to see the four-legged soldiers, especially after all the tales I had heard about the lives they had saved. War dogs had dragged wounded men out of firefights, sniffed out booby-traps and land mines before their handlers triggered them, and exposed saboteurs dressed in American uniforms. Their reward consisted of a scratch behind the ears and another bowl of rice which might contain something that approximated meat.

The bus weaved its way through the maze of single-story buildings. I glanced down at my watch. Twelve thirty-eight.

"Hey Sarge." I looked up at Foyt, followed the specialist's finger that pointed toward a large object in the distance. "Is that what you were wanting to see?"

There, shining in the midday sun, was a stretch DC-8. The silver fuselage gleamed, and through the glare I could barely make out the large red letters that spelled out Flying Tigers. Its tail was a deep blue, almost black, and carried the same name painted vertically in white. The ground crew were like ants scurrying below the four engines that hung beneath the wings. It was beautiful.

"There's your Freedom Bird, gentlemen," said Foyt. His statement was greeted with a rousing round of applause and cheers.

From the back of the bus, one of the guys yelled, "Hey man, I'm not short, I'm gone, baby!" and the applause and raucous yelling got even louder.

The bus had suddenly grown smaller, filled with buoyant jubilation. I grinned, then broke into laughter. The dark questions that had haunted me earlier were washed away by the joy I shared with those around me.

The bus came to an abrupt stop in front of the terminal and our driver leaned out the window to speak to one of the ground crew. Like a traffic cop, the crewman signaled with his arms and pointed directly toward the plane. Foyt steered the bus in that direction and his passengers erupted with boisterous yells and whistles.

Every soldier was standing, one hand clasped firmly on the straps of his duffel bag, when Foyt stopped the bus beside the stairs leading to the plane. He opened the door and a burly Air Force tech sergeant stepped up into the bus.

"Listen up!" The sergeant waited for the noise to die down. "This here is an eighty million dollar plane, and the pilots are nervous that Charlie might decide to use it for mortar practice. So here's what we're gonna do. Get your asses off the bus and on the plane, grab a seat and buckle in, don't be choosy 'bout which seat you plant yerself in, 'cause it's wheels up in ten minutes. Clear?"

"Clear!" It was yelled with one voice, and the tech sergeant backed out of the bus. I stepped forward immediately, dragging my duffel behind me. My boot hit the tarmac a shy second after the Air Force sergeant's, and then I was running toward the plane. I threw my duffel bag onto the conveyor leading to the baggage compartment and climbed the stairs. I was inside the aircraft before I ran out of breath.

It was like stepping into another world. There was a soft whisper of cool air sighing out of the overhead vents, and a gentle rumble of engine power from the floor. My eyes hadn't adjusted from the midday sun to the dim interior, but I didn't wait as I stumbled down the aisle. I found the first available window seat and sat down.

The tech sergeant be damned, there was something I had to do. I reached up and unscrewed the nozzle on the air conditioning vent, then closed my eyes as the frigid air blew into my face. It was like a cold and refreshing shower flowing over me, washing away the heat and humidity and grime of Vietnam. It was a touch of home, the first in a long time, and I bathed in it.

When the sweat had dried from my face, I leaned back in the seat. Even that was refreshing. A cushioned chair! Like a kid at Christmas, I flipped open the tray in front of me and let it drop down toward my lap, then put it back up and did it again. Only after I caught a sideways glance from one of the other soldiers walking past did I consider how I must look.

"Can't help it," I muttered to himself as I put the tray back into its upright position. "I'm going home!"

After that, I occupied my time by looking out the window and watching the buses unload. That soon became boring, so I alternated between glancing at my watch, adjusting the air vent, and watching the same amazed and joyful look appear on each soldier as they boarded the plane.

I had just glanced at my watch and was adjusting the seat belt when a voice spoke from beside me. "Well, if my eyes don't deceive me, I'd say that's Sergeant Moffett sitting by that window. Damn, Sarge! I thought you'd be back in New York having a beer by now."

I looked up to see the grinning face of Lonnie Anderson, one of the guys from the hooch. It was difficult to keep a straight face as I replied, "So did I. Had a little haircut problem with a nasty-ass Master Sergeant in Long Binh that sort of slowed me down."

"Now why doesn't that surprise me none?"

Part Irish, part American Indian from Arizona, Lonnie had dirty blonde hair, stood about six foot three, and weighed at least two hundred thirty pounds. In spite of his size, Lonnie had been one of the quieter GIs in the hooch. He had never gotten involved in the crazy antics that the rest of the guys had pulled. Mostly he had kept to himself. But there was something about his demeanor that had told everyone not to piss him off.

As Lonnie eased into the seat next to me, it made me feel good to know that the two of us would be making the trip home together. I waited until my friend was situated, then reached out and pulled the man into a bear hug. We slapped each other on the back like brothers who hadn't seen each other in years.

"Cutting it close, weren't you?" I asked as I felt the engines begin to rev. "Any later and you would've missed the plane."

"Nah. Long as that door was open, I had plenty of time." Lonnie motioned with his head toward the front. There was a slight pressure on the ears as the hatch closed, sealing Vietnam out of our lives.

The lights flickered as the aircraft was disconnected from the generator outside and took up the electrical burden with internal power. The engines began to whine faster, then shifted to a throaty roar. There was an abrupt lurch that tossed me toward the seat in front of me, and then the plane began slowly moving forward.

For a moment the sound of the engines was drowned out by an explosion of cheering and clapping. I watched the landscape move past my window as the plane taxied toward the runway.

The giant aircraft lurched forward again when it reached the runway and lined up for take-off. The intercom chimed, and a calm voice spoke. "Good afternoon, gentlemen. This is your captain. I would like to welcome you to Flying Tigers airlines."

I ignored the rest of the pilot's greeting as I watched a pair of F-4 Phantoms pass overhead. Their landing gear was down as they turned toward the opposite end of the runway. I followed the planes until they passed out of sight.

My mind returned to that day fourteen months ago when I had made this trip in reverse. I smiled, remembering the feeling over the long months that this day would never come. Yet here it was, and in just moments Vietnam would become only a collection of memories.

My reverie was broken by the scream of engines as both Phantoms flashed past my window. They were on the ground. I watched as they veered off the main runway in unison and taxied toward their hangars.

As if in reply, the four engines on the DC-8 screamed into full power. "Okay, boys, let's go home!" said the pilot.

There was another lurch, this time pushing me back into my seat as the pilot released the brakes. Acceleration and gravity grabbed me and held me back against the cushion as we rumbled forward, rapidly building up speed. My stomach flip-flopped for a moment when the ground dropped away below us. Then the wings bit into air and we were flying.

The applause and cheers began again once the plane was airborne. Lonnie and I joined in the celebration. Vietnam began falling behind us, and none of us would regret it if we never saw the country again.

Yet something made me look out the window. Perhaps it was the slow bank and turn of the airplane, or perhaps it was something else. I glanced down toward the buildings at the edge of the runway. With a start, I realized that I was looking at the hooch I had lived in for so many months.

Not all of the boys down there would make it home. I knew that, and there was a part of me that abruptly felt bad for cheering. I knew I shouldn't feel guilty. I had served my time, hadn't I? I deserved to go home, didn't I? Yet suddenly I felt a strong burden of guilt…as if I had escaped a death sentence and, in doing so, had abandoned my friends to take my place.

The war-torn country slowly fell away from me. Below at that very moment, I knew there were soldiers fighting in the jungle. Many of them would never get to see their own Freedom Bird, would never get to feel the joy all of us on this plane were feeling.

Some would be injured out there. They would lay in the mud as the battle raged around them. Boys, mostly. Young boys who would be terrified, uncertain whether it was safe to call out for help while their blood slowly drained away. The lucky ones might have a buddy nearby who could get to them and slap on a lifesaving pressure bandage. Or at the least, they would have someone there to hold their hand and tell bald-faced lies that everything was going to be alright.

And some of them would die alone.

Not all, I told himself. Many would be stabilized by medics, medevaced to a field hospital and eventually shipped by air ambulance to treatment centers outside the U.S. They might not get back stateside for months, but eventually many would make it home. I repeated it in my mind like a twisted version of Dorothy in Oz. Many would make it home.

But not all. I couldn't wipe away the image that formed in my mind. A pine box stacked atop another pine box, loaded by forklift into the belly of a cargo plane. That would be the bird which carried many of my brothers below back to the States. And home, what home for that soldier when the box was unloaded? A brief moment under the sky, the coffin with the stars and stripes draped carefully over it. A lone bugle sounding forlornly on a distant hill, and then nothing but the cold dark earth.

That was the way that many of those below me would find their way home.

"Penny for your thoughts, Moff."

I realized that tears were trickling down my face. I focused my thoughts on one thing. By fate or chance or guardian angels from above, I was a fortunate soldier. I had served my time, and I was going home.

"Just thinking," I replied to Lonnie. I scrubbed the tears from my face, then turned to face my friend. "I hope those kids will be okay."

Lonnie nodded, then turned his head. For a brief moment, I thought I saw companion tears on the soldier's face.

"This war is far from over. I hope they make it home safely." I turned back to the window, offering time and privacy to the soldier beside me.

"I was thinking the same thing." The giant Irish-Indian cleared his throat, paused, and then spoke in a stronger tone. "It's not like they're at a firebase somewhere. They'll be okay."

"Yeah. I know. It's pretty safe at the hooch."

"Uh-huh." There was a moment of silence, and then the giant's humor returned. "You know, if they don't use helicopters to run for pizza, or get involved in currency schemes, or impersonate officers to party in Saigon…they should be fine."

I turned back to face Lonnie and gladly took the bait. "Now what kind of idiot would do stuff like that, anyway?"

"Oh, let's see. Couldn't possibly be a sergeant I know who seemed determined to lose a few stripes and go directly to LBJ, now could it?"

"Long Binh Jail? Nobody in their right mind would want to visit there. I hear it's a hole."

Lonnie might not have participated in the crazy schemes thought up by the guys in the hooch, but he knew that I had. Smiles returned as the bantering began. Laughter came shortly afterwards.

It soon became apparent that other entertainment would be minimal on the flight. The pilot had announced that our first stop would be Yokota Air Base near Tokyo, with a flight time of eight hours.

The gleaming silver Freedom Bird slowly began to lose its luster. It was actually a DC-8 cargo plane that had been retrofitted with just the basics for passenger use. The drink choices were coffee, juice or milk, and there were no movies. Unless one wanted to watch the clouds float by outside, or to ogle the few cute stewardesses walking up and down the aisle, then there were two choices. Talk, or sleep.

Lonnie and I opted to talk. The hours passed quickly as we razzed each other about things we had done. It turned out that Lonnie hadn't been above a prank or two during basic training, like the shoe polish placed inside the brim of the drill sergeant's hat or placing the Captain's bars sideways on his ball cap. They were relatively harmless things, yet the bunkmate who had snitched on him had made Lonnie very leery of participating in the shenanigans done by the guys in the hooch.

The punishments during basic training had been severe. They had kindled an anger for the service that, after a year in Vietnam, now bordered on barely concealed disdain. His time in country had made him hard, and his dislike for authority had only grown.

"I put in my time, Moff. Did my bit for God and country, and now I'm going home." Lonnie looked away, motioned to one of the stewardesses. "The minute we walk out the gate in Oakland won't be a minute too soon."

"Amen to that, brother."

Lonnie grew quiet after that, as if he had opened up too much. The stewardess arrived and my companion ordered more coffee. I asked for orange juice, and we both sat in silence and waited for our drinks.

I turned away and gazed out the window, leaving Lonnie with his own thoughts. The world outside had changed during the hours we had talked. Earlier there had been nothing below us except the vast expanse of the blue Pacific ocean. Now, instead of water, it seemed as if a crimson landscape of clouds had appeared. There were hills and valleys that extended across the horizon, all bathed in the red fire of the setting sun.

It was beautiful, magnificent, breathtaking. Most of all it was peaceful, leaving me with a sense of being in transition. Behind me lay Vietnam with its wooden huts, mud streets, war-torn jungles, disease and poverty. Before me lay the States, with electricity in every room, flush toilets, modern conveniences and technology. For the moment, though, I was in neither. It felt as if I had stepped outside of time and place and floated with angel wings above the earth.

I didn't know how long I sat there watching the sun slowly sink below the horizon. It was a mindless, unthinking period. I had been caught up in nature's wonder and didn't even realize time passed.

A shiver went through me, and I became aware again. The sun had fallen below the clouds, casting the world in darkness. Cold air had started to seep into the plane, and my feeling of peace and comfort had faded. Outside had become a void, an empty blackness that left me with the sensation of falling.

I pulled the window shade, sealing the cold emptiness outside. My orange juice had arrived without me realizing it; Lonnie had lowered the serving tray and left it for me. The seat beside me was empty.

I sipped the juice slowly, savoring the way that the ice felt on my tongue. Funny, the little things that one could miss without even realizing it. Ice cubes. Something that you could just pull from the fridge, pop out of the tray, and drop into your drink.

The orange juice was almost gone when pressure started to build in my ears. I knew we were descending even before the pilot spoke over the intercom that we would be landing at Yokota soon. Lonnie came back to his seat and buckled in. The attentive stewardesses worked their way through the cabin, collecting trash and checking on seatbelts and stowed trays.

The landing was uneventful, and we welcomed the chance to get off the plane and stretch. The bar in the terminal was closed, but the snack bar offered sandwiches and sodas. There wasn't enough time to order anything from the grill. Too many soldiers in line, and the first boarding call had been announced by the time Lonnie and I had made our way to the counter and ordered. It was a quick meal, hastily chewed and swallowed, and then we headed back to the plane.

Plane and passengers had been refueled, and my fellow soldiers had regained some of the energy and jubilation they had shown after boarding at Bien Hoa. It dissipated quickly after the plane had taken off and reached altitude. The pilot announced that it would be eight hours to Anchorage, Alaska, and had turned off the cabin lights to let the soldiers sleep.

Lonnie had no difficulty drifting straight into sleep, but I was too restless. I listened to the constant thrumming of the engines, the whisper of air from the vents, and whispered voices nearby. A stewardess, noticing I was awake, delivered several cups of coffee at my request.

It didn't take long for the liquid to work its way through my system. I stood and worked my way quietly past Lonnie without waking him. The plane made it difficult to walk as it swayed back and forth, and occasionally up and down.

When I reached the front of the plane, there was already a line for the toilet. One young private pounded on the door. "Hey buddy," he was saying. "You don't have to burn this honey pot. Just jiggle the handle and it flushes!"

The pilot announced that we were climbing to get out of some turbulence. I took my turn and after a bumpy ride that nearly tossed me off the seat, surrendered the toilet to the next in line.

The plane continued bouncing as I walked down the aisle. Its unpredictable motion left my stomach doing flip-flops every time the aircraft dropped or rose. An abrupt sideways lurch left me grabbing for anything to hold onto. I was only too glad to reach my seat.

The vibrations in the plane slowly stole the energy from me. Without realizing when it happened, I fell asleep. I woke many hours later to the pilot's announcement that we were making the final descent for landing at Anchorage.

I raised the shade and looked out the window. Stars glittered in the night sky, and far below us I could see warm yellow lights twinkling from houses and street lights. The journey continued in darkness, yet for a moment heaven and earth blended. It seemed as if I was floating in a sea of sparkling diamonds, each a beacon of hope for a new dawn and home.

My thoughts were interrupted by the whine and thump of landing gear unfolding. Lights on the ground grew brighter, and soon I could make out individual streets and occasional buildings in the city. The plane leaned on its side and I could see the lights of the airport below me. Then it leaned again as the pilot lined up with the runway.

Wheels hit the tarmac and the engines screamed as the plane quickly lost speed. Buildings flew by my window at a rapid pace, and then slower until finally the world outside solidified. A short taxi to the fuel trucks waiting at the edge of the runway, and then the pilot announced that we were free to disembark the aircraft.

June in Anchorage sounds pretty comfortable, but it was four in the morning and forty degrees outside when the plane arrived. The terminal stood two hundred yards from where the plane refueled, and all of us were clad in nylon jungle fatigues. Gear made for extreme heat not the pre-dawn chill of an Alaskan morning. For us the temperature felt like it was below zero.

Even though the cold was penetrating, it had been eight hours on the plane since the passengers had walked on firm ground. Some soldiers milled around at the base of the stairs leading from the plane, laughing and joking. Lonnie and I decided to join the group who made a dash for the terminal in the hopes of finding hot coffee.

The heater in the small terminal and control tower building was working. Thankfully, the snack bar was open. The troops nursed coffee to keep their hands warm while some smoked their cigarettes. We all talked about the subject foremost on our minds…what we were going to do first after becoming a civilian again. It was a conversation that had been well-rehearsed during our time in Vietnam, and ranged from getting drunk to getting married and everything in-between. The soldiers teased and joked with each other, often providing suggestions for improvement on the idea or good-natured ribbing about why a soldier wouldn't be able to accomplish the task he had set for himself.

It was a similar camaraderie that I had felt with the guys from the hooch, and it surprised me. Sure, we had the fact that we were all soldiers from units in Vietnam, yet there was a brotherhood which seemed to surpass that common trait. Perhaps it was because we had all served, all been in the same war, eaten the same army chow and tasted the same mud.

A memory rose in my mind, perhaps a poem I had read or something I had heard. I couldn't recall who had said it, but while standing there in the early morning hours talking with men I had never known, I understood what the words truly meant. We few, we happy

few, we band of brothers. I didn't know why that thought had aris-
en, couldn't put my finger on it—but it rang true, and I knew that
I was going to miss it.

A private arrived then with the message that the ground crew
had finished refueling the plane and that they were ready to board.
I placed my thoughts on hold as the group made our wild dash back
to the aircraft, all laughing and joking despite the chill air.

I was buckled in and the plane taxiing toward the runway
before my thoughts returned to their previous track. The image of
the friends I had known in the civilian world, when I had worked
for the shipping industry, came to mind. I had thought myself close
to many of them, yet now I saw that those friends would never be
able to touch the unbreakable bond that had formed with soldiers
I had known.

We band of brothers. Brothers were family, and perhaps that was
the difference. I had lived with the guys from the hooch, and we had
been around each other almost every hour of every day. The most
intimate hopes and darkest fears, who snored and who talked in
their sleep… all of those things and more had become a part of my
life. I knew more about the guys I had served with than I would
ever know about my friends back stateside. We had become family.

It wasn't something that could be experienced in the civilian
world. There, one's friends were made during the eight-hour day
and most were forgotten upon going home. I had friends waiting for
me back in New York, but I was leaving part of my family behind.
It was a precious realization and—while it saddened me to think of
leaving them behind now—I knew that if I ran into one of the guys
from the hooch sometime in the years to come, we would greet
each other as if time had not passed.

Once again the plane rose from the ground surrounded by
darkness. It banked toward the southeast as it gained altitude and
then leveled off. I immediately sensed a difference in the atmosphere of the cabin. I looked around and listened, trying to discover what had changed that would account for the increased energy
and activity.

During the flight from Yokota, the cabin had grown cold. It had
been as if the frigid darkness outside had somehow seeped into the

plane and infected the passengers. We had grown quiet then, isolated in our own thoughts. Some had reached for blankets to fight off the chill, and others had distracted themselves from the lonely dark by engaging those beside them in conversation.

Yet this time there seemed to be something different about the flight. Perhaps it was the hot coffee from the terminal that kept it at bay, or the jokes and laughter we had shared with the other soldiers there. It could have been the pilot's announcement that the last stop on our journey home was Travis Air Force Base near Sacramento, California. Whatever the reason, it was obvious that the plane was alive again, as it had been when the soldiers had first boarded at Bien Hoa.

I smiled to myself and turned to gaze out the window. In the distance, the far horizon was beginning to glow with the first touch of dawn.

WELCOME HOME

The last leg of the journey was completed in daylight. Warm sunshine pouring through the windows seemed to renew everyone's spirits and banish all but one final underlying tension. There remained a concern, a fear almost, in the soldiers' minds as we drew closer to Sacramento. I was not the only soldier without immunity to it.

We had been in Vietnam, separated from family and friends, fighting the country's war against an opponent who could be brutal, heartless and cruel. Sometimes the battles had not been for any grand ideal...had not been for country, or defending freedom, or fighting communism. Many times it was simply a struggle for survival, of one man shooting madly into the jungle in order to kill the man at the edge of the tree line who was trying to kill him.

There were a few soldiers on the plane who were lifers, determined to make the military a career. Others had volunteered from a sense of duty or patriotism. Most had been drafted, yanked out of their homes and jobs by a random lottery of numbers. Some didn't care about the war, others opposed it...but we had all reported for training, and had all served our time on a foreign shore.

We knew about the discord at home. When it was available, we had devoured stateside media...newspapers and magazines, radio, even television. We had seen the stories and pictures about crowds protesting the war, students demonstrating at colleges who burned flags and spat on the soldiers who had survived their tour and wanted nothing more than to be welcomed home.

I had read the latest Time magazine cover story. Its caption had announced in bold letters, "The Military Under Attack." It had featured pictures of demonstrators holding signs which said, "Bring the GIs Home NOW," "Since Talks Began, 10,000 Dead," "One Million Vietnamese Dead. Stop This Genocide NOW."

One small section of the story had hit me especially hard. "For those about to become Viet vets," it read, "homecoming promises to be quiet. Unlike my World War II counterpart… an alumnus of the inconclusive Vietnam War can expect little more than a grateful welcome from his family, an occasional harangue from a college cousin, and a few questions or silence from everyone else."

The shadowy question and fear that floated in the cabin was what to expect when we stepped off the plane. Would there be flags waving, a band playing… or would there be an angry mob chanting insults? One was what all of us soldiers hoped for, yet feared would be absent; the other was what we feared would be waiting for us and hoped would be absent.

But the greatest fear of all was that we would simply be ignored, that there would nobody there to greet us at all. Our sacrifice—if nothing else, the simple fact that we had survived—would go unnoticed.

Like the Vietnamese villagers, I thought. Would the American people also refuse to raise their heads to acknowledge the soldiers on the buses as we went by? Would they grant the troops nothing more than the status of ghosts? To be praised or ridiculed, that was one thing…but to be completely ignored, that was a painful fear to consider.

After nearly twenty hours of flying, the jet's engines started to slow over Sacramento. The pilot spoke over the intercom, voicing the announcement that we had all been waiting for. "Good morning, men. We'll be landing at Travis Air Force Base in about thirty minutes."

He explained that buses would take the soldiers to Customs and on to the military separation center. Then he cleared his throat and continued, "Let me be the first to say 'Welcome home and thanks for serving our country.'"

It helped to chip away a tiny piece of the fear, but not enough. Lonnie voiced aloud what the majority of us had been thinking. "Don't get too hyped up on this 'welcome home' stuff, Sarge. Except for our families, there's nobody down there who likes us. We might as well get used to abuse."

"Thanks, Lonnie, for those words of encouragement." I grinned to let the giant beside me know that I was just teasing. "The happiest day of my life, and it's gonna end with a terrible let-down."

Lonnie shook his head. "Hell, it ain't that bad, not by a long shot. Way I look at it, this is the best day of my life. No more brass yanking my chain...now that's something to really look forward to."

"You hate it that bad?"

The burly man looked over at the cup of coffee resting on the folding tray, then glanced sideways at me. "Time to lay off the lifer juice, man. It's starting to get to you. Next thing you know, you'll be telling me that you want to re-up or something."

"Are you nuts? Me, a lifer? Get real." I made a game of reaching for my coffee, grabbing my wrist with my other hand and pulling it back. I shook my head. "I've had enough of this man's army."

"Then you know why it don't matter to me if every Playboy bunny is waiting to greet us when we hit dirtside. They ain't gonna hand me my discharge papers, and that's the only thing that matters."

"And what're you going to do about the protesters? You saying they don't matter either?"

"Nope. Don't mean a thing." Lonnie tugged at his shirt. "We'll be out of uniform soon enough. Just let your hair grow long, and no one will ever care where we've been."

"Like they care now." The words carried a bitterness to them that I hadn't even been aware was inside me. I had verbalized the fear, taking it a step closer to becoming real.

Yet something within me fought it. The fear that others would mock or ignore me—what anyone thought of me—had never truly mattered before. It went against the core of who I was. I had always taken everyone at face value, had always looked for the best in people. Even in the worst of situations, people could pleasantly surprise you.

I made a decision. Unless I was confronted with a difficult situation, I wasn't going to go looking for trouble. Always waiting for someone to say something derogatory, always being on the defensive... that was no way to live life. If it happened, it happened. Until then, the world was still a terrific place full of many wonderful people.

"Excuse me, sir?" My train of thought was interrupted by a beautiful young stewardess. She motioned toward my cup. "We'll be landing soon. Are you finished with that?"

I downed the remnants of coffee and handed her the cup. Before she could say it, I put my tray up and shifted my seat into its upright position. She thanked me politely before moving on to prepare the other passengers for landing.

The big DC-8 landed smoothly at Travis on a typical sunny California morning. The soldiers were standing, ready to disembark, before the front exit had even been opened. Lonnie and I led the mass of impatient soldiers down the stairs.

My first act upon clearing the stairwell was to keep a vow I had made months before. I knelt and kissed the hard airport ground. It was done with such exuberance that I cut my upper lip, a small price to pay for such a feeling of joy to be home again.

The Customs inspectors were waiting for us. Yet it wasn't a case of first come, first served—this was the army, and military tradition had to be maintained. The soldiers were told to form a mass formation. Then the front rank stepped forward with their duffel bags, opened them and went through the tedious process of inspection.

I made it quickly through Customs and started stuffing all of my gear back into the duffel bag. Beside me I heard the inspector ask a soldier, "Do you have anything to declare?"

"I declare I'm HOME!" the man responded enthusiastically.

The inspector's smile was plastic, as if he had heard the response a million times before. He motioned toward the soldier's duffel bag. "Yes you are, son. Now if you would please empty out your bag onto the table…?"

I sealed my bag, shrugged it over my shoulder, and started walking toward the waiting line of buses. I couldn't help smiling. Maybe it was the California air rich with the scent of summer, or the manicured lawns, or the dress-right-dress permanence of the buildings. I didn't know what it was, but the air base had nothing in common with Bien Hoa.

Then it came to me. There was no foreboding sense of fear here, like what I had grown acclimated to in Vietnam. Airmen walked in the open without concern of snipers. The aircraft were parked in neat rows, never having been targets of mortars or rockets. The base was free and open, and it was exhilarating.

I climbed onto the bus. The smile never left my face as I waited patiently for everyone to clear Customs. The inspectors were quick and efficient, and soon the buses were heading for the Oakland Army Base where the soldiers would officially regain the wonderful rank of civilian.

The reception station at Oakland seemed designed to remind everyone how the army viewed us. We were non-entities, things, walking pieces of meat with a number to identify us. We were separated into groups by the first initial of our last name, and constantly reminded to remain with our group. The calls of "Next!" from bored civilians soon grew monotonous, and then gradually irritating.

It took twenty-four hours for me to work my way through the maze of offices and lines and questions. I was immunized against every disease that could be contracted from the jungle; many of the vaccinations were duplicates of ones I had received only weeks before. There were mountains of forms to complete, and even fitting for new uniforms regardless of the fact that I'd be getting into civvies at the first opportunity. I had my last army chow consisting of steak chased down with the traditional army drink of choice... Kool-Aid. Somehow I managed to get through it all with barely two hours of sleep.

I was working my way through the final outprocessing stations to receive pay, my plane ticket, and my discharge papers. A familiar voice called out to me; I turned as Lonnie joined me in line.

"You're looking sharp," I commented as we stepped to the next station. It had been a long day with only catnaps for sleep, and I could tell that the tall soldier beside me was running out of patience.

"Yeah, haven't been in dress greens since we went on R&R what, six months ago?"

"Well, that was the last official R&R," I agreed, laughing. There were other trips I had taken that hadn't been sanctioned, but Lonnie didn't join us on our escapades to Saigon.

I handed the Specialist behind the desk a copy of my orders, then waited patiently for the man to rummage through a large filing cabinet to find my plane ticket.

"Here you are, Sergeant," the Specialist said, pushing an envelope toward me with one hand and a clipboard with the other. "Tickets from San Francisco International to New York City. Just sign here, please."

I signed, picked up the tickets and moved forward for my last time to draw pay in the army way. I saluted the pay officer who sat behind the desk and extended another copy of my orders. "Sir, Sergeant Moffett reporting for pay!"

"At ease, Sergeant." The captain glanced at the orders, turned to pull money from the safe beside him, and counted out the cash onto the table. The guard behind the pay officer stared at me with disinterest, the loaded forty-five caliber pistol holstered at his side a quiet reminder that soldiers should only take what they were owed.

I picked up the money and placed it in my wallet as I stepped to the final station. I presented another copy of my orders, and the civilian behind the desk handed me a large white packet.

"This is your DD form two-fourteen, Sergeant, showing your term of service and date of discharge. Please confirm that the dates on it are correct."

I glanced at the document, verified the dates, and nodded. "Looks right to me."

The civilian spoke in an emotionless voice, as if he had memorized his speech. "I'm to remind you that you are still on active duty until your arrival at home station and expiration of the date on your orders. Please conduct yourself accordingly by remaining in uniform and comporting yourself as befits a soldier of the United States Army. Thank you from a grateful nation. Next, please."

I waited for Lonnie, who grinned like a kid at Christmas when he received his discharge papers. I watched the smile slowly fade, replaced by an angry look at the civilian's rote speech. Before the burly man could respond, I stepped in. "So, are you heading to San Francisco International?"

Lonnie clenched his jaw, then let me lead him away from the final outprocessing station and toward the door. "Yeah. You?"

"Same. Want to share a cab to the airport?"

"Sure thing."

It was always a bad sign when Lonnie spoke in monosyllables. He had been looking forward to receiving his discharge papers and immediately becoming a civilian. His orders had him in travel status for two days, and now he had to stay in uniform until he got off the plane in Phoenix.

We walked the short distance to the cab stand where a long line of yellow and white checkered cabs were waiting. The driver of the first cab opened the trunk, and we threw our duffel bags into it.

"Hey, are you guys going to the airport?"

I turned to face the owner of the strange voice. It belonged to an Army captain who marched toward us.

"Yes, sir!" exclaimed Lonnie with an enthusiasm that meant, "and not one second too soon!"

Perhaps the officer only saw an opportunity to split the cab fare with us. I would never know. Without another word, the captain threw his duffel on top of ours, then pulled open the taxi's back door and made a move to jump in ahead of us.

That was too much for Lonnie. He had tolerated a day of regimented bureaucracy at the outprocessing station, with only the expectation of receiving his discharge to keep him from losing his temper. He might still be in uniform, but as far as he was concerned he was out of the Army. There was no need to put up with it anymore.

Lonnie picked up the officer's bag and flung it onto the sidewalk. As he slammed the trunk, the burly soldier yelled, "I said we were going to the airport. I didn't say anything about you coming with us!"

The officer pulled his foot out of the cab and looked at us, total disbelief written all over his face.

If the captain had offered to share the tab, then I would've invited him along. There was nothing else to do, now that Lonnie had issued his challenge. It simply wasn't wise to piss off someone that big, and I didn't want to have to pull him off the officer.

We didn't wait to see what would happen next. We jumped into the taxi and told the driver to step on it. As the cab sped away, I looked back. I compared the shocked look on the officer's face to Lonnie's satisfied smirk.

"It's a good thing we've already been discharged," I commented. "Otherwise we'd be headed for the stockade instead of the airport."

Lonnie wasn't contrite in the least. "Served him right, the pushy bastard. Just who in the hell does he think he is, anyway?"

The cab cleared the front gate without any military police show-ing up in pursuit, and I began to laugh.

"What's so funny?" Lonnie was definitely still defensive.

"You."

"What do you mean?" His question carried a Doberman-like warning tone.

"Took you awhile, Lonnie, but I'm glad to see that you finally joined the guys from the hooch. Just wait until I tell Brunetti about this one!"

It took a moment for the tall man to see the humor in the situ-ation, and then he joined in the laughter. The cab driver kept glanc-ing up at his rearview mirror as if he had two maniacs in the back, but we didn't care. We were free of the rules and regulations, and Lonnie had given a parting shot to the authorities that was classic.

We arrived at what should have been a teeming San Francisco International airport about eight in the evening. It was deserted. A helpful skycap filled us in. "Air traffic controllers' strike in thirty minutes."

Only one flight was leaving before the strike. As chance would have it, it was Lonnie's Air West flight to Phoenix. We shook hands, then wrapped each other in a bear hug. I watched as the big man walked toward the boarding gate. A final wave farewell, and then I was alone.

My flight had been cancelled. The last tie to the brotherhood that had grown in Vietnam had just passed out of my life. What a welcome home, I thought, starting to feel sorry for myself.

The misery only deepened. I learned that all hotels at the airport were full. Even downtown San Francisco was booked solid. The chairs in the waiting area weren't the most comfortable beds, but I had spent nights in worse places.

Or so I thought, until they started turning lights off and closing the airport. I slung my duffel bag over my shoulder and walked through the exit. I dropped the bag at the curb and sat on it, no clue what to do next.

A taxi pulled up and the driver rolled down the passenger win-dow. "Hey, soldier, you need a place to stay tonight?"

Sure, I thought. Go to some cheap joint and get rolled for my take-home pay. Or I could sleep on the concrete here and wait for who knows how long until the planes were flying again. Not the greatest of options. Then again, I had survived fourteen months in Vietnam, so I took a chance. "Yeah. Got any suggestions?"

"I know a small motel in San Rafael," the cabby replied. "It's clean, safe and cheap."

I grinned, stood and grabbed my duffel. After Vietnam, those three words sounded pretty good. "Okay, let's go."

It turned out that the cabby was a chatty kind of guy, which was a good thing. Otherwise I would've been asleep five minutes into the ride. The driver never asked if I had just come back from Vietnam, and he never mentioned anything about the war. Instead he talked about what had been happening in the local and national news. He was a fount of information, chatting about everything from a possible war between the Chinese and the Soviets to America putting a man on the moon sometime in the next month.

Part of my mind listened to the cabby while the other took in my surroundings. There was still a surrealistic sense to being out of the jungle and back stateside. The night sky was a black bowl overhead, the stars drowned out by the glow of San Francisco. The street lights and tall buildings were a sparkling panorama, and I couldn't completely believe that it was real.

The sensation of it all being a dream slowly faded as we crossed over the Golden Gate Bridge and left the city behind us. An hour later, the cabby pulled to a stop in front of the motel entrance.

"Listen," the driver said as I climbed out of the cab. "There's a fair chance the President may step in and force the controllers to go back to work. There's been some talk about it."

I pulled the duffel bag from the back seat and then leaned back in the window, listening. I could tell—contrary to what I had been led to expect of the civilian population toward Vietnam veterans—that the cabby was really trying to help.

"If that happens, there's no use for you to be sitting in San Rafael." The driver pulled the brim of his cap back, showing more of his face. "So, how about this. If word comes through tonight, I'll show up at the motel at eight tomorrow morning and blow my horn. This motel has no phones, so be ready. You don't want to miss the morning flight out."

I nodded. "Don't worry. I'll listen for the horn and be ready."

"If the strike is still on then I won't be seeing you, so good luck." With that, the cabby waved and drove away.

I turned to face my home for the night. The driver had been right about the motel, there was nothing fancy about it. It was a two-story building laid out as a large "U," with parking spaces in front of each room on the first floor. The exterior was in dire need of a new coat of paint and there were a few bricks missing from the walls. Several letters were dark on the neon sign by the street, but the word "vacancy" glowed invitingly.

I stepped into the lobby. It was small and sparsely furnished, with a cigarette vending machine and a water fountain on one side, and the interior stairwell on the other. The night clerk was awake watching the black and white television that rested on the counter.

We negotiated briefly on the price of a single bed for one night, decided thirty dollars would be fair, and I received my room key. I stepped up the stairs and walked the short distance from the lobby to the room. I had no great expectations, just the hope that the sheets were clean and the shower worked.

The room was a pleasant surprise. It was a decent place with shag carpeting, a dresser and two nightstands, and a queen-sized bed that seemed to call seductively to me. After the hooch, twenty hours on a plane, and the endless lines at the military separation center, it seemed like a palace.

I closed and locked the door, dropped the duffel by the nightstand and flopped backwards onto the bed. It was magnificently soft, and I mentally debated with myself whether to just get undressed and climb beneath the sheets or to get up and shower first.

Then my stomach rumbled. It had been only six hours since it had last been fed, so the rest of my body attempted to ignore it. Then it rumbled again, with insistence. I swore softly to myself; my stomach was still on Vietnam time, and thought it needed breakfast. With a groan I got up and wandered back to the lobby to ask the desk clerk for a decent place to eat within walking distance.

"Well, there's not a lot of choices." The clerk glanced at his watch, then shook his head. "There's actually only one place open, the Northern Inn. But it's good. Very good."

The man leaned over the counter and pointed down the street. "See the road out front? Just follow it for about a quarter mile. You'll see a path coming from the right. That leads straight to the restaurant."

The California night air was warm, but to one acclimated to jungle humidity it actually felt chilly. I was glad for the wool Class-A jacket as I followed the desk clerk's directions. It was an easy walk, but once I had found the place then I began having second thoughts.

The parking lot was full. Most of the vehicles bore elite hood ornaments like the Rolls Royce, Mercedes, Cadillac, and other expensive cars. I peered into the giant picture window that faced the parking lot, then shook my head.

Everyone in the dining room was dressed in formal attire. The women wore long gowns with diamonds and pearls. The men sported tuxedos. I looked sadly down at my own uniform. True, they were dress greens appropriate for formal military dinners, but they didn't exactly match the dress code of those dining inside. And what would happen when a Vietnam vet wandered into their little soiree?

The last thing I needed was a bunch of raised eyebrows turning toward my uniform and me. I shrugged my shoulders and started to head back to the motel. Perhaps there was a vending machine with peanut butter crackers.

As I turned away, a well-dressed man hurried toward me. "Excuse me, sir," he said, smiling. "I'm Michael, the Maitre d'. May I help you?"

"No thanks," I replied, trying not to show my disappointment. "I'm not properly dressed for your restaurant."

I gave a half-salute and began walking away.

"Wait a minute! Are you just coming back from Vietnam?"

The shadowy question and fear from the flight, of what to expect from the civilian population, had returned. I had kept it at bay with my decision to see the best in people and not be afraid of what they thought...but I found that I was afraid after all. Would the man behind me respond with praise, or with disdain, or simply turn away and ignore me as if I was a ghost unworthy of being noticed?

The reply was said neutrally as I turned to face the maitre d'. "Yes, I am."

"Well," the man said, smiling again and holding out his arm, "as far as I can see, you're dressed fine. Come on in."

I hesitated, as if waiting for the punch line of a cruel joke. Yet the man's smile never wavered, and his gesture toward the restaurant door seemed genuine. Neither he nor the cab driver had actually said welcome home, but that was the warm message they sent. I stepped forward.

The maitre d' led me to the front door, opened it and said, "Have a good evening, sir. Why don't you have a drink at the bar, and I'll hold the next open table for you."

I stepped through the doorway and looked around. It was a typical roadhouse design, very nicely done—a bar and lounge area at the front, the restaurant beckoning beyond. One highball, I told myself as I stepped toward the bar. One highball, and then dinner. Just like old times. My first real step back into civilian life.

Most of the barstools were taken, but I found an empty one next to two elderly ladies. They obviously belonged to the Cadillac society I had seen inside. Both wore mink stoles, and they both had layers of pearls around their necks. Diamond bracelets and rings completed the ensemble. At least if they ignored me, it would have nothing to do with the war zone I had just left or the uniform I was wearing. Treating me as if I was invisible would come from a far older cultural bias. I was comfortable as I ordered a martini.

It came as a shock when the feather-light hand touched my arm. I turned to see both ladies looking at me. They introduced themselves as Elsie and Sarah and asked the traditional questions of what's my name and where was I from; then they asked the dreaded question. Was I coming back from Vietnam?

Once again the fear tried to take form, but the warm greeting and sincere words from the two women quickly banished it. We began to talk. It was tentative at first, as if they were afraid to touch on any subject that might be sensitive or cause me any harm. Then it grew stronger as I answered their questions honestly and on occasion with straightforward bluntness. They asked about Vietnam, and were truly interested in what I had to say about the country and its people. There were problems in that country, all three of us agreed, just as there were problems that the war raised in the States.

The two women may have been gray-haired, but they were sharp and funny. As the evening progressed and I sipped my way through my martini, we told stories and laughed at each other's jokes. There was a warmth and comfort that surrounded us, and I began to feel at home.

The conversation grew somber as I ordered my second drink and the ladies started reminiscing about World War II. There had been no class distinctions in that war compared to Vietnam, no attempts by families who could afford college keeping their sons safe from the battlefield by sending them to school instead. The burden of war had been shared by all families, rich and poor. The joy or heartache of homecoming had been shared as well.

It was obvious to me that the two were lifetime friends. They shared many things in common with the other. One of those was that both knew firsthand the true sadness of war. Each had lost a son in the Pacific.

The ladies expressed their opinions of how the Vietnam soldiers were being treated when they returned home, and that was the only time there was anger in their voices. They talked about how their sons would've felt to have come home and then been treated that way, ignored or insulted about their service to the country. It was an insult to every soldier who had worn a uniform… and it was an insult to their sons. They would have none of it. So when I had sat down beside them looking lost and concerned, they had known what they had to do.

They welcomed me home. It was a long, pleasant evening, but I never did make it to the dining room. As I raised the glass to finish off my third martini, the olive bounced off my nose and then my head bounced off the bar. Jet lag, lack of sleep, and alcohol on an empty stomach had all decided to meet inside my head at the same moment.

The next thing I heard was a car horn blowing. "Shut up!" I grumbled, gingerly placing a soothing hand to my pounding head. There was a moment of disorientation as I wondered why someone was honking their horn outside the hooch.

I opened my eyes and looked around. I was still in uniform, sprawled across a large bed. My brain started to clear and the past days came into focus. This wasn't Vietnam, it was the motel in San Rafael and I was still intact after passing out at the bar. But how did I get here?

The horn kept blowing. It was a constant irritant, a reminder of something. What was I supposed to remember about a car horn? Finally the answer came through the hangover haze. That was the cab, which meant the controller's strike was over. Planes were flying and I could go home!

Grabbing my hat and duffel bag, I fairly flew downstairs to the front desk. I placed the key on the counter and rang the bell to call the desk clerk from the back office. The horn blared outside again; I leaned briefly out the door, motioning to the cab driver that I would be right out.

I turned and walked back to the front desk. The man behind the counter picked up the key, noted the room number, and began preparing a receipt. It wasn't the same man who had negotiated the room rate last night.

Two negative thoughts ran through my mind as I reached into my pocket. The first was whether the night clerk had mentioned the negotiated rate to his shift replacement. The second was whether I had made it back to the room with anything left in my wallet.

I opened my billfold and counted the money, then counted it again. Not a dime missing. There were the same number of bills as had been there when I had walked into the restaurant. It didn't make any sense.

"Were you on duty last night?" I asked the desk clerk.

The man grinned. "Oh yeah, I was here."

"Did you see me come in?"

"Sure did." The grin turned into a laugh.

I was confused, both by the money that should've been used to pay for my bar bill and by the desk clerk's odd behavior. "What's so funny?"

"Well," he said, trying to suppress his laughter, "About one in the morning, this nineteen forty something Rolls Royce pulled up outside." A chauffeur—this was one sharp-dressed dude, gloves and all—well, he got out and walked around the car. He opened the back door and that's when you came tumbling out."

The man used his hands, pantomiming the action. "That driver was something else. He just snagged you—right before you would've hit the ground—and threw you over his shoulder."

"Then," he added, still chuckling, "these two little old ladies got out wearing the fanciest get-ups I've seen around here in a long time. One was holding your hat, and the other had your jacket. They said you'd had 'a little too much to drink' and they wanted to make sure you got to your room okay."

"Then what happened?"

"Well, I let them into your room with the master key. I watched while they put your jacket on you. It was like you were dancing." The clerk laughed again, either at the memory or the bewildered look on my face. "The chauffeur held you up by the armpits while the women put you back into uniform. Then they gently laid you across the bed."

The man shook his head in amazement, still chuckling softly as he finished the story. "We came back downstairs, chatted for a bit. Then they got into their Rolls and left."

I ran the events of the previous evening through my mind. I realized there was something missing. "Did they leave their names by any chance?"

"Nope. Just said to tell you good luck and that they were real proud of you." The desk clerk extended the receipt. "Oh yeah, one more thing. They paid your motel bill."

The cab driver picked that moment to lay on the horn again, pausing only to motion madly at his watch. I snagged the receipt and thanked the clerk, then grabbed my duffel bag and headed out the door.

"You're cutting it close," the driver said as I slipped into the back seat, "but I'll get you there in time."

The man was true to his word. We made it to the airport with fifteen minutes to spare. I thanked him and gave a twenty dollar tip, and then I rushed to catch my flight. A short delay to check my baggage and claim my boarding pass, and then I was on the plane and seated once again by a window.

As the plane rose into the air and banked to show me the Golden Gate Bridge below, I had time to consider the events of the last twenty-four hours. It all seemed too fantastic to be more than a dream, yet here I was on the last leg of my journey home. After all the fears that had haunted me, it had turned out to be quite a welcome home after all. I had been truly blessed.

I returned to New York in one piece. Once there, I planted my feet firmly on the ground, got my head straight and went back to my job in the shipping industry. It was several months later, as I recounted special memories for my father, that I spoke about the cabby and the little old ladies with their Rolls. There was a questioning tone in my voice, as if the incident had not lost its dreamlike quality and become real for me yet.

My father listened to the story, then nodded. "Ya know, son, you should find a way to say thanks to those gals. Rich people like those don't need material things. But if you could locate them and send them a note, I'm sure it would mean a lot."

I considered it over the next several days. I argued with myself that it was silly to spend my time and money just to thank several strangers that I had known only briefly. The more I thought about how much the actions of those strangers had meant to me, the more I realized that my father was right. Their acts of compassion and charity had been given to a stranger as well. At the very least, I should make an effort to contact those good people who had helped me.

Two months had passed, and it was a shot in the dark to find people who might remember me or the elderly pair. The first step, I decided, would be to contact the inn where we had met. I decided that I would place my call on the same day and time of the week when I had arrived at the bar. That would be my best chance of reaching the right employees who could assist me in my search.

San Rafael information provided the telephone number for the Northern Inn restaurant. I dialed the number and a voice answered after just one ring.

"Northern Inn. This is Michael. May I help you?"

"Good evening. May I speak to the bartender, please."

"Certainly, sir. Hold on one second."

I waited on hold for several minutes and was about to hang up when a voice broke the silence and said, "Lounge bar, this is Gregg."

"Hi, Gregg," I replied. "My name is Pat Moffett. I was in your bar several months ago. You might remember me, I was the one in Army dress green uniform. I had just come back from..."

"Vietnam!" Gregg exclaimed. "I can't believe it's you! Guess you made it back to New York okay?"

"Yeah, I did. Thanks." I sighed deeply in relief. It seemed my hunt had begun with a promising start. The voice on the other end of the phone belonged to the bartender who had served our drinks.

"I hope you gave up on those martinis," Gregg teased with a quick laugh. "They're really not your kind of cocktail. Stay with drinks that have milk in them, you'll be better off."

"Maybe I'll grow into martinis under different circumstances," I replied with a laugh of my own. Then I focused on the purpose of my call. "Do you remember those two little ladies I was with at the bar?"

"Remember them? Are you kidding?" The bartender's words were disappointing at first, but then my hopes rose again when the man continued. "Classy gals like that are hard to forget; they're etched in my mind forever."

"Well, I'd like to get in touch with them so I can thank them for what they did. Maybe you can help me."

"Sounds like a great idea. Where do I fit in?"

"Well, I thought since they were regulars at the restaurant that you might know how I can reach them. A phone number or address, or even a note you could give them the next time they come in."

The voice on the other end was silent a moment. "Pat, I hate to burst your bubble, but they aren't regulars here."

I didn't know what to say. I had assumed, from the way that the bartender had acted around them, that the two women had frequented the restaurant and bar often. It was disappointing, and I didn't know what to say next.

Gregg saved me by saying, "You guys were definitely memorable, and all the staff here has talked about you. But I can tell you that nobody here has ever laid eyes on those women before that night, and we haven't seen them since."

"What? I can't believe that."

"I'm not kidding. There's no trace of them at all." Then Gregg added an afterthought. "By the way, even though we have a ton of expensive cars in this town, those ladies hauled your ass out of here in a 1945 Rolls. If that car existed in Marin County, we'd all know about it. Like them, it's too unique and classy not to be noticed."

I was stunned. The one lead that I had wasn't turning out the way I had hoped, and the task seemed impossible. I really didn't know what to say.

"Hey, ya know what, kid?" Gregg asked. "God probably saw that you were having trouble with the last leg of your journey, and He sent a couple of angels to help you along. That must be it because frankly, those women do not exist in San Rafael."

It was meant as a jest, but Gregg's words caused the nagging sense that it had all been a dream to return to my mind. The real world simply did not work that way, where two people would reach out in friendship to comfort and care for a complete stranger.

"Hey, sergeant," Gregg said, interrupting my thoughts. "I gotta go. My waiters are backing up at the bar. If you're ever back in town, stop in. Never know, those two might show up just 'cause you're here."

"Thanks, Gregg," I replied, "I appreciate your help."

"Sure thing. Take care, and stay away from those martinis!" With that the receiver went dead.

I hung up the phone and sat down on the edge of my bed. I looked out the window, staring at the star-filled night, and thought about what the bartender had said.

I had served fourteen months in a country torn by war, and had returned with only a shrapnel scar on my rear. Others I had known and worked with had come home bearing deeper and more dis-abling scars from an unseen enemy. Some had not returned home at all. Was it just chance or sheer blind luck that had left me relatively unmarked?

I recalled the sense of transition on the flight home, of having stepped out of time and place. The band of soldiers had moved through darkness toward light, from war to peace, and everyone on the plane had carried their own fears of what waited for them when they landed.

Mine had been that the time served for my country, the terror and joy I had felt in Vietnam, all of that would go unrecognized or ridiculed when I returned home. It had, now that I thought about it. Family and friends and coworkers had simply accepted me back without questioning or mentioning the fourteen months I had spent away from them. There had been no ridicule, but neither had there been much mention of it. Had I arrived home without the air traffic controller's strike interfering, then my fears would have come true.

I hadn't really thought about it before. The actions of those around me now would have hurt me deeply, would've made my sacrifice seem insignificant. Yet it hadn't mattered to me before now.

It hadn't mattered, because I had been welcomed home before I ever stepped off the plane in New York. Three complete strangers had appeared as if miraculously sent. The cabby, who just happened to be at the airport. All the hotels in San Francisco had been booked solid, yet that stranger had known a place where I could spend the night.

That situation had then led to meeting the two mysterious elderly ladies. They had removed my fears, comforted me with their humor and laughter. Then, when I had drunk myself into a situation where anyone could rob me, they had seen me safely back to the motel and had gently put me to bed. Their final act of kindness— paying for my room—had raised in me a sense of obligation to find and thank them.

I had tried, and the result had been as if the two ladies had never existed. They had appeared briefly to watch over me, and then disappeared. I doubted that I would ever find them, and I realized at that moment that I no longer felt the pressing need to do so.

Could they have been angels from Heaven? Maybe. Perhaps the universe unfolds as it should, and the life of one person is simply a single thread of a greater pattern woven by an unseen but benevolent force. The thread of that person crosses those of everyone he meets each day, and the threads of their lives cross his.

I considered the image that rose in my mind. It was of a single thread, frayed to the point of breaking. Yet surrounding it were other threads, wrapped carefully and lovingly to give strength to one who needed it.

Perhaps they had been angels who had watched over me during my tour, and who had brought one fortunate soldier safely home. I didn't know, but it felt right…and I promised myself then that I would do the same, that I would reach out to provide strength and comfort when I found another who was frayed to the point of breaking.

I stood and walked to the window. The night sky was filled with stars, and I whispered my words to the heavens above. "Thank you."

Maybe the angelic ladies heard me, wherever they were. I didn't know, but it filled me with warmth to think so.